Praise for *Abiding the Long Defeat*

"Evangelizing in contemporary western culture is a challenge. Conor Sweeney offers a unique approach to this difficult issue by looking to the wisdom embodied in J.R.R. Tolkien's epic work *The Lord of the Rings*. In particular, he compares the 'the ring of power' with the temptation for Christians to employ modern techniques in evangelizing. The author argues that, to be authentic, evangelization must be focused on a genuine relationship with the person of Jesus Christ, for which there is no 'short-cut' or easily packaged option."
— THE MOST REV. JULIAN C. PORTEOUS, Archbishop of Hobart

"The first Christians were known as 'Followers of the Way.' *Abiding the Long Defeat* aims to rediscover that way within the fabric of a baptismal, evangelical, and sacramental economy. It traces a lowly, hidden, narrow path, consciously out of step with the trendy, upbeat, and ostensibly glorious. But it is no typical travel guide. Conor Sweeney exposes ossified, superficial, decadent, and gnostic trends in contemporary Christianity. He teaches us to think on our knees: in prayer before God, in company with the saints, in light of the eschaton. Bold and original, even prophetic, this book helps us maintain steadfastly Catholic sensibilities and the conviction of our ultimate power to prevail when all else is crumbling to ruin."
— ADAM G. COOPER, John Paul II Institute for Marriage and Family (Melbourne)

"To understand contemporary, post-modern culture, one needs a grounding in the history of ideas going back to at least the fourteenth century, which is precisely what the author does by taking his reader on an intellectual history tour down the ages in the manner of a fire-side chat. He shows how certain ideas have created the culture of post-modernity, and then offers advice on how Christian hobbits can survive this culture without losing their faith. Though thoroughly Christocentric, the work draws upon Tolkien's imagery as well. It will have broad appeal to both professional scholars and intelligent laity alike. Perhaps most of all, it will be read by young Catholics eager to learn how the world got into its present disenchanted hollow. And there is even something for those who think themselves more elf than hobbit."
— TRACEY ROWLAND, University of Notre Dame (Australia)

"*Abiding the Long Defeat* is a bracing book meant for thoughtful pastors and priests, monastics and laypeople. The author takes his cue from J.R.R. Tolkien's sobering confession that Christians are not meant to conquer a world ruled by the Sauronic forces of the Prince of Darkness Grim. No, we are called to be joyful partisans in fighting 'the long defeat,' winning in the end by losing in the near term. For this interim life of valiant struggle, Sweeney provides a careful analysis of our post-Christian culture, engaging its major advocates on their own turf. Yet he offers also a fine hobbitic guide—drawing upon our best Christian theologians—that grounds our witness in a deeply sacramental Faith of baptismal and penitential life."

—RALPH C. WOOD, Baylor University

"It is not our choice whether to commence this journey. We are already underway, for we are inheritors of the earth cracks in scholasticism and the earth quakes of modernism. But Conor Sweeney's noteworthy book does not just beat up the bad old secularist; rather, it asks what responsibility we Christians bear. It provides a GPS location on our trek to Mordor, where the Ring of false power must be destroyed. A faithful hobbit can succeed if he stays true to the relation that forms the Christian self: baptismal adoption. Baptism does not spare us the journey, nor guarantee our success; but the liturgical fellowship of faith *can* uphold the traveler. A wonderful insight into the demands of evangelization."

—DAVID W. FAGERBERG, University of Notre Dame

"Tolkien described *The Lord of the Rings* as 'a fundamentally religious and Catholic work.' In his latest book, Conor Sweeney shows us how to take Tolkien's work as a guide to evangelizing ourselves and others. He shows us that humility is hobbit-sized, life is an adventure, and the powers of darkness, though powerful, can be defeated. All who are hobbits at heart will take courage from reading this wonderful book."

—JOSEPH PEARCE, author of *Frodo's Journey: Discovering the Hidden Meaning of The Lord of the Rings*

Abiding the Long Defeat

Abiding the Long Defeat

*How to Evangelize Like a Hobbit
in a Disenchanted Age*

CONOR SWEENEY

Angelico Press

First published in the USA
by Angelico Press 2018
Copyright © Conor Sweeney 2018

For information, address:
Angelico Press, Ltd.
169 Monitor St.
Brooklyn, NY 11222
www.angelicopress.com

978-1-62138-357-4 paper
978-1-62138-358-1 cloth
978-1-62138-359-8 ebook

Book and cover design
by Michael Schrauzer
Cover illustration by Michael Schrauzer
"Selfie Couple" modified from "Say Cheese" by "dolanh" from flickr.com

For Dad and Mom:
who raised me in a hobbit culture

Blessed are the timid hearts that evil hate
that quail in its shadow, and yet shut the gate;
that seek no parley, and in guarded room,
though small and bare, upon a clumsy loom
weave tissues gilded by the far-off day
hoped and believed in under Shadow's sway.
Blessed are the men of Noah's race that build
their little arks, though frail and poorly filled,
and steer through winds contrary, towards a wraith,
a rumour of a harbour guessed by faith.

J. R. R. Tolkien, "Mythopoeia"

Contents

Acknowledgments

THE WRITING OF THIS BOOK OWES AS MUCH TO others as it does to any inspiration which may have made its way unbidden into my consciousness. Thanks first to Diana Mascarenhas and the ICPE Mission in Auckland, and to John and Celia Kennedy and the John Paul II Centre for Life, Christchurch. Their invitations to speak became the first rough draft of the book. An invitation from Tom Gourlay and the Christopher Dawson Society in Perth occasioned more grist for the mill. The warmth and hospitality shown by all is fondly remembered. Thanks also to David Mills for publishing a version of a chapter in *Ethika Politika*.

I am grateful to all those who read bits and pieces of the manuscript during various stages of its evolution. Dr. Colin Patterson and Dr. W. Chris Hackett offered helpful feedback on the first rushed draft, while Dr. Anna Silvas, a true master of prose, gave the text a thorough and constructive going-over for which I am deeply obliged. Thanks also to Associate Professor Adam Cooper, Dr. Matthew Tan, and Dr. Owen Vyner for comments on various parts of the text. Specific gratitude goes to Vyner, whose liturgical and sacramental expertise has in no small part shaped aspects of my baptismal reflections. I also gratefully acknowledge Rev. Dr. Joel Wallace for his encouragement regarding some of my central ideas. Of course, any deficiencies in the text are my own.

To Zohra Esperal and Dominic Meese respectively I reserve special appreciation for organizing reading groups to discuss the book. I am grateful for intelligent discussion with them and all participants—Helenka Pasztetnik and Reina Kido; Tony and Lesa Meese, James O'Farrell, Samuel Green, Michael Mathai, and Robert Dugdale.

To John Riess and the good folks at Angelico Press, thank-you for your willingness to take this project on. It has been a pleasure working with you.

I am particularly indebted to my colleagues at the John Paul Institute for Marriage and Family, Melbourne — the late Professor Nicholas Tonti-Filippini, Bishop Peter J. Elliott, Professor Tracey Rowland, Associate Professor Adam Cooper, Dr. Colin Patterson, Dr. Owen Vyner, Dr. Gerard O'Shea, Anna Krohn, Rev. Dr. Pascal Corby, Dr. Anna Silvas, Rev. Dr. Joel Wallace, and Colonel Toby Hunter. It is hard to imagine being part of a warmer and more collegial academic environment. Your friendship is greatly valued. To my students — kudos for your willingness to wrestle with the more challenging aspects of the postmodern condition with me.

I also thank God for the John Paul II Institute for Marriage and the Family, and the opportunity to have served there. Pursuing the truth under its mantle has been the utmost privilege. The anthropological vision it has sought to propagate at the behest of its founder will, I think, form the long-term foundation for a new praxis of resistance against the worst forms of the death of God which are perhaps already upon us. For me, this vision embodies the very best of what it means to be a Christian and offers the hope of not merely *clinging* desperately to faith, but infinitely deepening and strengthening it.

At the heart of this book is my conviction of the central theological significance of filial and nuptial love. Baptismal adoption immerses the self into an eternal relation of love defined by the most profound kind of totality, fruitfulness, and fidelity. But this is not pie-in-the-sky stuff. It begins and is given shape here, now, in the liturgical and sacramental forms of the Church. I am thus immensely thankful for my own domestic church, for the gift of my wife Jaclyn and our 5 children, Finnian, Elle, Thea, Oliver, and Ava. Through them the Mystery has been made urgent and concrete for me in all its existential blessedness, delight, tension, and suffering. It is a gift to abide the journey with you.

Finally, to my parents, Mark and Janet: thank-you for abiding *me*, and for the experiences and sacrifices that made possible a revealing of faith strong enough to resist the power of the Ring.

John Paul II Institute for Marriage and the Family, Melbourne
April 2018

Preface

"I am looking for someone to share in an adventure that I am arrang-
ing, and it's very difficult to find anyone."
   "I should think so — in these parts! We are plain quiet folk and
have no use for adventures. Nasty disturbing uncomfortable things!
Make you late for dinner!"

J. R. R. Tolkien, *The Hobbit*

THE DIALOGUE QUOTED ABOVE TAKES PLACE
in the first chapter of J. R. R. Tolkien's *The Hobbit*. The great wizard
Gandalf approaches the apparently simple hobbit Bilbo Baggins
with the invitation to take on a job as burglar for a group of dwarves seeking
to reclaim their gold and kingdom from a fearsome dragon. Bilbo's initial
response is to recoil from anything that might disturb his comfortable
existence in his hobbit hole in the Shire, but in the end he is persuaded
and thus begins Tolkien's telling of the adventures of Middle Earth.

This book invites the reader — particularly, your average humble Christian hobbit — to something similar. Not an adventure concerning gold and
dragons, but one of deeper confrontation with the question of faith and
evangelization in the increasingly troubled and declining predicament of
Christianity in a secular or "postmodern" world.

Tolkien once noted that from the point of view of the Christian — who
knows that "the world in its present form is passing away" (1 Cor. 7:31) —
history is more about the story of defeat and decline than it is about victory, at least on any purely human scale of calculation. He wrote: "I am a
Christian, and indeed a Roman Catholic, so that I do not expect 'history'
to be anything but a 'long defeat' — though it contains (and in a legend
may contain more clearly and movingly) some samples or glimpses of
final victory." Or, in other words: "The kingdom will be fulfilled, then,"
says the *Catechism*, "not by a historic triumph of the Church through a

progressive ascendancy, but only by God's victory over the final unleashing of evil, which will cause his Bride to come down from heaven" (CCC 677). This present book asks, and seeks to *understand*, whether or not and why it might be the case that we are today in the midst of what is perhaps a particularly acute cycle of the long defeat of history.

To think of history as a long defeat, and to suggest that perhaps Christian faith today faces a certain kind of institutional, cultural, social, and political decline or even death is not to give in to crude forms of dystopian pessimism or fatalism. It is rather to recognize, within the ultimate perspective of a world passing away, the existential reality of the drama of good and evil, of the perennial capacity of human freedom to reject the face of Jesus Christ and to set up worlds opposed to his offer of salvation. In other words, it is to be cognizant of our own capacity to wittingly or unwittingly side with the powers and principalities that seek to hasten Christ's temporal defeat.

It is to thus perceive that there are no guarantees in history — no guarantees in progress or politics — even if the *final victory* has been promised and already won in Christ. And it is to acknowledge that within cycles of decline our personal ability to abide the long defeat and to faithfully retain, internalize, and proclaim faith may be severely challenged. The suggestion I will entertain herein as a possibility is that behind even well-intentioned and confident doctrinal certainty, devotional fervor, or evangelical zeal lies a deeper, more often than not unexamined ignorance and insecurity that we carry as the inheritors of a faith buffeted by *centuries* of turmoil.

The question we must face is this: do believers have what it takes to *faithfully* abide, confront, and engage the kinds of challenges faced by living faith in a post-Christian age without giving ourselves over to the temptations and corruption of the ruling Ring? My sense is that years of living in Minis Tirith or in Gondor, under siege by the dark lords of this world and let down and sold out by many of our own compromised leaders, takes its toll. Even when faith is present, it necessarily bears the wounds and scars of years of confusion, deception, flight, battle, intrigue, temptation, and trauma. And so I suggest that in this light it is *we ourselves* who may be in need of the most primary kind of conversion and evangelization.

The point of this book, therefore, is to try to rediscover a deeper perspective on the faith that in many ways may appear to be faltering, if not *failing*, before our very eyes. To do this, we will descend into the critical depths of the intellectual history, ideas, and practices that frame our world today and which thus implicitly shape and influence what we take both faith and the evangelical task to be. To go on this adventure is thus to at least temporarily leave the comfort of our own presuppositions about faith and evangelization and embark on a quest into the wild reaches of the history of the Christian West and beyond.

What I hope will make this journey less unsettling, however, is that we set out with companions, with what we might call the fellowship of faith — a fellowship that I think still holds all of its original power and promise if only we can find a way to rediscover it in its authentic fullness. By baptism, we have been immersed into the trinitarian fellowship of the Father, Son, and Holy Spirit. Because of this fellowship, we do not walk alone on our journey. We walk with Christ, in the Spirit, as children of the Father, with brothers and sisters in the communion of the Church. Our journey into the wilderness is thus not without hope and a reference point, even if — when — we pass through dark mines, high mountains, and desolate plains, and quail beneath all-seeing eyes of evil.

In the end, if we give ourselves to the quest, we may discover a deeper revelation of the Mystery and our part in it. We may discover, in a word, a new perspective on *our own faith*, and thus a deeper insight into the shape of the evangelical task.

The writing of this book was occasioned by a four-part series of lectures I gave to a general audience in Christchurch and Wellington in late 2014, which was loosely focused on the theme of postmodernity and evangelization. This forms the basis of the first four chapters. An address given in Fremantle in 2015 that took up the themes of the New Zealand lectures and would be published on the website *Ethika Politika* later in the same year forms the heart of the final chapter. All of this material has been substantially modified and reworked, with much new content added. Chapters 5 and 6 are entirely new.

The aim of this book is to present a semi-popular account of the topic, one that is as lively and accessible as possible. I have tried to avoid undue employment of specialist language, excessive referencing, and the curse of endless academic qualification of terms and ideas. At the same time, I have tried to resist dumbing down the narrative to a point where the complexity of ideas and history is not given its full due. These aims are of course never easy to balance, but I hope that two of the main overarching themes of the book serve them well.

These themes are baptism and the literary world of Tolkien's Middle

Earth, in the latter of which hobbits feature prominently. Both serve to lend a certain concreteness to our project of approaching the question of faith and evangelization in a historically conscious key. Hobbits immerse us into the thought-world of Tolkien's timeless accounts of Middle Earth, accounts replete with deep insights into the complexity of the human condition and quest for meaning. This gives us a literary, narrative frame in which to place and put illustrative flesh on many of the key intellectual ideas and historical events that have shaped the history of the West. And central to my argument about hobbits is the claim that they will offer specific inspiration for what the most effective kind of evangelization today might be.

Baptism is an equally concrete phenomenon in its own way. If hobbits are a way into the rich thought-world of Middle Earth, the horizon of baptismal adoption gives us an equally rich and primordial way into the mystery of faith, one that resists stripping this mystery of its narrative structure and thereby turning it into an abstraction that stands outside of the believer. As a child of God the Father in the Son, you yourself are part of the story. You are "related" to him by adoption. His story is your story. The narrative does not stand at a distance from you: you are in it, tasting, touching, and feeling it. Faith is thus not just a collection of propositions and ideas "out there." Rather, it is a dynamic and concrete reality that the baptized find themselves already immersed in. I thus use baptism to frame a much more "embodied" and "sensory" sacramental description of faith from the inside, one that I hope the reader will find both rich and accessible, and one that I think is a crucial yet underappreciated perspective with infinite possibilities for the reframing of the questions of faith and evangelization today.

In terms of the scope of the book, I do not claim that it in any way represents a doctrinal treatise or an exhaustive account of the ideas explored. I do not intend to say *the* word on faith and evangelization in all their dimensions. Nor do I purport to systematically articulate the full theoretical and practical bases upon which a rationale for renewal might be expressed and enacted. Rather, my goal is to provoke a kind of existential first "immersion" into the foundational, usually hidden themes that underwrite the question of faith within our "postmodern condition." The main objective is the big picture: what faith looks like in the long historical sweep, within and according to the enduring baptismal center, in the perspective of history as a long defeat. This demands something more than a simple repetition of rote theological formulas or principles. It precludes the assumption that people will already have the basic tools in their tool kits. And it forbids us from jumping too quickly to systematic perspectives without considering their broader historical context. My hope is that by this our imaginative capacities may be expanded so as to help us transcend the many factors that presently inhibit our full immersion in the mystery of faith.

And so I welcome the reader on this adventure. I am convinced that in the end it will be worth making you late for dinner, and I promise that you will make it back. What I cannot promise, however, is that the adventure will not change you. I only hope that when you return to your hobbit hole you will bring with you some degree of conviction that doing very great and noble things depends first on doing very small and simple things in fidelity and love.

Introduction

This is the hour of the Shire-folk, when they arise from their quiet
fields to shake the towers and counsels of the Great.
   Some believe it is only great power that can hold evil in check.
But that is not what I have found. I have found that it is the small
things, everyday deeds of ordinary folk that keep the darkness at
bay. Simple acts of kindness and love.
                        J. R. R. Tolkien, *The Fellowship of the Ring*

T HE MAIN GOAL OF THIS BOOK IS TO EXPLORE
what the task of evangelization might look like today. But this
will take us deep into the very question of faith itself against the
backdrop of a "postmodern" situation.

What is presented here is loosely drawn from two main sources, one
more professional and the other personal. First, much of the content
is adapted from a course I taught during my time at the John Paul II
Institute for Marriage and Family in Melbourne, Australia on "The New
Evangelization and Postmodern Culture." The course took an historical
or "genealogical" approach to questions of truth and meaning, beginning
from a contemporary social and cultural context seemingly more and
more marked by what Friedrich Nietzsche called the "death of God." We
would then trace the ideas and events of this context back to their historical
sources and causes in order to seek a deeper perspective on how all of us
who inhabit this context today might better grapple with its challenges.
Students typically described this as an eye-opening—if challenging—
experience that helped them find their own bearings in both their faith
and their experience of various facets of contemporary society and culture.

The second source for this book lies in my own areas of specialization
in continental philosophy and the theology of sacramentality, two areas I
brought into dialogue with each other in my doctoral dissertation. On the

one hand, I have always been interested in the big ideas, the "existential" themes of the meaning of life that are in today's postmodern world more pressing then ever: Who am I? Why am I here? Where am I going? Why is there suffering and evil? Why is there something rather than nothing?

On the other hand, I am convinced that the answers to these eternal yet urgent questions can only be found, not by separating ourselves from others, shutting ourselves in a dark room alone with our thoughts, but rather by entrusting ourselves to others, by opening ourselves to a living dialogue with the realities and experiences that wound, confront, and nourish us the most.

More often than not, attempts to wrestle with questions of ultimate meaning have been premised on escaping experience and history in order to discover what is timeless and eternal in a realm of ideas beyond the world, a realm thought to be distinct from experience and history. A dualistic escape from the world in one form or the other, whether philosophically or psychologically, has always been a temptation. But I have become more and more convinced that the answer to the "big questions" that transcend the world cannot be answered by running away from the world, running away from others. The truth that this approach yields may not be enough to face the existential intensity that comes with living in history and in relationship. Instead, I have been inspired by the quite simple image of the first exchange of a smile between a mother and her child as the primordial paradigm of truth and meaning as always given "inside" the experience of love.

This intuition belongs to my interest in sacramental theology. The sacraments forbid us from escaping the world and the other in order to explain the world and the other. They forbid us from escaping relationships, escaping history, escaping the body, and finding refuge in the realm of "pure" ideas. They commit us to discovering truth in and through the other, in and through relationship, in and through the body, in and through love. They commit us to *this* world, even as they call us to the next. They show us the next world, in order to allow us to become in *this* world living presences of love, living beacons of joy and hope, living icons of God's own love, through and within the experience of love.

Anyone who has shared a first smile with their infant child will grasp that the fullest meaning is to be found, not only by a second-order "explanation" of the experience by other categories outside of it, but by simply dwelling joyfully in the experience itself, and in this, discovering a piercing wound of transcendence that calls you to commit yourself entirely to love, to something that transcends the individual self.

Ultimate meaning, then — the answer to life's "big questions" — is for each person disclosed *within* the small, the (apparently) insignificant, the embodied; *within* experience and relationship, not outside of it. Meaning is discovered, we might say, *within* the "smile" of Jesus Christ, shared with us most personally in baptismal adoption, where we become living children of God the Father, sharing in Christ's own sonship. The sacraments and liturgy — at least when they are not bastardized caricatures of their proper form (and unfortunately, today they so often are) — thus relocate us in an intimate, personal, new world of faith, and in this world transmit the "smile" of the deeper language of sacrificial love — the deeper truth, the deeper reason, the deeper explanation of meaning.

In a word, my own story has led me to seek the big in the small; to seek "reason" by always starting in "faith"; to seek "truth" in love; meaning in both joy and suffering. For the Christian, then — and this is a teaser, by the way — answers to the perplexing issues and questions raised by what I will describe as our "postmodern" context can only be discovered through a constant re-entrusting of the self to the "smile" of Jesus Christ in sacrament and liturgy, by a constant conversion and re-conversion of self to the "smallness" of faith, to the foolishness of the Cross (cf. 1 Cor. 1:18), to the things that defy normal "rational" explanation. And so, as Pope Benedict XVI once said, *the new evangelization must begin in the confessional.* In this, it will be a call as much for *our own evangelization* as for the evangelization of others.

None of this is to say that faith is a magic formula, a way to avoid critically engaging with the new questions, challenges, and crises of the day. Faith does not commit us to a ghetto. Rather, faith takes the center of the Church to the heart of the world. It provides a way into situations and problems that would otherwise chew us up and spit us out. Faith is the ongoing encounter with a person whom we may not know or understand fully, but whose loving presence kindles a trust, clarity, and inspiration that transcends "facts," one that exposes a real truth that has the power to convince and transform us even if we do not know all the details. This is why the uneducated person can always truly encounter Christ in the liturgy, sacraments, and Scriptures when they are faithfully celebrated or venerated.

Faith, expressed through and embodied in love, is the relationship from which all true knowledge can then be genuinely attained. Faith, then, is precisely the fruit of a sacramental, baptismal belonging to the Father in and through the relationship of Christ with his Bride, the Church, that grounds and illuminates our contact with the world and with others.

And so, what I would like to share with you in this book are some aspects of my own experience wrestling with questions of ultimate meaning in and through the lens of baptismal entrusting. Within my own particular, necessarily partial, wounded, and limited experience of the universal dramas of existence and of faith, I hope that I can shed some small ray of light on what faith and evangelization call us to amidst the existential challenge of our own confrontation with Tolkien's "long defeat of history."

The reader should note well that the basic lens of what follows is auto-biographical in the more precise sense that I speak first and foremost *to myself*, from inside my experience of the demand that faith places *on me*. That is, the sometimes direct and sharp character of my stress on the way faith places unyielding existential demands on the believer derives from my conviction that before we can — perhaps in the name of pastoral sensitivity or prudence — somewhat more gently lead *other* souls to the threshold of the mystery, we must be prepared to unflinchingly confront the fire of the Gospel's most pressing and urgent demands for *ourselves*. Before I speak to others, I must speak frankly to *my own* pride and hard-heartedness. I must judge my own failure to follow Christ and to love others with the measure of *His Love*. I must judge my own tendency to abstract daily from my baptismal promises.

What follows is not therefore a work of "pastoral" theology, at least as it is often understood today. It is rather a candid and possibly disturbing first-person confrontation with the human condition born out of my own experience and addressed to it. In an age of so-called "trigger warnings," mine would be that faith is dangerous. It must provoke an urgent confrontation with the deepest and darkest possibilities of the self. It must at some point force me to pick sides in the cosmic battle for my soul between the forces of good and evil. It must jolt me to awareness that I am called to consciously join in this battle, that humming and hawing on the sidelines or excusing myself on the basis of weakness is not enough.

I hope that there is still room in the Church for such an existential and evangelical approach to the things of faith, one that is permitted to confront — without flinching or apologizing — the full, objective measure of Christ's personal address to the self.

The first chapter of this book will introduce some of the main motifs of our contemporary cultural situation. In it, I attempt to come to grips with the experiences of meaninglessness, rootlessness, superficiality, mediocrity, anxiety, violence, and despair that seem to characterize our "postmodern condition" by beginning to trace them to some of the significant moments and developments in the history of the Christian West. I begin to show how we can no longer take it for granted that the faith we think we possess is in fact faith properly speaking. In fact, it might be the case that the faith we profess and practice is being held hostage in myriad ways by a foreign power that has, it seems, subtly eroded the very possibility of belief itself, and thus the possibility of bearing faithful evangelical witness to the world. I propose here that the ethos and disposition of Tolkien's hobbit may provide an imaginative analogy for a fruitful re-framing of the question of faith and evangelization today.

The second chapter will trace various genealogies of the history of the West, employing a kind of archaeological method that asks: "how did we get here from there?" This approach seeks to exhume ideas within their historical context and follow their genesis and mutations through various historical phases. The purpose of this is to show that ideas are never "pure" or self-grounding, but always linked in some way to ideological and material conditions. They always embody or represent some effect of necessarily contingent and relative ways of looking at the world and they always presuppose certain cultural practices, external imperatives, and motivations that mean they are therefore never neutral in how they stand in relation to God or others. In other words, this exercise helps us to see that there are always historical and "belief" motivations guiding how we view and interpret the world, what we take to be "rational" or "irrational," what canon of values we adhere to, how we treat others, how we worship God, etc.

Chapter three completes the genealogical journey begun in chapter two by looking at how historical ideas are played out for us today in our own contemporary social and cultural narratives of secularization. That is, when we look at the world today as it is represented in various secular accounts of the person, society, the good, etc., we can detect the various worldview commitments and presuppositions governing such accounts. This is to say that it matters quite a lot whether one presupposes a Christian account of reality based on our creation by a loving God or an agnostic (or openly atheistic) view of our origins and destination. We will see here that the way a society is set up and the values that it endorses *are never neutral.* In our own time, we will see that what we could call liberal secularism is as much a metaphysical and "religious" and therefore *non-neutral* account of reality as are the Christian claims that contend with it.

On one level, this might all seem like a moot point. After all, the devout Christian might say, of course atheism and secularism are "bad"; no one needs to tell us that. What this knee-jerk response misses, however, is the fact that we are ourselves very possibly unaware of the extent to which we have been implicitly formed by a whole range of presuppositions and practices that do not necessarily fit very well with faith. Again, and still more uncomfortably, we may also discover that what we in fact call *faith* has itself perhaps become something of a caricature. And so in this chapter I will attempt to make sense of the deeper commitments that certain practices necessarily commit us to, to show that beliefs, ideas, and practices are never neutral or rationally (or irrationally) self-evident.

This will set the stage for chapter four, which will begin to develop a constructive response to the challenges raised in the first three chapters. Here, we focus on the challenge of violence, a common trope explored by postmodern thinkers who accuse Christianity of being at heart a violent imposition on the free flux of reality. If ideas are historical, if all accounts of rationality are in some sense "situated" or a matter of perspective, what then of the Christian claim to universality? Is it not too perhaps just another violent attempt to control reality and as such barely different from any other play for power, indeed, more *offensive* than any other?

As we will see from this chapter and chapters two and three, postmodernity presents Christianity today with a *crisis of legitimation*, both inside and outside of the Church. Is what Jesus claimed and what the Church claims true? Our personal crises may not be underwritten by the claim writ large that "there is no meaning." But we might feel the weight of an overwhelming cultural feeling that of this meaning, as Nietzsche said, "there are no facts, only interpretations." In this, we suspect and fear, if only deep in our hearts or as a disturbing thought from time to time that we hastily dismiss—if not a much deeper existential unease—that Christianity is all an illusion, a ruse, a great deception, just one more play of power that terminates in violence, exclusion, and corruption. While there is no generation of Christians who have not struggled with such questions, we now live at a time when unbelief rather than belief is the cultural norm that jostles for our allegiance in the majority of social practices that we partake in. Perhaps "God is dead"—if not *really*, then at least in our churches, in our hearts, and in our practices—as

Nietzsche said. This chapter will seek a frontline confrontation with such an argument.

Chapter five is the systematic heart of this book. It centers on the theme of baptism as the fundamental answer to the postmodern condition. Baptismal adoption is a prominent theme throughout the entire book, but here it comes to the fore in a much more sustained way. I suggest that the ultimate answer to the postmodern condition is to be found here, in a mystery whose real power seems so often to be taken for granted or reduced in its truly positive ontological and existential significance. Baptism is the gift of divine adoption which completely and utterly changes the horizon of the self's pursuit of meaning by recreating that individual's reality in the cruciform and resurrected shape of a participation in Christ's divine sonship, in and through the mediation of the Church. One must therefore approach fundamental reality differently — *very* differently — in the light of baptism. The radicality and far-reaching scope of baptismal transformation has, I think, not yet been fully realized and reclaimed by today's faith discourse, and part of the aim of this chapter in particular and this book in general is to sketch a vision of the deeper possibilities afforded by the perennial newness of baptismal faith.

Armed with a new baptismal framing of existence, chapters six and seven apply the constructive principles of the preceding two chapters to the practical question of the shape that the task of evangelization should take within the context of the pathologies of a postmodern world. Is evangelization possible in these circumstances, and if so, what might it look like? Chapter six considers the possibility and limitations of "virtual" or "Facebook" evangelization, while chapter seven resumes our motif of the hobbit in earnest. I conclude that if evangelization is indeed to be true to genuine *baptismal* faith, and therefore *effective* as genuine faith, it must begin from and take shape according to the unassuming smallness and outwardly *ineffective* vocation of the hobbit, which I submit is a deep and convincing embodiment of the heart of a functioning baptismal existence. Unlike the way of power and force embodied in the Dark Lord Sauron, the way of the hobbit embodies a joyful embrace of the goodness of creation and the horizon of salvation and redemption lived in hope, the way of baptismal prayer and worship, loving self-gift and sainthood. In this, it is, I will argue, the *only* way to personal and then (maybe) cultural salvation.

By now, you might suspect that I favor an approach to evangelization that at its heart is quite "small," at least from the perspective of the world.

We do not need yet another shiny program or strategic plan, another committee or synod. We do not need to be more "rational" as much as we need the intact mediation of a feeling, tasting, and savoring kind of encounter and of practices that kindle our trust and our love from *within* a loving embrace, a relationship, a *smile*, that pierces and wounds us to the heart. This is nothing less or more than faithfulness to a baptismal approach grounded in the fertile soil of the Gospel itself and embodied in the liturgy, an approach that begins in and is shaped by a more radical gift than a creature could ever expect or anticipate: divine adoption.

It is here, in the baptized experience of hobbits, that postmodern violence and despair can be overcome, where we can become faithful witnesses for Christ—and where we can abide the long defeat.

ONE

The World is Changed

It is sad that we should meet thus only at the ending. The world is changed, I feel it in the water, I feel it in the earth. I smell it in the air. I do not think we shall meet again.

J. R. R. Tolkien, *The Return of the King*

THIS POIGNANT, SPINE-TINGLING DESCRIPTION sets the scene for what we can describe as the "postmodern condition" of our own world.[1] In the context of Tolkien's Middle Earth, Treebeard the ent utters these words evoking a world that is slowly but surely losing what we might call its "mystical" or "enchanted" character. At the end of the *Lord of the Rings*, Middle Earth enters the Fourth Age, a time marked by the waning of an explicitly "supernatural" reality, a kind of "dying of the light" in a world originally animated by spirits, angelic powers, magic, etc. Non-human beings—such as elves, dwarves, and ents—either decrease in power or leave Middle Earth altogether. This is embodied in Lady Galadriel's statement: "I will diminish, and go into the West…."[2] The elves leave the shores of Middle Earth, never to return. Middle Earth now belongs to men, and men alone. *The world is changed.*

Without trying to force the analogy too much and without being too dystopian, we might be said to feel something similar in relation to our own world and age. We might sense that the world has indeed changed. It seems to have lost the vital élan, the divine spark, the spiritual presence, the perspective of wonder, a living memory of its origins and organic unfolding. It has been "de-mythologized," stripped of any deep meaning other than the visible, the observable, the testable, the measurable. When

1 Cf. Jean-François Lyotard, *The Postmodern Condition: A Report on Knowledge*, trans. Geoff Bennington and Brian Massumi (Minneapolis: University of Minnesota Press, 1984).
2 J.R.R. Tolkien, *The Fellowship of the Ring* (New York: HarperCollins, 2011), 476.

1

we look at things, we see only surfaces, material things as they present themselves to our eyes. We do not consider their essential relationship with other things; we do not care if there is more to them than first appearance, beyond "scientific" analysis, unless this can be seen to further our instrumental needs and motivations.

From enchantment to disenchantment

To employ the terminology of the famous German sociologist Max Weber (1864–1920), we have shifted from an "enchanted" world to a "disenchanted" world.[3] In an enchanted world, existence is perceived to be animated and punctuated by the presence and activities of gods, spirits, demons, the divine, etc. In such a world, people imagine themselves to be part of a dramatic cosmic interplay between divine freedom and human freedom, a world of a struggle between good and evil. Their behaviors and practices thus reflect an effort to live within the rhythm of this perceived enchanted world, something embodied in the central role played by sacrifice, ritual, and worship in daily life.

Within a disenchanted world, by contrast, we find that we need no longer invoke anything outside the world in order to explain it. We no longer need the crutch or (as Karl Marx put it) the "opiate" of religion to give us meaning, to get us through life. We no longer need to ritually adapt our behaviors and practices to conform to some supposed supernatural being or beings, some cosmic drama beyond the horizons of finitude. Rather, we can look to ourselves, to our own minds, to "science," to "progress," to answer all of the important questions.

For the English philosopher and statesmen Francis Bacon (1561–1626), the first "true knowledge" only becomes accessible to us when we strip away the essentially superstitious notion that there is anything "beyond" the strictly observable and quantifiable.[4] In other words: do not waste your time with the question of where something may have come from. Simply work with the reality in front of you, and put it to practical use in making the world a better place.

This has been described as a shift from a contemplative worldview (in which, as for Plato and Aristotle, the contemplation of the good is the

---

3 Cf. Max Weber, *The Protestant Ethic and the Spirit of Capitalism*, trans. Talcott Parsons (New York: Scribners, 1958).

4 Cf. Francis Bacon, *The New Organon and Related Writings* (Indianapolis: Bobbs-Merrill, 1960).

ultimate human activity) to an active worldview (in which the ultimate good is demonstrably productive, utilitarian, instrumental, material). Apply "knowledge" in order *to change the world* (that is, make it a more comfortable, convenient, equitable, just, livable place), not to attune yourself spiritually to a beckoning presence behind it. The true "children" or achievements of knowledge are practical, not contemplative.

The philosopher David Hume (1711–1776) famously argued that any contemplation of a reality beyond the world was quite simply a waste of time and a deception: "commit it then to the Flames: For it can contain nothing but Sophistry and Illusion."[5]

A de-mythologized faith

In a religious setting a similar principle of reduction was used to try to get to the heart of what Christ really said and taught. The German Lutheran theologian Adolph von Harnack (1851–1930) suggested that in order to get the heart of the Gospel message, we needed to strip away the "husk" of Christ's teachings (historical, miraculous, ecclesial or "superstitious" elements) in order to reach the true "kernel" (the "rational" or "human" elements).[6] This provoked a movement of de-mythologization or rationalization within Christianity, forming the basis of today's liberal theology, which sees things such as a genuinely incarnate divine being, a determinate morality, or an ecclesial context of faith as accretions upon true religion that we "enlightened" Westerners should now have the courage to relegate to an antiquated past. Christ did not *really* show us the true face of God. He did not *really* marry his bride the Church. He did not *really* show us a radical path to holiness. He did not *really* offer us full conversion and transformation. No, he just brought us the "idea" of God and shared a certain moral ideal, a "rational" program of social justice and reform, perhaps; he is a great guy, a good example, an historical inspiration, and all that.

"Salvation," then, is a subjective and relative state of mind, a perpetual process of aimless wandering or directionless journeying rather than a *condition* of radical transformation, a radically new way of living in the world.

---

5 David Hume, *An Enquiry Concerning Human Understanding and Other Essays*, ed. Ernest C. Mossner (New York: Washington Square Press, Inc., 1963), 158.

6 Cf. Adolph von Harnack, *What Is Christianity?* trans. Thomas Bailey Sanders (Philadelphia: Fortress Press, 1986).

Allegiance to other gods

This new, "disenchanted" world thus has as its driving motivation the notion that we can be happy, good, or "rational" without invoking any magical or superstitious "God principle" or prostrating ourselves before any deity. Such a world belongs in its first robust historical articulation to the "Enlightenment," which itself belongs to the broader cultural and historical phenomenon of "modernity." We are all "modern" in that we live lives structured by a certain separation of Church and state, a bracketing and policing of social conversations about the good life and life after death, an arrangement of social life that does not involve any robust public reference to the beyond, and a basic rhythm of daily practices that are bereft of any reference to "something more," something beyond the visible.

We thus discover that many of the practices and activities in which we take part daily are committing our allegiances not to God, but to something else. The vast majority of "normal" things that I do every day in the "modern" world bear no real relation, embody no particular witness, and articulate no great defense of the presence of "something more" to life than its mere surface. It is entirely possible to do "normal" things, such as marry and have a family, celebrate national holidays, participate in social and political discourse, work a job, etc., without ever being obliged to reference or even think about God, except perhaps in a merely nominal and increasingly archaic and soon-to-be-offensive way ("God bless America"; "God bless the Queen"; "God keep our land"; "God defend New Zealand").

"God," if we still invoke him at all, may only belong, properly speaking — in any meaningful sense — to a vague and unexamined sense of transcendence to which I may devote a small, private, cognitive, and increasingly irrelevant allotment of time on Sunday morning. In other words, at the end of the day, God has very little to do with the majority of my waking existence. Canadian philosopher Charles Taylor has remarked that Christians of the medieval age would likely regard us "modern" Christians as "blasphemous and licentious."[7] Most of the social rites and rituals that we take part in are properly modern, premised on a practical separation between heaven and earth, soul and body, and the like that our "enchanted" ancestors would not be able to comprehend.

Of course, we may, as Christians, try our best to make a "secular" moment a "religious" one, by deliberately forcing ourselves to mentally

---

7 Charles Taylor, "Two Theories of Modernity," in *Hastings Centre Report* 25 (1995), 31.

link it to God, by looking for God in it *despite* the fact that in itself, it may proclaim a very different allegiance. But who among us has not felt the hollowness of such endeavors? While being compelled to cultivate a religious sensibility in an otherwise secular environment may help some people never to take faith for granted, the vast majority of us seem to simply give way to, and find ourselves shaped by, the deeper allegiance that our social and cultural actions reflect. It is almost impossible to live in the "modern" world and not become it. It is difficult — if not impossible — in thinking in accord with modernity, and asking and answering questions according to its terms, to avoid *becoming the role* that we might tell ourselves we are only playing.

In a word, we can describe a quintessentially "modern" horizon or worldview as one in which God, transcendence, and ultimate questioning have no real place. They have been banished to the increasingly under-attack margins. More broadly, within modernity anything that is not ostensibly "scientific," "analyzable," "logical," "provable," or linked with an enlightened conception of a universal human reason distinct from tradition and religion is therefore irrelevant, superstitious, and untrue. Appeals to an order of reality beyond what is analyzable in the lab — what is capable of being weighed, measured, and quantified — or to a freedom oriented by a vigorous notion of some transcendent good have no weight and merit no credence. Within these conditions of modernity it becomes very difficult to even imagine or visualize what it might mean to organize the many facets of your existence around a more "enchanted" sense of reality. The bottom line, therefore, is that within the conditions of modernity, you will never be able to find the questions and answers that may get you out of it.

In the meantime, perhaps most of us will be content to live a superficial faith within what is at least for some still a quite comfortable world that keeps us fed, housed, and clothed, and which distracts us from ultimate questions with a wide array of entertainments, pleasures, amusements, consumptions; endless doings, endless noise, endless escapes from reality. But if we attend more closely, if we look more deeply, if we confront ourselves more honestly, we may discover something disturbing.

Postmodern prophets

Danish philosopher Søren Kierkegaard (1813–1855) argued that the person who has not made an existential response to the weight of meaning pressing down on him will find himself unable to escape despair.[8] That is, everything that he does, every strategy he employs to mask the question of *infinite* meaning, will simply send him further into the pit of despair. We always act surprised when someone unexpectedly commits suicide or commits some horrible act of violence: "He was such a good person. There was no indication that he was going through something that might have provoked this. I just do not understand how he could have done this." The reality is that we have become masters at masking our own despair, both to others and to ourselves. But despair always gets its revenge. And perhaps we ourselves, even as "believing" Christians, might be closer to the brink than we would like to admit.

For Kierkegaard, *existence must be confronted, appropriated, owned.* "Listen to the cry of a woman in labor at the hour of giving birth — look at the dying man's struggle at his last extremity, and then tell me whether something [that is, existence] that begins and ends thus could be intended for enjoyment."[9] The world proposed by modernity is a hollow shell of existence, a world in despair, a world that has lost hope, a world that no longer tries to ask and answer the truly important questions. As such, it is a world that is dying. "And when the hourglass has run out, the hourglass of temporality," says Kierkegaard, "when the noise of secular life has grown silent and its restless or ineffectual activism has come to an end, when everything around you is still, as it is in eternity, then eternity asks you and every individual in these millions and millions about only one thing: whether you have lived in despair or not."[10]

Kierkegaard voices perhaps the first most full-throated critique of the brave new disenchanted modern world. He finds at the heart of this world an inner insecurity and instability born of its deliberate and comprehensive deadening of the existential horizon of human questioning. And so we may begin to feel a grave sense of betrayal. We may begin to feel extremely uncomfortable and unsettled. We may feel our anger rising at the way the modern story has duped us.

We may thus find ourselves at a crossroads, confronted with a number

---

8 Cf. Søren Kierkegaard, *The Sickness Unto Death: A Christian Psychological Exposition for Upbuilding and Awakening*, trans. Howard V. Hong and Edna H. Hong (Princeton: Princeton University Press, 1983).

9 Søren Kierkegaard, *The Diary of Søren Kierkegaard*, ed. Peter Rohde (New York: Philosophical Library, 1960), 25.

10 Kierkegaard, *The Sickness Unto Death*, 27.

of possible responses: 1) we can inject ourselves with stronger drugs and recommit ourselves to the values of the modern world, to unconfronted despair; 2) we can seek some revitalized, positive way to again find solutions to our existential crisis outside of the conditions of modernity (faith?); 3) or we can chuck everything and live a radical existence of self-determining freedom, giving the middle finger to all attempts at the articulation of meaning, all strategies that attempt to dull the raw edge of existence.

If Kierkegaard himself was able to take the route of faith, there was another figure after him who radically embraced the third option. It is this tragic figure in particular who shows us what a "postmodern" world — a world *after* modern certainty and instrumental reason — might look like. He speaks to a generation that has not been able to find a way out of the existential crisis of legitimation provoked by disillusionment with the despair of modernity. This man is German philosopher Friedrich Wilhelm Nietzsche (1844–1900).

Nietzsche is often dismissed by Christians as a raving lunatic, a degenerate "nihilist" and immoralist, a "sinner" to the nth degree. He is also dismissed by anyone who still believes in the modern story. But these dismissals miss the point quite profoundly. For what Nietzsche rants and raves against first and foremost are the idols that we create and nurture in order to dull the sharp edge of a broken human existence that at its heart cannot be understood or controlled. Like Kierkegaard, Nietzsche cries out against unexamined despair, against "coping strategies," against therapeutic deceptions that mask our own confrontation with our despair, that block any possibility of a deeper, more authentic form of existence. Perhaps more than any other his critique of modernity is worth taking seriously.

Nietzsche casts his withering gaze at both Enlightenment man and Christian alike, accusing them both of trafficking in forms of false consciousness and myopic delusion about what in fact they are professing to believe or disbelieve. To Enlightenment man he says, you may claim not to believe in God, but this is not to say that you do not still believe in some "god." You believe in an autonomous rational principle that functions as a god, one that provides a solid ground and explanatory framework for what is real. Your god is what you call "reason." You still believe there is an ultimate story that explains everything, by which you can manage and categorize all things. It is just that you have connected it to a principle of sufficient reason with a purely rationalist measure for truth, one now based on purportedly empirical laws or methodologies.

But, says Nietzsche, this merely represents a later, more degenerate stage of a basic failure to confront existence in all of its uncontrollable rawness and horror: no matter what you do, everything ends in death. For all we can see, every human claim about meaning, high or low, rational or irrational, cannot escape the grave. Death visits the righteous and unrighteous alike. All that is distinctive (and for Nietzsche, particularly repugnant) about Enlightenment man is that he has consciously turned his gaze from existential or higher things and fixated all of the energies of his still-voracious desire to know and explain upon a lower level of reality, i.e., reasons, causes, or grounds based on or extrapolated from purely immanent premises and directed to practical ends. But with this, man has simply narrowed and constricted the range of his vision. Significantly, he has excluded any aesthetic, artistic, or religious sense that might break his iron grip on his own airtight principles or keep him open to a more "uncanny" approach to the riddles of life and death.

In the end, Nietzsche finds that the condition of being human (bound by time, space, context, temporality, finitude, psychology, desire, etc.) has a funny way of destabilizing, relativizing, or disproving what we want to be the freestanding, unpolluted, and indisputable universal truths of reason. Alasdair MacIntyre remarks that the greatest irony of the Enlightenment was that its central goal of establishing a mode of universal rational justification (in this case, for morality) independent of authority and tradition has in fact only multiplied disagreement exponentially. He remarks that "in five swift, witty and cogent paragraphs" of his 1882 book *The Gay Science*, Nietzsche "disposes of both what I have called the Enlightenment project to discover rational foundations for an objective morality and of the confidence of the everyday moral agent in post-Enlightenment culture that his moral practice and utterance are in good order."[11]

Here, Nietzsche derides Enlightenment man's pretensions about having discovered some universal law through his reason. He tells this man: "Your judgement, 'that is right' has a prehistory in your drives, inclinations, aversions, experiences, and what you have failed to experience; you have to ask, '*how* did it emerge there?' and then also, '*what* is really impelling me to listen to it?'"[12] He mocks this man for his pretensions to pure reason:

11 Alasdair MacIntyre, *After Virtue: A Study in Moral Theory* (London: Duckworth, 1990), 113.

12 Friedrich Nietzsche, *The Gay Science*, trans. Josefine Nauckhoff (Cambridge and New York: Cambridge University Press, 2001), 187.

"the firmness of your moral judgement could be evidence of your personal wretchedness, of lack of a personality; your 'moral strength' might have its source in your stubbornness — or in your inability to envisage new ideals."[13] Finally: "You admire the categorical imperative within you? This 'firmness' of your so-called moral judgement? This absoluteness of the feeling, 'here everyone must judge as I do'? Rather admire your selfishness here!"

MacIntyre looks to the shrilly "emotivist" character of today's moral discourse as ample proof of the prophetic character of Nietzsche's critique.[14] Self-assertive protest and indignation — not enlightened rational discourse — have become the dominant modes of moral utterance in a social community that is no longer bound together by fundamental shared norms and values.[15] All we really have today are the shrill, unsupported, and unexamined assertion of Rights! Tolerance! Freedom! Justice! Fairness! Equality! But, inasmuch as no truly rational foundation or consensus has been able to be adduced for such assertions, all we really have are claims no more true than the belief in "witches and unicorns."[16]

In this, Enlightenment man's pretensions to serenely "scientific" *total* knowledge generated by the measure of the strict conditions of his autonomous reason sets him up for a particularly monumental fall into absurdity and *irrationality*, for in so doing he has effectively tied the measure of reason to his own incorrigibly historical, contextual, and psychological condition. For Nietzsche, if there is no ultimate bar or measure beyond this condition — some real "God" — then all man will have in the end are his own wishful projections or his juvenile tinkering with the physical building blocks of the universe. No God, no reason. This for Nietzsche is Enlightenment man, the last gasp of a universal truth-seeking endeavor that began with Plato. There can be no transcendence or ultimate truth if man is not capable of transcending himself; or better, you might say, if something or someone does not transcend *him*.

What makes Nietzsche so important is his recognition that the modern project to ground a universal truth in some pure measure beyond the contingent, temporal, and historical could only end in failure, with far-reaching consequences. It is in this context that, amidst all the apparent sophistication, confidence, success, and progress of a nineteenth-century

13 Ibid., 188.
14 MacIntyre, *After Virtue*, 23–35.
15 Ibid., 71.
16 Ibid., 69.

modern world, Nietzsche cut across the grain and declared that *God is dead*. He told the tale of a madman who bursts into a village and asks frantically: "Whither is God?" After enduring the jeering and mocking of the villagers, the madman pierces them with his eyes and answers his own query: "I will tell you. We have killed him—you and I. All of us are his murderers.... God is dead. God remains dead. And we have killed him."[17]

With this, Nietzsche proclaims the failure of modern man's attempt to ground truth according to the measure of his own sufficient reason. In truth, man has neither a God nor a reason beyond his own contingent self. Enlightened man is of course unwilling to accept this, but Nietzsche tells him anyway: God *is* dead. You are trading in illusions and lies. Nietzsche's subsequent embrace of historicism and a radically perspectival notion of reason and truth "beyond good and evil" is the product of his recognition that if God is in fact dead, then so too is the possibility of a universal reason, truth, or morality. Nietzsche is thus the inheritor, unmasker, and undertaker of a failed tradition, a failed experiment premised on how far you can get without God.

But the Christian does not escape Nietzsche's ire in all of this. The Christian God is dead as well. "It is still recounted how on the same day the madman forced his way into several churches and there started singing his *requiem aeternam deo* ['grant God eternal rest']. Led out and called to account, he is said to have replied nothing but, 'What are these churches now if not tombs and sepulchres of God?'"[18] While Nietzsche actually admired the man Christ—"there was only ever one Christian, and he died on the Cross"[19]—he thought that what historically and institutionally went by the name Christianity was simply an earlier version of the same psychological need for order and explanation that had come to drive Enlightenment man. His critique of Christianity is biting, relentless, and total. Be that as it may, he keenly understood that contemporary Christians no less than moderns had long since abandoned belief in a truly transcendent foundation for their belief in nature, reason, and morality.

Capturing well the difficulty of maintaining the "enchanted" foundation and character of faith within a progressive and enlightened age, he asks:

17 Nietzsche, *The Gay Science*, 119–20.
18 Ibid., 120.
19 Friedrich Nietzsche, *The Anti-Christ*, in Friedrich Nietzsche, *The Anti-Christ, Ecce Homo, Twilight of the Idols*, trans. Judith Norman (Cambridge: Cambridge University Press, 2005), 35.

"When on a Sunday morning we hear the bells ringing we ask ourselves: is it possible! this is going on because of a Jew crucified 2000 years ago who said he was the son of God. The proof of such an assertion is lacking."[20] Even more evocatively:

> A god who begets children on a mortal woman; a sage who calls upon us no longer to work, no longer to sit in judgment, but to heed the signs of the imminent end of the world; a justice which accepts an innocent man as a substitute sacrifice; someone who bids his disciples to drink his blood; prayers for miraculous interventions; sin perpetuated against a god atoned for by a god; fear of a Beyond to which death is the gateway; the figure of the Cross as a symbol in an age which no longer knows the meaning and shame of the Cross—how gruesomely all this is wafted to us, as if out of the grave of a primeval past! Can one believe that things of this sort are still believed in?[21]

How much more true this might feel for us today in an even more advanced stage of the death of God, where enchantment and mystery have retreated even further into the shadows.

The believer may of course quibble with Nietzsche's fundamentally dismissive account of faith—considering the possibility of faith *after Nietzsche* might be another way to describe the aim of this book. But what he did effectively unmask was the *empirical fact* that by the nineteenth century belief and truth were already in crisis, already laced with the poison of their own decline or demise, even if neither Enlightenment man nor Christian man could yet confront it. As the madman recognizes,

> "I have come too early ... my time is not yet. This tremendous event is still on its way, wandering; it has not reached the ears of men. Lightning and thunder need time; the light of the stars needs time; deeds need time, even after they are done, in order to be seen and heard. This deed is still more remote to them than the remotest stars—*and yet they have done it themselves!*"[22]

20 Friedrich Nietzsche, *Human, All Too Human: A Book for Free Spirits*, trans. R. J. Hollingdale (Cambridge: Cambridge University Press, 2005), 65–66.

21 Ibid., 66.

22 Nietzsche, *The Gay Science*, 120.

In other words, then, Nietzsche identified us all as killers and hypocrites well before we were prepared to admit it. We have now for centuries been using a "god-principle," a "hollow man" kind of god in order to avoid facing the real truth about ourselves. And if a "real" God exists, we have long since lost any chance of genuine contact with him through our creation of counterfeit alternatives.

Nietzsche thus forces us to confront the reality that *modernity and everything mapped within its horizon is already nihilism*; that our beliefs and practices are framed by a more fundamental commitment to existential emptiness, nothingness, and meaninglessness, and managed by our therapeutic fictions.

Unmasking our own idolatry

Another important thinker said something similar. German philosopher Martin Heidegger (1899–1976) suggested that the God that we might say we believe in is in fact seldom much more than a god who is a "first principle," a Deistic or "Watchmaker" God who gets everything going and then sits back and lets us do our own thing. "Will Christian theology," asked Heidegger, "make up its mind one day to take seriously the word of the apostles and thus also the conception of philosophy as foolishness?"[23] Like Nietzsche, Heidegger observed a disconnect between what Christ actually said and how most Christians actually think and act.

Might this not apply to me? Is the God that I profess to worship a person who accompanies me existentially throughout my life? Does He communicate something more to me than mere "principles" or "suggestions"? Does He unsettle and reset my desires and purify me for real relationship with Him and with others? Is God more than an idea that gives me solace, energy, or a nice warm feeling, and that essentially lets me do my own thing?

We might discover that we have been worshipping a God whom we do not think ever *really* appears as the living reality of a person present to us, so that it does not really matter what we do and say, whether in bedroom or liturgy. Or we may discover that we have been reading the Scriptures more as an abstract moral or devotional guidebook and less as a means to a dramatic encounter with a real person, with the Christ who is in his

---

23 Martin Heidegger, "The Way Back into the Ground of Metaphysics," in *Existentialism from Dostoevsky to Sartre*, ed. Walter Kaufman (New York: Meridian Books, 1975), 276.

person and his call to us "the way, the truth, and the life" (Jn. 14:6).

And it is at this point that we cannot ignore the fact that perhaps we are guilty of breaking the second commandment — "Thou shalt have no other gods before me" (Ex. 20:3). Keenly recognizing this, Kierkegaard made the following observation: "The Bible is very easy to understand. But we Christians are a bunch of scheming swindlers. We pretend to be unable to understand it because we know very well that the minute we understand, we are obliged to act accordingly."[24] Or, "Christian scholarship is the Church's prodigious invention to defend itself against the Bible, to ensure that we can continue to be good Christians without the Bible coming too close."[25]

If the Father is something other than the "living God" (cf. Ps. 42:2; Mt. 16:16), if Christ is something other than the living Son of God, if the Spirit is something other than the Gift of the Father and Son who shows us the face of God, then we are free to follow the "wide gate and broad road that many enter," but which the Gospels tell us "leads to destruction" (cf. Mt. 7:13). And so, like Peter and Thomas, we have denied Christ. Like Judas, we are the betrayers of Christ.

We thus see with such figures as Kierkegaard, Nietzsche, and Heidegger a profound unmasking of the corrosive mediocrity, insecurity, and falseness of the modern world and perhaps of our own complicity in it as well, both as a church and as individuals. Their critiques alert us to the possibility that Christianity cannot simply blame the big bad world (secularism) for the present situation. *For we ourselves may be part of the problem.* Our next chapter will begin to try to show how this is so.

Suffice it to say, then, that "secularity bashing" is not enough. For saying that the problem exists solely "out there" can merely be a way to deflect criticism of ourselves. We can congratulate ourselves that it is not *we* who are corrupt and degenerate, it is the world. It is not us who need fixing, we tell ourselves; it is the world and others who needs fixing. And thus we avoid a genuine confrontation with the real, with candid soul-searching, a true turning to the One who is always there calling us. We are probably more compromised than we know.

---

24 Søren Kierkegaard, *Provocations: Spiritual Writings of Søren Kierkegaard*, ed. C. E. Moore (Farmington: Plough, 2002), 201.
25 Ibid.

Describing the postmodern condition

Returning to our narrative, we can now start to understand what the phrase "postmodern condition" might be all about. Though we live in the "modern" world — a world of scientific and technical surety and progress — we increasingly feel disturbed, uneasy, and homeless within this brave new world. The "postmodern condition" is a marker for this sense of unease with the story of modernity.

At its heart it refers to what French philosopher Jean-François Lyotard (1924–1998) called "incredulity towards meta-narratives."[26] We find that we no longer believe "big stories," ultimate explanations for why something exists, what it is good for, and why it may be good for us. For as French philosopher Paul Ricoeur (1913–2005) pointed out, the very foundations of consciousness and selfhood have been unsettled by the destabilization of modern foundationalism. Ricoeur identified Marx and Austrian father of psychoanalysis Sigmund Freud (along with Nietzsche) as the great foundational "destroyers" of the possibility of certitude unhindered by a deeper insecurity and suspicion.[27] Together, Ricoeur described them as the "masters of suspicion." Each takes up the consequences of the death of God in modernity, unmasking what must be the "false consciousness" of a self that still tries to operate under the assumption of some foundational meaning accessible to it beyond the purely immediate and instinctual. Each reduces the self who remains to an amorphous collection of sub-rational drives, instincts, and urges premised on the baser motivations of sexual desire, power, will, resentment, and the like.

With Nietzsche, Marx, and Freud, and others, then, we might begin to suspect that everyone and everything has an angle, that everything that we have been told is logical or rational is actually a mask for a more primitive play of power, actually the deception of one's own desire or an ideological stratagem of another to get you to conform to this or that imperative. This may be true of our relationship to religion and Christianity, nation states, elites, politicians, institutions, corporations, etc. For example, when we discover the lengths to which contemporary advertising goes to detect, manipulate, and exploit our desires, we might feel our suspicions are confirmed.

---

26 Lyotard, *The Postmodern Condition*, xxiv.

27 Paul Ricoeur, *The Conflict of Interpretations: Essays in Hermeneutics*, ed. Don Ihde (Evanston: Northwestern University Press, 1974), 148.

And so we might very generally describe postmodernity as a condition of general loss of confidence in universal or ultimate explanations of reality. The state of insecurity that this provokes thus feeds into what is often named a "crisis of legitimation"[28] — what happens when the subject realizes that it may not in fact be possible to rationally ground and thus defend his nearest and dearest beliefs. In this sense, it could just be called a crisis of belief.

The postmodern condition has therefore also been described as a condition of radical "hermeneutical suspicion." That is, the attitude of the person who has lost confidence in reason and is undergoing a crisis of belief must treat everything and everyone as a potential lie or threat. Now, if one has given up on the possibility of universal truth, one might seek as much relative and limited meaning as possible in specialized disciplines or in the solace of family and relationships. And so the postmodern condition might be described as fostering the embrace of "little" stories rather than "big" stories, of rationalities rather than Rationality. Meanwhile, those not fazed by the end of universality and not satisfied with the limited meaning of small stories might, like Nietzsche, instead celebrate nihilist despair as the self's liberation from all restrictions, limits, and lies. The celebration of death, then, becomes mainstream in postmodern despair.

In it all, we may discover that we have reverted to the state of a surly, disillusioned, and rebellious teenager. We no longer believe or trust parent-figures (Church, state, etc.) — and more often than not *with very good reasons*. Any Christian who has lived through or been made aware of various betrayals and abuses by ecclesial leaders will have warrant to be suspicious or, sadly, be threatened by a deep loss of faith. Is the institutional Church out simply to protect itself and its "assets" and status? Has the Church given up on its deeper spiritual mission, its call to holiness? Has the Church forgotten how to embody faithful and serious worship, to be faithful to Christ's sign of contradiction (cf. Lk. 2:34), to speak against all corruption to power (including its own), to resist bureaucratic, economic, and political imperatives, to speak in more than sociological terms?

These are perhaps the essential questions for our relationship with the institutional modes of the Church today. But, within a position of radical

28 This term was originally used by German sociologist and philosopher Jürgen Habermas to describe the loss of confidence in institutions and leadership. Cf. Jürgen Habermas, *Legitimation Crisis*, trans. Thomas McCarthy (London: Heinemann Educational, 1976).

postmodern skepticism — within a "hermeneutic of suspicion" — we may find ourselves paralyzed, unable to free ourselves from the paralysis of the age.

Embracing the death of God

And so perhaps we find ourselves deeply unsettled, even as Christians. What if our faith is not deep enough to sustain us in times of challenge and crisis? Maybe our faith has been reduced to clinging desperately to devotions, reason, nature, dogmas, and creeds, not because we know them to be true, but because we fear the consequences without them. It may be the case that in clinging to such consoling or "solid" things we start to conceive of faith as less than an encounter and more as an idea or technique.

But if faith is not built on something other than fear and the need for security, it risks morphing into deeper despair and even something more sinister. The strain may become too great, the dissonance too profound. And so we may find ourselves slipping into nihilistic despair and lethargy, into a spiritual and existential numbness that may eventually terminate in a more militant, more confident, more uninhibited embrace of the void.

We have here the radical Nietzschean response to the apparent meaninglessness of existence. For Nietzsche, the death of God, the purging of our idolatry, and the end of therapeutic deception are not to be mourned or lamented. As the madman says, "there has never been a greater deed; and whoever is born after us — for the sake of this deed he will belong to a higher history than all history hitherto."[29] Nietzsche does not cower in the face of a world that has lost meaning, a world in despair. He laughs in the face of meaninglessness and despair. He makes it the occasion to discover new values, to turn the prevailing account of the world on its head.

Nietzsche's master-class, the *Übermenschen* (supermen or "overmen"), defy reason, convention, pity, weakness, resentment — all the values of the "slave" or the "herd," those modern souls incapable of laughing in the face of the void, of giving themselves over to a joyful embrace of meaninglessness. The lyrics of a 2004 Green Day song, "Jesus of Suburbia," capture this kind of existence well: "To live and not to breathe, is to die in tragedy." To live according to the dictates of therapy is to waste a life that could otherwise be lived in freedom and spontaneity, in search of ever-new and ever-more-transgressive experiences and pleasures. In this, the Nietzschean discovers authenticity, not by a Kierkegaardian leap back into

29 Nietzsche, *The Gay Science*, 182.

faith, but by a radical, self-defining act of freedom; pure will, the "will to power." And so the postmodern condition, taken to its extreme, ends in the absurd, the violent, the insane, and in the celebration of death itself.

While many of us may not experience a crisis of meaning like that described by Kierkegaard or Nietzsche, the long and short of the story I have tried to tell here is that in our so-called "postmodern condition," the world really has changed in a significant way. If for an "enchanted" world belief was the norm, for our "disenchanted" world disbelief is the norm. There have always been crises of belief; what we are witnessing today, however, is a crisis of belief and hope on a massive social scale, including in our faith communities — the "masters of suspicion" have done their work well. "Their critiques," says American philosopher Rick Roderick (1949–2002), "have become a common possession of our culture, and they have cut off one of the reservoirs [faith] within which we might find a coherent meaning for our life."[30] It is not that after postmodernity belief in something becomes entirely impossible. Rather, Roderick explains, the masters of suspicion have ensured that faith must now exist under the marks of confusion, insecurity, and complexity.

Our postmodern condition thus leaves a gaping hole, a radical condition of homelessness, instability, and insecurity that is therefore also an opening for the will to power, force, self-interest, violence, and ideology. It would be one thing if a lack of belief merely manifested as cynical self-interest or resignation. But instead, the instability and insecurity produced by the failure of deep meaning also manifests in the emergence of new idolatries of "identity." Our need to believe in *something*, our need to control and order reality, our experience of alienation in the horizon of the modern, and our fear in the face of the emptiness of the void and the capacity for evil in human hearts is no longer checked by a belief in and experience of an overarching order of truth and goodness, and so we direct our allegiance to subsidiary communities of more "tribalistic" belief and belonging that today coalesce around new permutations — on both the Left and the Right — of politics, religion, race, class, gender, and the like.

In fact, Nietzsche himself would probably look upon many of these shrill forms of "identity politics" today as little more than new therapies for the

---

30 Rick Roderick, "Paul Ricoeur: The Masters of Suspicion," in *The Self Under Siege: Philosophy in the 20th Century*. Audio Cassette, The Teaching Company (1993), at http://rickroderick.org/301-paul-ricoeur-the-masters-of-suspicion-1993/.

herd, misguided collective attempts to retain some semblance of meaning and belonging after the death of God. For him, living freely in the face of the void was rather a form of individualism premised on an interior, almost "spiritual" detachment from groupthink or identity politics of any kind. For example, Nietzsche was opposed to antisemitism and nationalism. Properly conceived, the superman pursues an embrace of the void on his own, eschewing collective expressions of assertion and activism.

Nevertheless, we should not be surprised when the instability which Nietzsche helped to unmask and for which he was incapable of furnishing a genuine solution finds its most universal expression in shrill expressions of collective fear and ideology. Today we seem to be witnessing a kind of recrudescence of the Marxist category of struggle in some parts of the Western world with the recent emergence of new protest groupings and causes ("Occupy," "Black Lives Matter," "marriage equality") whose activism seems directed to a more or less wholesale deconstruction and overthrow—sometimes violent—of the norms and structures of a seemingly patriarchal, racist, and economically and socially unjust past and present social and cultural order. Meanwhile, these are matched by opposing movements which assert an identity grounded in post-Christian notions of race and nation (i.e., the "alt-right").[31]

In his perhaps freshly relevant critique of modern capitalist technological society, German-American Marxist philosopher and political theorist Herbert Marcuse (1898–1979) spoke in the 1960s of the need for a "Great Refusal"[32] of that social and cultural status quo, to utterly resist "false words and wrong deeds" that "contradict and counteract the possibilities of liberation."[33] That is, within what Marcuse saw as the absolute struggle of the *truth* of liberation against the *lie* of the modern order, there could be no dialogue or *rapprochement*:

> Indiscriminate tolerance is justified in harmless debates, in conversation, in academic discussion; it is indispensable in the scientific enterprise, in private religion. But society cannot be indiscriminate where the pacification of existence, where freedom and happiness

31 Cf. Matthew Rose, "The Anti-Christian Alt-Right: The Perverse Thought of Right-Wing Identity Politics," in *First Things* (March 2018), at https://www.firstthings.com/article/2018/03/the-anti-christian-alt-right.

32 Cf. Herbert Marcuse, *One Dimensional Man* (London: Abacus, 1972).

33 Herbert Marcuse, "Repressive Tolerance," in Robert Paul Wolff, Barrington Moore, Jr., and Herbert Marcuse, *A Critique of Pure Tolerance* (Boston: Beacon, 1970), 88.

themselves are at stake: here, certain things cannot be said, certain ideas cannot be expressed, certain policies cannot be proposed, certain behaviour cannot be permitted without making tolerance an instrument for the continuation of servitude.[34]

Note: *anything that does not serve the goal of "liberation" need not and should not be tolerated.* We see this attitude today in the new imperative not to tolerate or dialogue with "hate," namely any feature of perceived racial, sexual, or economic oppression or discrimination causally linked to Christianity or capitalism. There is a reason why the vaunted values of tolerance and free speech in liberal democracies do not always cut both ways today.

This is not of course to deny that some forms of identity politics are born from genuine conditions of alienation and injustice. It is in many cases to *agree* with aspects of a critique directed towards a degenerate modern secular liberal order that truly *does* represent forms of oppression, injustice, and violence; in chapter three I will develop an interpretation and sustained critique of this order. But it is also to claim that none of the problems inherent in such an order can be resolved within the context and presuppositions of a postmodern condition where God is dead, where no order beyond politics and will exists, and where Christianity has ceased to draw on the central reality of the redemption offered in Christ.

And so, in short, we discover that in our postmodern condition despair has been unmasked. Violence has gone mainstream. *The world is changed.* We have at last the real prospect of a Nietzschean world where God is dead, where reason has been subsequently stripped of its power, and where raw power and force typify social discourse. In this context "the proofs of the truth have lost their cogency," says von Balthasar. We may still voice our closed and theoretical accounts of truth in disciplines like the empirical sciences, where "syllogisms may still dutifully clatter away like rotary presses or computers which infallibly spew out an exact number of answers by the minute." But, Balthasar continues, "the logic of these answers is itself a mechanism which no longer captivates anyone. The very conclusions are no longer conclusive."[35] Or, the conclusions are weaponized to serve the ends of ideology.

---

34 Ibid.

35 Hans Urs von Balthasar, *The Glory of the Lord: A Theological Aesthetics*, vol 1: *Seeing the Form*, trans. Erasmo Leiva-Merikakis (San Francisco: Ignatius, 1989), 19.

All of this means something for the way that we go about envisioning and mobilizing the so-called new evangelization and our own confrontation with faith; it is to these points that I now turn, if only provisionally.

The postmodern challenge to faith

Taken together, everything that I have been articulating here complicates how we assess the question of faith and the task and pursuit of evangelization. Today we can no longer presuppose that people (including ourselves) have had a genuine encounter with the practices of faith. We can no longer assume that we collectively live our lives according to some overarching principle called "reason" that could somehow serve as a bridge or a "way in" to our hearts. In the wake of the "masters of suspicion," belief is under the constant mediation of doubt and insecurity. We are dealing, in short, with the myriad of fractured, wounded, disjointed, unreflective, forgetful, suspicious, and ideological states and motivations that constitute the postmodern condition.

Certainly, many fragments of truth are still retained, many touch-points and openings, for the human heart theoretically never loses its capacity and restlessness for truth. But the general woundedness of human hearts within a context punctuated by the death of God, the radical denial of both faith and reason, the loss of confidence, means that we cannot simply presume that what worked once will still work now.

American Orthodox theologian David Bentley Hart has suggested how Christianity paradoxically makes atheism and nihilism a real possibility for the first time in human history, inasmuch as the revelation of the face of the living God in Jesus Christ makes a determinate "no" possible, even as it also makes possible a determinate "yes."[36] In other words, the appearance of an incarnate God on earth sets up a dramatic confrontation between good and evil. "Christianity, with its cry of 'no other god,'" says Hart, "is in part responsible for the nihilism of our culture. The gospel shook the ancient world to its foundations, indeed tore down the heavens, and so helped to bring us to the ruin of the

---

36 Cf. David Bentley Hart, "God or Nothingness," in *I Am the Lord Your God: Christian Reflections on the Ten Commandments*, ed. Carl E. Braatan and Christopher R. Seitz (Grand Rapids: Eerdmans, 2005), 59. This piece was originally published at *First Things* under the title "Christ and Nothing" in 2003, at https://www.firstthings.com/article/2003/10/christ-and-nothing.

present moment."[37] Hart calls Christianity the "midwife of nihilism, not because it is itself nihilistic, but because it is too powerful in its embrace of the world and all of the world's mystery and beauty; and so to reject Christianity now is, of necessity, to reject everything except the barren anonymity of spontaneous subjectivity."

This means that the rejection of Christ risks perpetuating a new kind of darkness and violence. The one who rejects Christ does not easily slip back into innocent paganism. No, the rejection of Christ more readily translates into a vigorous resistance against the truth, goodness, and beauty that Christianity so effectively made its own. If what Hart says is true, when an entire culture begins to embrace the social and cultural death of God, the outcome will not be peaceful secularism (i.e., "the end of history") but stronger and more subversive forms of insecurity, transgression, violence, and evil. As the power that brought down the pagan gods seems to die out in our hearts, so too does our capacity to resist evil. You could say that this is precisely what we now face in a much more urgent way in our present postmodern condition. *The world is changed.*

As I see it, we stand today at a critical point in the history of Christian faith and Western culture. We can either recover the living foundations of Christian belief and faith, or we can head to the cultural and social abyss created by the rejection of Christ.

Unfortunately, at precisely this juncture we seem to face an exhausted, corrupt, and self-destructive Christianity, bereft of its own living culture, seemingly worn-out and preoccupied with false priorities, torn by divisions and unfaithfulness quite shocking in their depth, unable to respond effectively or evangelically to the increasing chorus of voices raised against it (more often than not from *within* it). We find ourselves on the defensive, struggling for words and reasons for what we believe. Most disturbing of all, we find that we too belong to the postmodern condition; we too are part of the crisis; our faith too is disturbed.

Evangelizing ourselves

When faced with all of this, where are we to turn? We might eventually come to realize that we ourselves are as much in need of evangelization as the "world." *This, I suggest, is the wrinkle that haunts many of today's efforts to mobilize the new evangelization.* We are perhaps as ignorant

---

37 Ibid., 69.

and insecure (maybe even deluded) as those we attempt to evangelize. At the very least, we bear the same wounds and scars as anyone else who participates in the practices of modernity and postmodernity.

Perhaps, then, at a deep level all of our programs, strategies, and techniques are hollow and empty of real content: perhaps all of our busy doing, all our sophistication, all our methods, are themselves cheap substitutes for a genuine encounter with the living God. Perhaps they merely mask our own crisis of faith, our own condition of unchallenged despair. Perhaps they even help to perpetuate the death of God.

I cannot yet tell you fully how I think the new evangelization might bear the best kind of fruit, for this must wait until we have confronted the post-Nietzschean challenge to faith. However, I would like to connect a few dots from what we have seen in this first chapter. My first point is this. Taking into consideration all that we have seen thus far about the postmodern condition, I submit, with Benedict XVI, that *evangelization must begin in the confessional*.[38] I mean this both symbolically and literally. We must face faith with a sense of our own inadequacy, a radical humility, and an awareness of our own shortcomings. We must face it with a genuine falling to our knees, a genuine taking-up of the task of conversion. We must, as it were, turn Nietzsche's critical gaze on our own selves.

Heidegger once quipped that "only a god can save us."[39] Indeed. Hart captures the pathos of our situation when, riffing on one of Heidegger's central claims, he argues that we live "in a very deep twilight indeed; ours is the time of the 'darkening of the world and the flight of the gods.' We are homeless in the world, standing over against it, and it is doubtful we will ever find ourselves at home again, at least if we are forced to rely on our own meager resources."[40] The question is always whether there is in the end something beyond our own resources.

Only in a renewed encounter with a God who truly gives himself, who truly redeems, changes, and sanctifies us, can we expect to discover a way out of the crisis of the postmodern condition. This is to say that the new evangelization must begin with *our authentic search for the face of this God.*

---

38 See Benedict's address to an event hosted by the Apostolic Penitentiary on March 9, 2012 in Rome, at http://www.ewtn.com/library/PAPALDOC/b16intforum.htm.

39 Heidegger said this in an interview in the German news magazine *Der Spiegel* in 1966.

40 David Bentley Hart, "A Philosopher in the Twilight: Heidegger's Philosophy as a Meditation on the Mystery of Being," in *First Things*, February 2011, at https://www.firstthings.com/article/2011/02/a-philosopher-in-the-twilight.

It must begin, that is, with the task of *our own re-evangelization*, with a renewed confrontation of our own selves. It must begin in the cultivation of a radically receptive, contemplative disposition that takes seriously our call to ongoing and transforming conversion, and that refuses to be satisfied with cheap alternatives. This is to recognize that it is only upon our knees that we will truly find ourselves — or better, that we will be found by an Other. It is only here that we will be found and named by a presence, by a Person who gives our lives a radically new direction, who transforms us into living icons of faith.

This, then, is my second suggestion. Evangelization will simply not work at the level of abstract ideas or devotional fervor, whether on the basis of reason or of faith. Something stronger is needed to penetrate to the existential core of the challenges facing faith in an age of the twilight of the gods, or indeed of the *death* of God. Simply following doctrinal formulas and principles will not be enough. When we give "reasons" for faith, these need to be made on the basis of the genuine and lived transformation afforded us in Christ, a transformation of which we ourselves — as baptized sons and daughters of God — have already tasted the first genuine fruits.

Hart argues that "Christian theology has no stake in the myth of disinterested rationality: the church has no arguments for its faith more convincing than the form of Christ; enjoined by Christ to preach the gospel, Christians must proclaim, exhort, bear witness, persuade — before other forms of reason can be marshaled."[41] Rediscovering the infrastructure and setting of this form must be the first imperative.

Today, particularly in a postmodern society that has given up on ideas and explanations, it is precisely the "organic" witness of a person who has internalized and who embodies the claims of Christ that will have the most power. Evangelization will thus be most effective at the level of a simple witness that shows the world that I really believe what I preach; that I am a living embodiment of the faith I proclaim. This is the way of the saint, the most effective evangelizer.

American Catholic theologian Michael Hanby sums this up nicely, remarking that "the act of love is incompatible with atheism."[42] This throws down the gauntlet, inasmuch as it requires us constantly to consider the

41 David Bentley Hart, *The Beauty of the Infinite: The Aesthetics of Christian Truth* (Grand Rapids: Eerdmans, 2003), 3.

42 Michael Hanby, "The Culture of Death, the Ontology of Boredom, and the Resistance of Joy," in *Communio* 31 (2004), 194, n. 31.

ways that we have failed and continue to fail in our witness to love. It forces us to face *our own* perpetual need to be evangelized. It requires us to live up to the great claim of love. It makes our words stand or fall according to how we have loved.

The revitalization of faith is thus not ultimately reducible to a program. Before faith can be effectively transmitted by formal pedagogical proce-dures, it must be manifest as a living personal presence; as the radiation of the Father's love in the most basic practices and exchanges of human relationships and culture. The heavy lifting of evangelization must take place here, or it will not take place at all.

How to evangelize like a hobbit

It is in this sense, then, that I think we can learn something profound from Tolkien's hobbits. The elf Lord Elrond keenly recognized that the truly great, the truly momentous, the truly valuable, begins in the very small, the simple, the lived, the very particular, and indeed, the *stubborn*: "Yet such is oft the course of deeds that move the wheels of the world: small hands do them because they must, while the eyes of the great are elsewhere."[43]

The way of the hobbit is insignificant when compared to the might of the world, of those who wield authority and power. But the way of power, the way of the world, is, as we should know, vulnerable, fickle, corrupting. The way of Sauron is the way of "coercive force," says American Baptist theologian Ralph C. Wood.[44] Sauron is the master identity politician: he lives and influences others by power, force, arrogance, and a constant and restless "doing" and controlling, manipulating, subverting, and corrupting all things and beings for his own ends.

Hobbits no doubt have their own particular failures and shortcomings. For example, the petty vices (i.e., envy, pride, greed, desire for status) that are to be found in every culture are present in hobbit culture as well. Bilbo and Frodo's own relatives, the Sackville-Bagginses, are archetypes of these tendencies. Moreover, hobbit culture as a whole is not immune to colonization by evil, as the final episode of the *Lord of the Rings* indicates.

And yet, Elrond's point is that there is something unique in hobbits that can translate into the highest and most effective virtue. Gandalf is

---

43 Tolkien, *The Fellowship of the Ring*, 351.

44 Ralph C. Wood, "'Sad, but Not Unhappy': J.R.R. Tolkien's Sorrowful Vision of Joy," *ABC Religion and Ethics* (June 2, 2014), at http://www.abc.net.au/religion/arti-cles/2014/06/02/4017211.htm.

constantly surprised by the hobbits' resiliency and courage, even amidst their weaknesses and failings. More than other peoples and races in Middle Earth, it seems, hobbits are the inheritors and possessors of a cultural ethos that gives them a kind of immunity to pride and the grossest ambitions of power and status. While it may seem entirely plausible to think that the floor of Hell is paved with the skulls of bishops, as St. Athanasius of Alexandria (296–373) is said to have quipped, it seems doubtful that one could find enough hobbit skulls for such a purpose.

Hobbits are under no illusions about themselves and their place in the world, nor are they particularly worried by their "small" place in it. Well-formed hobbits are not likely to be swayed by false prophets, "progressive" solutions, identity politics, Jesuitical casuistry, or bureaucratic or institutional idolatry. They prefer to stubbornly seek and cling to the authentic ways of simple living handed on by their ancestors. They are not easily attracted by quick fixes, easy solutions, or the allure of power contained in the Ruling Ring.

And so, says Wood, "Frodo proves to be a fit bearer of the Ring because he does not seek, but only reluctantly accepts his task." Of course, even he fails in the end, giving himself over to the power of the Ring at the moment of truth. But in this moment Frodo learns that at the end of the day, all is out of his control and power; in Christ, we are met with the one who overcomes our weaknesses, who intervenes and saves us, often by the most surprising means. "Frodo and his friends learn what for Tolkien is the deepest truth," says Wood, "how to surrender one's life to the good, how to 'lose' evil 'treasures' and thus how to live with moral and spiritual concentration...."

In this book I will argue that all our attempts to revitalize and proclaim the faith must resist the power of the Ring in all of its many shapes and temptations; we must resist the way of efficient force, the temptation of quick pastoral fixes, the coercive and reductive manipulations of political power (those of both Left and Right), slavery to bureaucratic process, empty catch-phrases and moralisms, and the corporate ethos embodied in things like "mission statements."

There is but one mission statement: "Jesus Christ, and him crucified" (1 Cor. 2:2). As Wood argues, "The great temptation is to take short-cuts, to follow the easy way, to arrive quickly. In the antique world of Middle-Earth, magic offers the surest escape from slowness and suffering. It is the equivalent of our machines." The postmodern condition makes it painfully obvious that there can be no short-cuts. There are no easy ways. There is no quick arrival. There is only the long way, the deep search, the slow encounter, the full *abiding*. The only way forward is the "road less traveled," the "narrow gate," the "way of love" — in short, the *baptismal* path.

Though the light of the world may seem to be fading, we remain the guardians of that light. Hobbits perhaps show the possibility of the rising of a new light. "For the time will soon come when Hobbits will shape the fortune of all."

TWO

Genealogies of Modernity

I do not expect "history" to be anything but a "long defeat."
J. R. R. Tolkien, Letter 195

IN CHAPTER ONE, I NOTED THAT THE WORLD HAS changed. We no longer inhabit an enchanted world. Rather, we inhabit a disenchanted world of terminal modernity, a world torn from the inside out by a postmodern anxiety and depression.

So, from our point of view as Christians, how did we get into this mess?

Dealing with discontinuity

This is, of course, an extremely complex question. And seeing as I have in the previous chapter implied that at least some of the blame is to be laid at the feet of certain tendencies within the historical Christian tradition itself, a short discussion of the relationship between tradition and truth is necessary before we jump into the vagaries of historical interpretation. One can also observe the pertinence of this discussion at a time in the Church when fundamental disagreements about questions of development (i.e., continuity versus rupture) are the rule of the day.

On the one hand, we believe that the Spirit has been given to us to guide the Church through the vicissitudes of history, to protect us from error, to safeguard the deposit of faith. To put your faith in the Church is to entrust yourself to a sure guide through the difficult periods of human history, the difficult times of our lives. Christ tells Simon: "you are Peter, and upon this rock I will build my church, and the gates of hell shall not prevail against it" (Mt. 16:18).

At the same time, a Spirit-guided Church is not a magic or mechanical formula that simply gives us all the answers or that prevents us, in our freedom, from asking the wrong questions, investing in the wrong ideas, imagining things that are contrary to authentic faith, or in some ages and circumstances seeming to almost lose the plot altogether.[1] It does not seem a coincidence that very soon after calling Peter the rock, Christ also calls him *Satan*: "he turned and said to Peter, 'Get behind me Satan! You are a hindrance to me; for you are not on the side of God but of men'" (Mt. 16:23). The assurance that the gates of Hell shall not prevail against the Church does not save us from temporal pain. Nor is it a guarantee that specific shepherds of the Church will not fail in their mandate of fidelity to the deposit of faith. Some may indeed be worthy of Christ's harsh words. Von Balthasar admits that "the whole Church cannot go astray for long in important matters. But even if the promised Advocate let the Church as a whole find or regain once more the right course, with what groping and stumbling does she find her way along this right path!"[2]

The teaching office of the earthly Church (the Magisterium) is not, especially in its ordinary function, infallible in the sense that it can see *all* things at *all* times, like the all-seeing eye of Sauron, so to speak. The Magisterium is not an absolute guarantee against all the ambiguities of historical interpretation, judgment, and possible distortions by the concrete leadership of the Church that mediates its teaching. It does not render us fully immune, in other words, from the effects of various kinds of failures of leadership or other dysfunctions of perception that may appear in this or that historical configuration. There have been some pretty dark episodes, and even failures, in the history of the Church.

Do not get me wrong: I believe in and submit to the authority of the teaching office of the Church. But at the same time, this should not mask a healthy and proper awareness of the way its legitimate charism is at times mediated by contextual limitations which may hamper its ability to speak

---

1   In an interview on Bavarian television in 1997, then-Cardinal Joseph Ratzinger was asked a question about whether the Holy Spirit specifically picks the man who emerges as Pope from the conclave. "I would not say so," he answered, "in the sense that the Holy Spirit picks out the Pope.... I would say that the Spirit does not exactly take control of the affair, but rather like a good educator, as it were, leaves us much space, much freedom, without entirely abandoning us. Thus the Spirit's role should be understood in a much more elastic sense, not that he dictates the candidate for whom one must vote. Probably the only assurance he offers is that the whole thing cannot be entirely ruined." In other words, there is lots of wiggle-room here for us to cause all sorts of trouble.

2   Hans Urs von Balthasar, "The Fathers, the Scholastics, and Ourselves," in *Communio* 24 (1997), 369.

clearly and prophetically. Sometimes it may overreach, other times it may be wrongly used or neglected by those entrusted with its care.

The challenge of history thus means to accept a certain degree of discontinuity and inconsistency in the march of faith. It must be to accept that certain ways of approaching an issue in the past may be seen, with the benefit of hindsight, as inadequate or limiting ways of thinking that become a problem which subsequent generations must revisit. And so there is need for a sometimes robust criticism of the Church's historical decisions and activities, often in relation to political powers and social norms, for example. None of this in principle means that core dogma and doctrines can legitimately "change" in the sense of flat contradictions or "creative" evasions of fundamental received teaching. If some suggest that doctrines might change thus, *beware*. It is rather about learning from both the successes and mistakes of the past and trying to bring them to bear in some positive way to our own historical appropriation of faith. It is about honestly recognizing how cataclysmic historical events—such as the Reformation, the Enlightenment, the Sexual Revolution, for example—can sometimes shape or expose the quality of our broader frameworks and presuppositions. This, I suggest, is part of the value of the kind of "genealogical" thinking that we will do in this chapter: it allows us to understand the relationship of ideas to their original and changing contexts in order to discern and assess their value for us today in our own context.

So we must therefore be prepared to always seek the deeper reality hidden beneath the tensions, dissonance, and complexity that accompany the task of living in history. That is, our default position when it comes to difficult questions and challenges should be to presume that underneath confusion and ideology there is always a truth that Christ is inviting us to pursue more faithfully. Our motivation must be to patiently and prayerfully seek after this truth, always willing to accept an answer that goes deeper than our desires or the spirit of the age.

To do this is to open ourselves to the "Spirit of truth" (Jn. 16:13), the one who seeks to lead us into a knowledge and understanding, not of the things of this world (cf. 1 Jn. 2:15), but of the things of the Father and the Son. And by this deeper point of entrusting we will discover a way to a more profound encounter with the truth.[3]

---

3 Note how John Paul II's response to the question of contraception in this case, rather than thinning it out, instead *deepened* and *enriched* our understanding of the sacramental

All of this means that the task of interpretation looks neither to some perceived ideal past state nor to some present or future earthly omega point. Recall Charles Taylor's point about how the medievals would likely view us as "blasphemous" and "licentious." But we need to be careful. While it is true that we have our faults, it is equally true that the medievals had theirs too. Though they made perennial insights, they had their own blind spots, their own historically inflected and informed preferences and enthusiasms inasmuch as they, like us, were limited by the particularity of their own space and time. This is just part of existing *in* time and space, rather than outside it.

If we are honest with ourselves, none of us would really want to go back to that world, even if there are aspects of that world that are true, good, and beautiful. Moreover, the past *as past* is always inaccessible to us. Yes, truth is eternal and immutable, an image of the very Triune God from which it comes. And yet we also "see dimly, as in a mirror" (1 Cor. 13:12). Each age sees dimly in a different way. No single age has a corner on truth, because no age can see everything from every angle.

This is as true for us as any other age, but the difference is that the present must weigh and measure both the past and the present simultaneously. We are called to *this* moment, even as we seek to preserve the good of the past while overcoming the bad. And so every generation must confront the faith in new ways, for history gives it to us as a responsibility and task that must be placed in the context of *this* world, *this* time, *these* historical challenges — for us, the world, time, and challenges of the postmodern condition.

In regards to the problem of tradition and truth, then, an *authentic* faithfulness to tradition must always be a properly *theological act*, one motivated by acquiring the wisdom and perspective of a deeper fidelity to Christ, something that can happen only through docility to the Spirit of Truth. This may of course be easy to state theoretically; what it looks like practically is another matter. And so the point of this chapter is to try to wrestle with some of the ambiguities of historical interpretation. There are no easy answers, and the task will always be incomplete. But I hope the exercise itself will start to get us thinking in different ways, even if provisionally, about some of the critical questions facing Christianity today.

---

character of spousal love. This is one example where a clear principle of both faithfulness to the tradition *and* the theological desire to go deeper produced an *excess* of theological meaning that we had not yet appreciated in its fullness.

Approaching the tapestry

In what follows, I will take you through a whirlwind tour of some major thinkers' genealogies of the history of Christianity, particularly in relation to the events that took us from the age of Christendom to the age of Enlightenment, to modernity, and on to our own postmodern-inflected modernity. Each of these thinkers picks up on some element of Christian theology in relation to the momentous events of history, and attempts to pinpoint where things went wrong, what this or that motivation or decision caused or facilitated.

Canadian Reformed theologian Hans Boersma evokes the image of a tapestry to convey this idea.[4] He speaks of the early Christian and medieval appropriation of the wisdom of the ancients, bringing faith into a fruitful dialogue with reason, as the "weaving" of the tapestry. He then refers to the "unravelling" of the tapestry in the late medieval period, where faith and reason start to part ways. In the "cutting" of the tapestry by the "scissors" of modernity, reason starts to usurp faith. Finally, he speaks of the task of "reweaving" the tapestry, of confronting the question of what went wrong, of discovering a new way forward.

In this chapter, I will discuss some of the threads of the tapestry and what provoked their unravelling.

Thinking within love

Let us return to our question: how, from a Christian point of view, did we get into the "postmodern" mess that we presently find ourselves in? How did we get here from there?

American Evangelical theologian Stanley Hauerwas makes a simple and provocative suggestion: he bluntly portrays postmodernism as "the outworking of mistakes in Christian theology correlative to the attempt to make Christianity 'true' apart from faithful witness."[5] Like Hart, Hauerwas thinks that what went wrong is that we lost confidence and gave up hope in the reasons that *faith as faith* gives us, in the "reasons" provided by our own baptismal encounter with Christ. You might say that we tried to make faith "sing" for a conductor named "reason," to make it rationally and

---

4 Cf. Hans Boersma, *Heavenly Participation: The Weaving of a Sacramental Tapestry* (Grand Rapids: Eerdmans, 2011).

5 Stanley Hauerwas, "The Christian Difference, or Surviving Postmodernism," in *The Blackwell Companion to Postmodern Theology*, ed. Graham Ward (Oxford: Blackwell, 2005), 147.

socially acceptable, to make it fit more comfortably with the powers and principalities. For both Hart and Hauerwas, this sours the notes, makes them either "flat" or "sharp," and thus destroys the possibility of a deeper harmony between faith and reason.

You might have guessed by now that I am sympathetic to this view. As I said earlier, the meaning of the mother's smile cannot be sought in anything but the smile itself. That is, to try to explain its meaning by categories other than love, trust, beauty, joy, and desire would be to render the experience mute, to constrict its pregnant fullness.

Now, one's quintessentially Catholic question might be this: do we not believe in both faith *and* reason? In other words, is there not a place for *reason as reason*, for reason as a preparation for faith (*praeparatio evangelica*), or as an explanation for faith? Is this not part of the authentically Christian heritage?

In certain respects, yes, this is true. We do believe in the capacity of the human intellect to encounter truth in a meaningful way. And reason in this sense has always played an important role in helping to express faith. However, perhaps historically we have had confidence in our thinking and comprehending capacities just a little too much or in the wrong way. Perhaps we have not considered carefully enough how reason is always led and framed by something. Reason is always inflected — it is always shaped by something. Reason can be intentionally or unintentionally crafted and manipulated to embody and legitimate our own desires, whether they be our desire for order and security, for power and gain, or for love and belonging. All of us have our allegiances pulled in many different directions from a wide array of sources, and from day to day we might not be aware of how vulnerable and changing our desires actually are. Moreover, what reason — no matter how developed or sanctified — can never give us is the encounter with the *historical* person of Jesus Christ.

I am not against reason as such; what I am against, however, is the Christian who acts as if he or she were not always already shaped by someone and something, and who is not therefore attentive to the way that these experiences shape their desires, their loves, their sense of the world, and their pre-understanding of what qualifies as "rational." Nietzsche was on to something important. Balthasar argued that conscious cognition and the reflective capacities of the intellect are always formed and shaped by a relation to an event/encounter and a "someone" that/who *precedes* and *frames* the working of the intellect. Knowledge, then, is always at its heart the product of an encounter with the other, not simply the function of discursive and abstract thinking.

For Balthasar, the primordial model of this deeply "eventful" or relational framing of reason and knowledge is found in the event of love between a mother and her child symbolized by the mother's smile. This is how he describes it:

> After a mother has smiled at her child for many days and weeks, she finally receives her child's smile in response. She has awakened love in the heart of her child, and as the child awakens to love, it also awakens to knowledge: the initially empty sense-impressions gather meaningfully around the core of the Thou. Knowledge (with its whole complex of intuition and concept) comes into play, because the play of love has already begun beforehand, initiated by the mother, the transcendent.[6]

We can note here how human thought is received from within the encounter of love. Its deepest ground is not in the thinking subject himself or in the "structures" of reality, but rather *from the other* and *in the other*, in dialogue with the particular historical person who stands before you in the flesh, who caresses you, who speaks to you, who lovingly draws out a response from you. It takes root in the subject from "inside" the experience of the radiation of a smile.

If reason is going to be its true self, what matters, then, is that the relation that frames and shapes it is one of love and gift, permeated by the unconditional radiance of love symbolized by a mother's smile. If it is, there is hope that reason will be able to perceive the world as hinting, however inchoately, at an *eternal* relation of love that might break the bonds of sin and death. There is hope that in and through the experience of a prior love the child will realize that its existence is real, that reality

---

6 Hans Urs von Balthasar, *Love Alone Is Credible*, trans. D.C. Schindler (San Francisco: Ignatius, 2004), 76. Elsewhere, von Balthasar explains it thus: "The child's 'I' awakens in the experience of a 'Thou': in its mother's smile through which it learns that it is contained, affirmed and loved in a relationship which is incomprehensively encompassing, already actual, sheltering and nourishing. The body which it snuggles into, a soft, warm and nourishing kiss, is a kiss of love in which it can take shelter because it has been sheltered there a priori. The awakening of its consciousness is a late occurrence, in comparison with this basic mystery of unfathomable depth." Hans Urs von Balthasar, *The Glory of the Lord: A Theological Aesthetics*, vol. 5, *The Realm of Metaphysics in the Modern Age*, trans. Oliver Davies, Andrew Louth, Brian McNeil, John Saward, and Rowan Williams (San Francisco: Ignatius, 1991), 616.

has meaning, and that being joined to the other is the fullest realization of reason, one that will infinitely expand and enrich its capacities.

If reason is *not* shaped by a deeper relation of love, by contrast, the danger is that it will perceive reality, not as hope, but rather as violence and despair. A child who has not received a smile, who is not loved, will be led to think that darkness exceeds light. Similarly, the powers of thought and judgement not sufficiently inflected by the priority of love will deceive themselves by making concepts, formulas, and structures the measure of truth. Reason in this sense will be led to see reality not in relations, but merely in substances. And it will thereby degrade our capacity to perceive the genuine depth and realism of the mother's smile that in fact constitutes and pervades our existence,[7] and furthermore the depth and realism of the historical event of the Son, the true constitution of our existence (cf. Col. 1:15–16).

Keeping in mind that the above suggestions are still provisional and will be further explicated in subsequent sections of this chapter, we can nevertheless advance the conditional hypothesis that it is precisely a departure from what American Catholic philosopher David C. Schindler, following Balthasar, calls a "dramatic notion of reason"[8] — one framed and born from the mother's smile — that leads to the despair and violence catalogued in this book's first chapter. To extricate the thinking, willing, and knowing self from its native soil in a loving relation to the other is to drive it first to abstraction and idolatry and then to suicide, i.e., nihilism.

The argument that I will begin to sketch here and take up again in chapter five is that in the end, the only effective way to prevent reason from committing suicide and the only way to recover a reason not held captive by the suicidal logic of the death of God that presently frames our modern and postmodern horizon is to re-conceive it from within the heart of *the* relation that forms the Christian self: the relation of baptismal adoption, *the* relation of a "smile" experienced in the time and space of the practices of the Church that truly constitutes and frames the self and its capacities.

---

7   See my argument about the capacity of the mother's smile to rescue reason from the impersonal conditions of truth understood as concept or structure in Conor Sweeney, *Sacramental Presence after Heidegger: Onto-Theology, Sacraments, and the Mother's Smile* (Eugene: Cascade, 2015).

8   David C. Schindler, "'Wie Kommt der Mensch in die Theologie?': Heidegger, Hegel, and the Stakes of Onto-Theo-Logy," *Communio* 32 (2005), 665.

Relating God and man

Of course, it is true that reason has played an important role in our tradition. The question to consider regarding reason is not whether it may not have a legitimate role to play in the understanding of faith and the pursuit of truth. The question is rather *which* reason we are talking about and *which* place we assign it in the whole mystery of human existence.

One thinker who is often regarded as having got it right was St. Thomas Aquinas (1225–1274), with his integration of faith with Aristotelian realist epistemology and metaphysics. In his 1998 encyclical on the theme of faith and reason, *Fides et Ratio*, St. John Paul II rehearsed a common refrain from recent popes when he referred to the "enduring originality" of Thomas's thought. "Thomas had the great merit," John Paul II said here, "of giving pride of place to the harmony which exists between faith and reason. Both the light of reason and the light of faith come from God, he argued; hence there can be no contradiction between them" (43).

The merit of Thomas's synthesis is often said to lie in the way his framing of reason is informed by his broader metaphysical achievements. He has often been lauded for avoiding dualistic and monistic interpretations of existence, charting a delicate path between the risk of thinking of the existence of individual beings merely as a ghostly or ultimately unreal participation in Being or divinity (into which it is collapsed) and that of reducing Being or divinity to the multiplicity of real existing individuals who have an existence independent of a divine reference point. Put differently, is reality "One" or is it "many"? Do individual beings (the "many") "exist" in their own right with an identity distinct from a divine being or process (the "One")? Are individual uniqueness and freedom in the end "mere shadow or illusion,"[9] merely part of the One? But before hearing Thomas's precise answer to this question and its import for the question of human reason, we need to tell a bit more of the back story.

Where Greek philosophy would always wrestle with the tensions of the One-many dialectic from within a closed understanding of the cosmos, early Christianity injected new life into the question by positing creaturely existence (the "many") as the free creation of a loving, trinitarian God (the "One") who in the Incarnate Son has (mysteriously, paradoxically) poured himself out beyond himself, creating beings who are destined to relate to him as sons and daughters (and who therefore

---

9 Boersma, *Heavenly Participation*, 37.

cannot truly understand themselves apart from the Father) but who, as sons and daughters, are therefore also distinct from him (and who therefore possess their own individual act of existence). By this, says Hart, "God and world alike were liberated from the fetters of necessity; God could be accorded His true transcendence and the world its true character as divine gift."[10]

In this, Christianity articulated the grounds for an understanding of existence both as "One" — everything derives from, depends on, and is destined for a return to God — *and* "many" — creatures have been granted a genuinely real and distinct existence as an act of gratuity on the part of the Creator who "makes room" for an "other" not strictly co-extensive with himself. Note that this principle has precedence within God himself, in whom a kind of otherness and difference is already present in the relation of the trinitarian Persons who, though each fully God, are nevertheless differentiated in the one Divine Substance by way of the mode of person.

The challenge for Christianity would be to keep this delicate unity-in-tension in proper balance. Historically, Christianity primarily conceptualized the relation of worldly being or "nature" to God by reference to Platonic and Aristotelian philosophy. If Plato emphasized the participation of worldly entities in the eternal forms, Aristotle stressed the integrity and powers internal to worldly entities. Very generally speaking, the Patristic period of Christianity tended to see in Platonic and Neoplatonic philosophy an apt vehicle to express how the creature's act of existence is at all times dependent on and a part of its divine source and how all creation must be interpreted dynamically in relation to this divine source. As Boersma explains, "One of the reasons Neo-Platonism has been so attractive to theologians through the centuries is that the Neo-Platonic view of the cosmos as 'going out' from God and 'returning' to him — the so-called *exitus-reditus* schema — was broadly compatible with Pauline Christianity."[11]

If there was a risk here, it was that this did not always adequately safeguard the *distinction* between God and man, nor did it always give due weight to the sheer historical novelty and significance of a God who becomes flesh in time and history as an *event*, who in Christ enters into an indissoluble relationship with it. Without a strong enough sense of the

10 Hart, "God or Nothingness," 67–8.
11 Boersma, *Heavenly Participation*, 5.

creature as given a truly distinct act of existence, the risk was that in the end the existence of the creature could just be pantheistically absorbed into divinity, or worse, abrogate the status of divinity for itself. From another angle, Balthasar speaks of how "spiritualization, presented in a thousand different colorations, is the basic tendency of the patristic epoch."[12] This tendency toward spiritualization, understood in the sense of an ethereal escape from the world, could lead in certain instances to a denigration of bodiliness and a downplaying of the sheer historical novelty of the Incarnation and the subsequent centrality of the particular ecclesial and sacramental transmission of Christ's presence in the world.

Belgian Catholic phenomenologist and religious philosopher Louis Dupré speaks of how

> despite a Christian concern to safeguard creation's integrity, Platonism left a clear mark on its early formulations, insofar as it located the image of God (God's proper dwelling place) primarily in the mind. The body, though not deprived of traces of the divine, belonged to a lower level that often conflicted with the soul's aspirations.[13]

Dupré recounts how confidence in the Platonic synthesis began to wane within the conditions of the decline and fall of the Roman Empire, and in the context of debates between the theologian Pelagius (354–420) and the great African bishop St. Augustine (354–430) on the nature of grace. Grand mystical visions of cosmic harmony and order were replaced by "a growing moral pessimism as Rome and its Occidental empire were disintegrating."[14] To the Pelagian emphasis on a fallen human nature that must work hard by penance and mortification to clean itself up, Augustine replies, no, what you really need is grace to purify this broken nature. While Augustine here correctly highlights nature's reliance on grace, Dupré argues that he shares with his Pelagian opponents a new pessimism about our capacity to more than *relatively* overcome its fallen tendencies here on earth. What we have, then, with the otherwise Platonically-inspired Augustine is something of a new pessimism regarding nature. Augustine affirms that all created things are good and come from God (*exitus*) and

---

12 Balthasar, "The Fathers, the Scholastics, and Ourselves," 375.

13 Louis Dupré, *Passage to Modernity: An Essay in the Hermeneutics of Nature and Culture* (New Haven: Yale University Press, 1993), 168.

14 Ibid., 33.

are destined to be made perfect in the Son and returned to the Father (*reditus*). But he also has a keen sense of how all of this is complicated by sin and fallenness. Place all of this in the context of the debate with Pelagius and the general decline and pessimism of the age, and Dupré's point is that a kind of shift in how these perennial themes are approached is taking place.

Thus a new accent on grace relative to nature slowly begins to emerge, a stronger sense that if nature is to be able to bear the weight of divinity, it must first be purified of its shortcomings. The new pessimism, coupled with what had always been Latin theology's somewhat less mystical and more practical approach to theology compared to the Christian East,[15] led to an increasingly muted role for the sacramental and mystical perspective of deification, i.e., existence as above all else — in its first and last movements — union with God through Christ. Though perhaps there was in this more Neoplatonic approach a risk of idealism and a tendency to *underestimate* the concrete challenge of sin and fallenness, the claim I am making in this book is that when wedded with a more baptismal and sacramental conception of what it means to be in Christ, the perspectives of divine adoption and deification are precisely the remedy for better addressing some the historical tensions concerning how nature relates to grace.

In broad strokes, then, new pessimism about nature and a practical concern with moral and juridical issues started to move Western theology out of the headspace of filial relation to the Father in Christ to a preoccupation with the healing and perfecting of human nature, one that risked abstracting this healing from the horizon of deification. The unity of God's grace began to splinter into something parceled out to various points of specific need in the creature. From this point of view, in relation to the problem of nature, grace began to be conceived primarily in "medicinal" terms, that is, as offering a healing that could allow nature to be its ideal self, but as natural. Here, the risk is that once healing nature is thematized, the broader goal and relation of this healing to deification could become downgraded.

One should of course clarify that this not to say that everyone immediately began thinking about grace in a purely instrumental way, nor that this new medicinal emphasis on grace was not in most cases framed by a greater recognition of grace as given for nature's ultimate destination

15 Cf. ibid., 32.

in God. Rather, what is important here is that imaginative space is being carved out for a kind of semi-autonomous conception of nature and man as having integrity and transparency distinct from a relation to God. What is produced here in the fifth century is by no means yet the fully autonomous thinking self of the Enlightenment who needs neither relation to others nor to God to reason effectively; but certain remote seeds have already been sown. Once the marks of the creature's deeper sacramental relation to divinity are rubbed off, it will be but a short step to conceiving the operations, objects, and ends of the intellect as purely secular in character.

To return to Dupré's story or "genealogy," we see him next account for the renewed optimism which began to characterize the 11th century. The gloom and pessimism that began the path to a more muted appreciation of nature as nature now morph into an unexpected confidence and optimism about nature as a new medieval order emerges. Culturally speaking, says Dupré, "The mood lightened, the vision concentrated, and for the first time a genuine Christian naturalism emerged."[16] This "new naturalism" inspired literary, scientific, and artistic perspectives typified by a sense of nature as a dynamic and primordial site of God's self-expression. "Christians once again came to trust the impulses of nature, and they began to pay attention to the subtler feelings and emotions of the soul."[17] Here, we still have a thematization of nature, but one permeated by a new sense of optimism and creativity rather than pessimism and reserve.

Philosophically speaking, this new emphasis on the integrity of nature as a reliable source and inspiration for meaning finds expression in St. Thomas's new synthesis of faith and reason, a synthesis in part inspired by a *ressourcement* of Aristotelian philosophy in Scholastic theology. While St. Thomas broadly retains the Platonic-Augustinian conception of worldly entities as structured by their coming forth from and their return to the trinitarian God (*exitus-reditus*), there is also a new sense of the rational intelligibility of nature and of the individual as bearer of a rational nature, something that strictly speaking did not require faith for its basic intelligibility — so that, for example, one could on the basis of uninflected reason recognize the ends commensurate or proportionate to human nature.

If Platonism linked creature to Creator by the notion of participation as a kind of mystical *via pulchritudinis* (way of beauty), Thomas employs

---

16 Ibid., 33.
17 Ibid., 34.

the more rationally clear and distinct Aristotelian notion of causality to supplement the idea of participation. As "efficient" cause, God is distinct from his creation as cause is from effect. This allows a clearer delineation of man as *different* than God, with the result that "God can no longer in any way be regarded as the being of things, except in the sense that he is their efficient, exemplary and final cause."[18] If efficient causality safeguards the absolute distinction between Creator and creature, "exemplary" and "final" causality ensure that, notwithstanding the distinction between Creator and creation, there is also a real similarity to and end in the God who has created man in his image and likeness in and through Christ the eternal Son, both God and man. That is, in both creating and saving man, God shares Himself with His creatures in a real way, even if He does not give His being or self per se.

And so God is in and behind everything as cause and sustaining source. The creature is intelligible only inasmuch as he recognizes that he is *not* God, but that he comes from, is related to, and destined for God. There is thus both fundamental dissimilarity (man is not God, and God does not need man to be God) and simultaneous similarity (man is from God and for God). God is therefore both transcendent and immanent.

What is new in Thomas is thus a more precise sense of the creature's distinction from God (causality), even if in Thomas this distinction ultimately serves to more adequately clarify the proper scope of the creature's relation to God (participation). One of the consequences of the shift to causality is that with the new sense of a clear distinction between God and man, Thomas grants a new measure of autonomy or created integrity to the creature and to nature. This is significant in that were one to either bracket out or reduce the necessity of exemplary and final causality, efficient causality could then become the means for a view of creaturely existence as merely given to itself and set in motion by a God who is a First Cause or Prime Mover and who remains operationally distinct from his creation, as will happen with Enlightenment deism.

But this is not to say that Thomas himself thought in these terms. Against a "neoscholastic" interpretation of St. Thomas dominant in the 19th and early 20th centuries, a movement in 20th-century scholarship — led by

---

18 Hans Urs von Balthasar, *The Glory of the Lord: A Theological Aesthetics*, vol. 4, *The Realm of Metaphysics in Antiquity*, trans. Brian McNeil, Andrew Louth, John Saward, Rowan Williams, Oliver Davies (San Francisco: Ignatius, 1989), 393.

French Jesuit Henri de Lubac (1896–1991)[19] — argued that Thomas never construed any legitimate autonomy of the creature or its distinction from God as grounds for the suggestion that after Christ one could construct an account of human nature and its ends in isolation from the historical reality of the creature's election and adoption in Christ. These thinkers thought there was little in Thomas that could justify a "duplex ordo" interpretation of nature and grace which posited two distinct ends for the human person: a natural end and a supernatural end. Moreover, de Lubac complained that far from protecting the "gratuity of grace," this trenchant distinction instead tended to foster a dualism between the temporal and eternal dimensions, one that was fast reaching its zenith in a worldly secularism that had begun to deny the supernatural altogether.

For example, Balthasar argues that St. Thomas still "attributes to human nature a single, supernatural goal. The natural goal of which he sometimes speaks, he regards as the best that a mortal man can achieve in this earthly life, but one which would never suffice to justify the existence and the particular nature of mankind."[20] Similarly, Dupré posits that "Aquinas never conceived of nature as an independent reality endowed with a self-sufficient *finis naturalis*."[21] In other words, in Thomas the sense of the creature as given an act of existence in its own right is still framed by a greater sense that this act only finds its fulfillment when it rests in God's existence. Within this synthesis, then, Thomas grants certain powers of intelligibility to the intellect while also continuing to claim that beatitude is in fact the proper end and fulfillment of its powers.

Nevertheless, even if one argues that the place for the creaturely (nature, reason) and the place for the divine (grace, faith) are correctly balanced in St. Thomas himself, it seems undeniable that in the end his synthesis, no less than the Platonic synthesis, bears similar fault lines and potential areas of ambiguity that could (and would) in the end be exploited for a conception of human existence that possessed its own ground and ends beyond a more basic orientation to a divine source and end. We have already mentioned the risk of the notion of causality being degraded to a conception of God as merely a First Cause.

19 Cf. *The Mystery of the Supernatural*, trans. Rosemary Sheed (New York: Herder & Herder, 2016).

20 Hans Urs von Balthasar, *A Theological Anthropology* (Eugene: Wipf and Stock, 1967), 82.

21 Dupré, *Passage to Modernity*, 172.

From another angle, Dupré thinks that Thomas does not fully overcome the Latin tendency to think of grace in medicinal terms, and as such, sees the continuing risk of construing grace merely "as a supernatural cure for a natural disease and, as such, as initiating a wholly different order of grace."[22]

This, when coupled with an Aristotelian confidence in the integrity and powers internal to worldly entities, could lead, first, to a closed understanding of nature, and then to a fully secular understanding once any remaining conditioning features of religious belief are sloughed off. The fact of the matter is that by as early as the 16th century, it was becoming commonplace to articulate an account of human nature in abstraction from that nature's supernatural finality. This would become a dominant interpretation of St. Thomas by the neo-scholastics or neo-Thomists up to the Second Vatican Council.

From a purely practical point of view, Dupré suggests that "the very complexity of the synthesis made it vulnerable to being distorted in one direction or another."[23] Or, as Catholic historian Christopher Dawson (1889–1970) remarked, "the completeness and symmetry of the Thomist synthesis should not blind us to the fact that it rests on a very delicate balance of opposing forces and different traditions which can only be maintained by a strict adherence to an order of ethical and metaphysical requirements that rests in the last resort upon an act of faith."[24]

Which raises the question: to what extent does the encounter with and justification of Christ stand or fall by reference to the second-order conceptual systems that we conceive to explain faith? After all, in *Fides et Ratio* John Paul II says that "the Church has no philosophy of her own nor does she canonize any one particular philosophy in preference to others" (49).

I am not saying that we should not grapple with the relation between Christian faith and worldly wisdom. Many such historical grapplings have been necessary and some have borne lasting fruit. Nor do I deny that some philosophies will have more to offer to faith than others. I am rather saying that we must always remember that our engagement with the thought-forms of worldly wisdom, no matter how nuanced and profound that wisdom might be, must always be performed from a more primordial point of contact, from within a more constitutive sacramental event

22 Ibid.

23 Ibid., 173.

24 Christopher Dawson, *Religion and the Rise of Western Culture* (New York: Doubleday, 1991), 177.

and relation of love that, strictly speaking, stands outside of the reason or knowledge capable of being generated by the measure of the thinking subject's cognitive powers.

Thinking must, perhaps, have as its deeper ground paradox, mystery, and relation; specifically, the paradox, mystery, and relation communicated in the baptismal movement of love that transforms the individual into a person, into a child of God the Father. This relation may do more to transform and reorder the structures of perceiving and knowing inherited from classical Greek epistemology and metaphysics than we have in the past appreciated. Perhaps we should take St. Paul more seriously when he says that "whoever is in Christ is a new creation: the old things have passed away; behold, new things have come" (2 Cor. 5:17).

At the deepest level, then, a question might be raised about Scholastic theology from the point of view of what we could simply call the "imagination." It might be asked whether a certain Aristotelian emphasis (distorted or otherwise) on knowing rather than loving ends up subtly undermining the properly deifying criteria for relation of the creature to God. There is always a temptation here to lodge truth in things rather than relations, to conceive of beatitude as primarily an intellectual act, rather than as something more akin to an affective experience.

My point is not that the classical philosophical insights that have helped to shape and express faith should be jettisoned. Rather, I think that there is scope to immerse and ground them more deeply in the living forms of a baptismal existence whose first referent is the ecclesial transmission of the Father's elective and adoptive love accomplished in the Son, by which as sons in the Son we are given the deepest internal access to a reality that transcends the normal capacities and scope of the created intellect. Certainly, the relative wisdom of reason and nature is not contrary to this ultimate gift; it is in fact its created preparation. Nevertheless, my central concern here has to do with how the person today, living amidst the ruins of the social and cultural death of God, might hope to realistically and meaningfully access truth and meaning in such conditions. And my conviction in this context, particularly in regards to either the lapsed or struggling Christian, is that a path to truth and meaning that more confidently begins by sketching a vision of existence unapologetically shaped by faith is in fact a more compelling and much-needed approach.

More constitutively, I want also to ask whether this contemporary crisis might provoke inspiration for a more uninhibited systematic articulation of the person according to the existential conditions of baptismal adoption, not only as an addition that "tops up" identity, but one that in fact reconstitutes it. By this, we may therefore retroactively outflank and overcome the very rationalist pretensions that provoked the death of God in the first place, thereby acquiring a better immunity from such pretensions in the future.

Finding reason through baptismal faith after the death of God

So, having been through this preliminary genealogical tour, what might we now be able to say about the specific problem of faith and reason that we started out with? As I have already indicated, to this day St. Thomas has often been appealed to as an example of how this relationship might be fruitfully construed. It remains the conviction of Catholic Christianity that there is a genuinely harmonious relationship between faith and reason. I do not contest this, except to say that the deeper factors that inform faith and reason's relation must always be the subject of ongoing scrutiny. I am thus happy to agree with John Paul II, who began *Fides et Ratio* by claiming that "Faith and reason are like two wings on which the human spirit rises to the contemplation of truth."

We must now ask, however, in the name of this deeper scrutiny, just what or whom the wings are attached to. Who is actually driving this thing? What is the body of the bird? What is the engine that keeps faith and reason working together? Put very simply, we could say that faith and reason only work together the way that they are meant to when they are attached to a living, breathing creature whose identity, whose orientation, whose motivations, whose allegiance have *already* been "branded" by a sacramental belonging to Christ, by the radical re-orientation provided by the *baptismal* marking of grace on the creature; and not, we might say, by any "rational" power internal to the thinking subject. We can "fly" only when the wings of faith and reason are attached to the sacramental center (the "smile") of our adoption. And we will therefore "crash" when this deeper sacramental core, this deeper existential belonging, breaks down or is called into question.

My point, again, is that unless the deeper, strictly *pre-cognitive* and *personal* conditions of belonging — that is, those that cannot be reduced to structures or thinking — are present and firing on all cylinders, then a tendency to an excessively stark separation of Creator and created will always be present in one way or another.

And so, my more precise proposal will be that an approach *to truth and meaning specified by baptism* — the faith of transformative encounter and conversion that comes with adoption as sons in the Son, the faith of experiencing the love of Christ concretely (not simply a cognitive faith reduced to the function of *ratio* assenting to propositions) — is precisely the ingredient that is needed today to lead both faith and reason to a deeper encounter with the truth. Joseph Ratzinger has argued that the encounter with truth is only possible within the deeper encounter of love. For him, it is precisely the personal encounter with the love of Christ that makes possible and provides the grounding conditions for an encounter with the truth as something more than an idea. In Christ, truth becomes a Person, and it is in the living experience of and dialogue with this person that this truth becomes accessible to us.

So, by what I would call *sacramental* or *baptismal faith*, then, I mean something distinct from both faith and reason if they are understood only in the sense of two certain powers or faculties that belong to "nature" and "revelation" respectively. By "faith" in this more fundamental sense, I refer to the gift of a primary relation to a Person, the encounter with whom enlightens our understanding and engages our freedom in new ways. The point is that without this new relation, without this new ground of identity, such illumination could not occur. Again, what is accented here is a *change of being* for the *baptized* person who thinks and believes. I do not pursue the truths of faith and reason as a neutral being, as someone who stands outside the realities to which they refer. By receiving the gift of adoption — a "family" relation to God, becoming a member of the trinitarian communion — the point from which we encounter and attain the truths of both faith and reason change. Even if we do not know it, we are by baptism already become, in a sense, a living embodiment, a real synthesis of the respective realities signified by the terms "faith" and "reason" or "nature" and "grace." Chapter 5 will take up this question in further detail.

For now, I want to suggest that according to this measure, new insight is given into how to read the history of Christianity in the West, specifically the story of its decline. One way of reading this history is to see it in terms of a simple story of reason being led away from faith. But it may also be a story of *both* faith and reason being led by a kind of perverse curiosity away from *love*, from that deeper sacramental encounter with Christ that remains grounded in and mediated by the most basic sacramental and liturgical life of the Church. From what we have seen so far, we could advance the proposition that the story of Christianity's decline may be read as a creeping, incremental departure from the existential horizon of the self's total immersion in the living forms of divine Love.

In this horizon, we could thus read decline in simple terms as a loss of baptismal consciousness. More specifically, it would therefore represent the loss of the deepest modes intrinsic to baptismal existence: the centrality of love, worship, and a revelation of existence under the aspect of the beautiful, i.e., an "aesthetic" or tasting and savoring appropriation of the truth, rather than a more strictly cognitive or intellectual one. And this would mean that at the core of this loss of depth is not simply a secular reason that attacks faith from the outside. Rather, I would suggest that every "secularizing" cultural or social trend can be traced back to a severance or mutation of the baptismal modes of love, worship, and beauty. I suggest that we can read the history of the West as the story of the religious and cultural problems created by the loss of the deeper perspectives of relationship, worship, and beauty.

It might be shocking and challenging for us to hear it, but this means that Christianity itself is in a certain sense responsible for the postmodern condition. The story of decline is a much a story of *our* failure as it is about an enemy outside of our community. Rather than letting this crush us, however, we should instead use it as an opportunity to go back and try to recover the deeper baptismal conditions of our relationship to Christ.

All of the above is more relevant than ever for we who live amongst the forms of the postmodern context of the death of God. Compared both to the Patristic context of Platonism and the Scholastic context of Aristotelianism, the situation today is different, the questions are new. We are at the tail-end of a long experiment that has given us the imaginative possibility and social reality of the death of God, an experiment that has failed in its capacity to offer us anything but greater despair and violence. I would say again, then, that above all else there is today a new need to highlight the originality of the horizon of truth and meaning given in Christ. In light of the history of the death of God, we are perhaps poised to more acutely recognize that no element of Platonic or Aristotelian philosophy can in the end supply us with what we *truly* need, especially in this historical moment.

In what follows, we will continue our narrative by recalibrating it in light of the perspectives of love, worship, and beauty.

The fate of love, worship, and beauty

What can we know outside of love? Actually, this is the most insidious kind of question that one could ever ask. For who cares what we can know outside of love? Knowledge without love is a somewhat impersonal bedfellow.

Now sure, we may get important and desirable "benefits" from this bedfellow, such as science and technology, the fruits of a certain stripping of knowledge down to its most basic material elements, taking it out of experience and putting it in the lab. None of us, if we are honest with ourselves, would want to lose all the benefits of this application, would want to go back to a pre-technological age.

If, however, we are honest with ourselves at a deeper level, none of us would want to define what *really* and *ultimately* matters except in terms of love. In this sense, the truly great thinking, the truly great knowledge — even if it is not the truly "scientific" knowledge as we today understand the word (for love can never be a "science") — is precisely the thinking and knowing born of love, and in this, the kind of thinking and knowing that matter most. This, I have submitted, is the "knowing" and "thinking" embodied in the loving smile exchanged between a mother and her child.

The French phenomenologist Jean-Luc Marion has remarked that "philosophy comprehends only to the extent that it loves — I love to comprehend, therefore I love in order to comprehend."[25] This becomes a radical, indeed revolutionary statement when juxtaposed with the history of Western thought, which we have begun to read as the progressive attempt to extricate the knower from a "loving" — that is, personally invested, participating, indwelling, committed, even "spousal" — relationship with knowledge. According to the logic of what became the dominant Western tradition, if we want to understand truly pure, truly universal ideas, we have to consider them apart from the adulterative effects of our desires, our loves, our historical subjectivity, our faith-commitments. Yes, it may have taken a long time for these tendencies to materialize, but now, amidst their present materialization, we are obliged to consider more critically the points of tension that produced them. In this sense, the encounter of Christianity with the wisdom of the ancients (especially Aristotle), while fruitful, had certain risks. For in the effort to show how Christianity could "fit" with or fulfill the wisdom of the world — to show how faith was not

---

25 Jean-Luc Marion, *The Erotic Phenomenon*, trans. Stephan E. Lewis (Chicago: University of Chicago Press, 2007), 2.

simply something that hung in the void, but that it had something to do with the natural desires of the human heart — there was always the risk that faith could end up being tied down to the measure of practical reason; that reason could start to dictate the terms upon which faith conducted itself.

As I have suggested, what was original to Christianity was the intuition that God — whom the more rationalistic threads of Greek philosophy had spoken of as the absolute being, the uncaused cause, pure thought, the highest principle — was something much more than simply a philosophical concept related to origins and causes. According to Ratzinger, in his still remarkable *Introduction to Christianity* (1968), what the revealed truth of Christ added to the philosophical understanding of God was the resolute conviction that God is not simply an abstract cosmic reality, but that he is Love (cf. 1 Jn. 4:8).

In other words, what is radical about Christianity is that it claims that *love is reason*, or that *the highest reason is love*. Reason does not therefore consider only abstract facts and ideas that hang in the void. Reason is rather born in the relation, that sacramental relation I alluded to earlier. Responding to the temptation to conceive of God in an overly philosophical way, Ratzinger observes: "We unthinkingly assume that pure thought is greater than love, while the message of the Gospel, and the Christian picture of God contained in it, corrects philosophy and lets us know that love is higher than mere thought. Absolute thought is a kind of love; it is not unfeeling idea, but creative, because it is love."[26] Therefore, the "rational" moment is to be found precisely in the "loving" moment, in being-with-the-other. True knowledge is the true knowledge of love, the experience of the mother's smile. True knowledge is wonder and gratitude and the joy and attraction of beauty.

The significance of a God who *is love* is thus both that He is beautiful and as such attractive, and worthy to be praised and worshipped. The God who loves, the God who suffers and dies for us, the God who redeems and sanctifies us is precisely the God who alone is worthy of worship, who casts down all other idols and impostors. Heidegger famously said that "man can neither pray nor sacrifice to [the god of philosophy]. Before the [uncaused cause] man can neither fall to his knees in awe nor can he

---

26 Joseph Ratzinger, *Introduction to Christianity*, trans. J.R. Foster (San Francisco: Ignatius, 2000), 147.

play music and dance before this God."[27] Nietzsche said: "I would believe only in a God who could dance."[28] Both point to the fact that if the G/god you say you believe in is only a philosophical proposition, then he is not worthy of worship, for he has not yet become a living, radiant, personal presence in your life.[29] The point is not that philosophical propositions are necessarily all dead ends. It is rather that if they are not eventually "restumped" by the horizon of worship, their truth will be left incomplete. Moreover, our broader point has been that after the death of God, philosophical approaches will be mediated by a new instability and insecurity.

But if He is a God of *love* who has revealed himself, then He is indeed worthy of our grateful, sacrificial, loving prostration before Him. Indeed, if He is a God of love — if He has established a genuine, loving relationship with us — then worship itself becomes our proper — and *only* — mode of existence in relation to this God, which in turn shapes a contemplative, grateful, steward-like response to our existence and to the whole of created reality, which can be read as pure gift, not something that is ours by right. Our existence and the world itself and all that is in it are gifts meant to be given back to God in gratitude, through the Son, in the Spirit.

Ratzinger suggests that when God led the Israelites out of Egypt, he did so not to give them "freedom" in what we might call the "American" sense — *viz.* freedom to be whatever you want to be — but rather in order to give to them the freedom *to worship him*.[30] In other words, in its deepest essence "freedom" is realized precisely in the act of a loving, receptive, grateful response to God. Anglican theologian Catherine Pickstock has argued that philosophy is properly completed only in doxology, that is, in worship.[31] For her, anything less is nihilism: the creation of secular

---

27 Martin Heidegger, "The Onto-Theo-Logical Constitution of Metaphysics," in Martin Heidegger, *Identity and Difference*, trans. Joan Stambaugh (Chicago: University of Chicago Press, 1969), 72.

28 Friedrich Nietzsche, *Thus Spoke Zarathustra: A Book for All and None*, trans. Adrian Del Caro (Cambridge: Cambridge University Press, 2006), 29.

29 While the more Platonic notion of divine beauty belongs also to Western civilization, this strain has tended to be superseded by more degraded Aristotelian notions of immanent science and mechanistic causality.

30 Joseph Ratzinger, *The Spirit of the Liturgy*, in *Collected Works: Theology of the Liturgy* (San Francisco: Ignatius, 2014), 7. See also Joseph Ratzinger, *"In the Beginning…": A Catholic Understanding of the Story of Creation and the Fall*, trans. Boniface Ramsey (Grand Rapids: Eerdmans, 1995), 30–32.

31 Cf. Catherine Pickstock, *After Writing: On the Liturgical Consummation of Philosophy* (Oxford: Blackwell, 1998).

substitutes for eternity. This is to say that philosophy must be implicitly a *theology* before it is a *logic*. Its guiding motivation must be wisdom and not simply syllogistically demonstrable non-contradiction.

Within the perspective of a deity understood as love, our worship of and obedience to God is not understood as an attitude of servile groveling or fearful adherence to an arbitrary law. Rather the One who is worshiped, the One who is obeyed, is One with whom you have a *filial relationship*. God is a loving *Father*; by baptism we are His adopted sons in the Son, generated, elected, redeemed, sanctified, forgiven, named, and loved by him. His reproofs and commandments are extensions of His love. God is therefore "beautiful": the glory that shines from His face in Jesus Christ is attractive, desirable, fulfilling, entirely worthy of praise.

To be a Christian, then, is to be consumed with the fire of a burning, passionate, even "erotic" (within proper analogical bounds, of course!) love for the beauty of God in Christ. For to have an eye for beauty is to be compelled, exhorted; to sense, to implore, to feel; to be impelled into relationship, into commitment to something, to an "other." It is to never stand outside the drama of existence as a merely disinterested, dispassionate, or detached observer. Beauty, to follow von Balthasar, is the visibility and desirability of the good and the true.[32] It is the deeper, more organic vision of the whole, a kind of "feeling" and "tasting" of reality that draws one deeply into the Mystery as a participant. Beauty is therefore in a certain sense the "grammar" of love, its mode of appearance, the compelling reason why being-in-relationship is good.

The scandal of a God who gives everything

Unfortunately, as I have begun to suggest, the implications of a trinitarian God who is Love, of a creation "breathed" into existence by the overflowing, self-giving fruitfulness of this love, of a God who is therefore more interior to me than I am to myself, a God worthy of worship, a God of sublime beauty who overwhelms us with His glory, who calls us through the attractive power of the beauty of love, were not always appreciated in their full radicality.

On one level, it is not surprising. For if God truly is love, if God truly becomes human like us, if God dies on the cross and makes Himself vulnerable and weak, if He suffers, if He desires our love and desires our

---

32 Cf. Balthasar, *The Glory of the Lord*, vol. 1.

salvation, can He really still be called the all-powerful, the transcendent, the all-knowing, the unchanging, radically *other* God? A God who *dies?* A God who "needs" us? For the systematic and philosophical mind, or for the mind fighting heresies, the imperative to downgrade the priority of revelatory categories of divinity in the face of pressing intellectual problems would always be a point of tension that, given the right conditions, could translate into a loss of the sense of the newness of a God revealed in Christ. Again, it will not happen overnight, but the points of tension are there.

The person: substance or relation?

A related vulnerability lay in a hesitancy to fully define the human person, the being created in the image of God who is love, as someone best understood according to the radical conditions of love given to them in Christ. Ratzinger has suggested that there is a need to expand the range of the Christian understanding of the person beyond what had been the standard account that lodged the image of God in the individual *as individual*.[33] That is, the main approach of the tradition has been to locate the imprint of the trinitarian God on us not first in our capacity to be in relationship with others, but inasmuch as within our own individuality we have the capacity to think, to remember, and to will (*intellectus, memoria, voluntas*).

Now, this capacity is understood by both St. Augustine and St. Thomas as a dynamic feature of the individual that in fact gives him the capacity for, and places him in, a loving relationship with God and others. Nevertheless, it may lead us to think of the individual capacity for thinking, remembering, and willing apart from a more original, loving relationship. That is, if you start with the person *as individual*, as first an abstract "individual substance of a rational nature" (the influential formulation of Boethius), you may find it difficult to understand how love — the moment of relation when the self seems to lose (but in fact gains) itself in the other — fits into this, or what it means to say that this individual is by baptism drowned — put to death — in the waters of baptism and raised with Christ as an adopted child, a *theological* person utterly defined by relation to the other, something that would seem to deeply challenge and qualify more naturalistic or substantialist descriptions of what it means to be human.

---

33 Cf. Joseph Cardinal Ratzinger, "Concerning the Notion of Person in Theology," in *Communio* 17 (Fall 1990).

Greater cognizance of the way relationality lies at the center of human existence makes it easier to see how the human person is intrinsically open to infinite supernatural fulfilment, a fulfilment already in a certain sense signified and mediated by the experience of finite relationships of love.[34]

Again, however, in this case the hesitancy to more freely embrace the category of relation is part of the difficulty of understanding how the apparent weakness, dependency, and vulnerability operative in love can be a perfection properly speaking. To accent knowledge as the intellectual act of an individual more than loving relation to the other makes it difficult to see how deeply the baptismal relation of the individual to the Father in fact constitutes and frames that individual's existence.

A fraying tapestry

By the high middle ages, with the rise of the university and the burgeoning of new "secular" disciplines of thought, the tears which had begun to appear in the theological and philosophical tapestry that Christianity had woven finally deepened. Both Platonism and Aristotelianism as handmaids to theology were on the way out. New metaphysical principles started to replace the models of participation and causality. A few of the key players here were Franciscans Duns Scotus (1266–1308) and William of Ockham (1285–1347) and Jesuit Francisco Suarez (1548–1617). Duns Scotus developed the notion of the "univocity of being" and Ockham advanced the idea of nominalism, while Suarez proposed the "extrinsicist" or two-ends theory of nature and grace.[35]

These developments are far too complex and painful to consider here in any detail. But, acknowledging the dangers of retroactively attributing guilt to specific historical figures, it suffices to say that at the very least the *effective history* of these somewhat abstract and conceptualist methodological approaches was that faith as contemplation and worship as response to love, as animated by the intellect's participation in a movement from and return to a trinitarian God (*exitus-reditus*), would come to be effaced by new interpretive standards. A host of quintessentially modern philosophical approaches and problems were born here, including neutral and static conceptions of Being, knowledge understood not as the mind's real

---

34 I will develop these themes in the light of a *baptismal* personhood in chapter five.

35 For an (admittedly challenging) account of all three of these themes and their progenitors, see Balthasar, *The Glory of the Lord*, vol. 4, 9–29.

participation in the object but rather as its "representation" or "mirroring" (the "mind-body" problem is born from this), particulars without universals, and nature and grace as distinct competing orders. In a word, to use Boersma's analogy, the tapestry of existence understood as "heavenly participation" was already beginning to come unraveled by the 13th century, well before more drastic developments in the Enlightenment period.

None of these subtle movements of secularization happened overnight, but these are key moments, watersheds of conceptual thinking, if you like, that gradually ushered in the transition from love to knowledge, from worship to autonomy, from beauty to instrumentality. At the deepest level, it could be argued that the biggest problem lay at the level of the imagination or the heart. We can consider again Hauerwas's sense that the loss of faith is due to "the outworking of mistakes in Christian theology correlative to the attempt to make Christianity 'true' apart from faithful witness." From this angle, philosophical questions and motivations begin to exert a strong pull in terms of how faith should be described.

For example, attempts to plumb the depths of God philosophically (often with legitimate motivations and under real pressures) start to move us further from the purview of a loving God towards that of a "thinking" God, and by extension, from a loving man to a thinking man. Eventually, God's absolute power and will began to be accented (as in voluntarism) rather than His love and His goodness. A new obsession with systems, formulae, propositions, dialectical arguments, and "possible-worlds" rationality started to reflect a new definition of knowledge not as personal relationship, not as the worshipful entrusting of the self to beauty, but as impersonal "scientific" exploration and explanation. The point is not that this latter kind of knowledge is per se unreal or false; the question is whether it can be countenanced in a manner that does not usurp its more originary source.

Highlighting the significance of a new home for learning in the university, MacIntyre has claimed that "what defeated Aquinas was the power of institutional curriculum."[36] He refers to how the standard of truth came to be "the achievement and sustaining of high levels of professional skill in the elaboration and use of logical and conceptual techniques."[37] Thought became professionalized and bureaucratized. And thus philosophy

36 Alasdair MacIntyre, *Three Rival Versions of Moral Enquiry: Encyclopedia, Genealogy, and Tradition* (Notre Dame, IN: University of Notre Dame Press, 1990), 151.
37 Ibid., 158.

artificially narrowed its scope of inquiry, detached itself from the living soil and genuine practices of mystical experience and worship. Knowledge as a specialized discipline gives the impression that knowledge is "scientific," that it can and should reach outside of the relative, contingent, and embodied. Such knowledge easily becomes idealist and formalistic, disengaged from the lived and empirical, as in the philosophical system of Immanuel Kant (1724–1804). It easily becomes merely conceptual and analytic, obsessed with logical coherence within a very narrowly (and arbitrarily) defined system.

Thus, the impression began to be given that in order to say who God is, I do not so much have to be invested in a relationship with Him according to the measure of love, worship, and beauty, as much as I need the right concepts and ideas of philosophy that I know how to arrange correctly. While in the pre-modern period during the decline of scholasticism we are still dealing with men of faith in the strongest sense of the term here, what nevertheless started to happen was the initiation of a shift from a more "religiously" stimulated approach to truth (*viz.* truth discovered in prayer) to a more "technical" approach to truth (*viz.* truth discovered by ticking the right boxes, thinking in the correct technical way, etc.).

In a word, what we call "reason" began to lose its properly theological motivations and doxological framing. It was coming to be conceived as a productive tool that, if wielded by the rational subject in the right way, could on its own terms discover the properly "scientific" truth of God and the mysteries of existence. As such, it began to scour out paradox and mystery as central to faith.

Balthasar observes that High Scholasticism's tendency to think that it could "give an appropriate answer to every inquisitive question, however untheological" has in the "theology of its imitators … multiplied beyond all bounds; the answers become more and more hair-splitting as the legitimate rational method of a Thomas is increasingly distorted into an unbearable rationalism by the overweening deductions of a 'theology of conclusions.'"[38] This in the end leads to an eclipse of the mystery and transcendence of God.

Balthasar is blunt about the consequences: "behold the door to atheism."[39]

---

38 Hans Urs von Balthasar, *Theo-Drama: Theological Dramatic Theory*, vol. 4, *The Action*, trans. Graham Harrison (San Francisco: Ignatius Press, 1994), 458–59.

39 Ibid., 459.

New rationalisms

As we move beyond the Middle Ages, this "scientific" approach to truth came to be embodied in robust form in the Catholic philosopher and mathematician René Descartes (1596–1650). Descartes deliberately tries to slough off any theological presuppositions for thinking, any affects or effects of a loving, praying, and worshipping self who discovers himself already called, already transformed by a presence received as gift. He famously shuts himself up into a dark room in order to discover truth. "I shall now shut my eyes, I shall block up my ears, I shall divert all my senses, and I shall even delete all bodily images from my thought or, since this is virtually impossible to achieve, at least count them as empty and worthless."[40] Upon re-entry into the light of day, Descartes thinks that he has "proven" both the existence of God and the existence of the world, *but on the fully rational, fully scientific basis* of autonomous consciousness.

With Descartes, then, the western world's thought categories changed. For what emerges from his dark room is a mathematically calculated world of forces, power, and will. There are two significant points here: first, it is now the rational subject who fully "proves" God from the powers of his unaided rational faculties (i.e., outside of a prior relationship); second, the God who is thus "proved" is primarily a God who is power, force, will, cause, numbers, and the like. In other words, for God to be "true," the subject himself must be able to prove God, and the God who emerges from the fruit of his rationalized mental exercise is not the Christian God. It is rather the God of deism, whose proper mode is not love but reason, causality, and will stripped of their transcendent referents and submitted to the new dualistic and mechanistic standards of the day.

And make no mistake; these are two very different G/gods. "God does geometry" is the way Ratzinger explains the mathematical and logical function that God plays in the cosmology of Galileo. As Ratzinger explains it, here "the knowledge of God is turned into the knowledge of the mathematical structures of nature; the concept of nature, in the sense of the object of science, takes the place of the concept of creation."[41]

The growing confidence in the powers of the unaided human intellect undoubtedly opened up vast vistas of opportunity. In a now unprecedented

---

40 René Descartes, *Meditations on First Philosophy*, trans. Michael Moriarty (Oxford: Oxford University Press, 2008), 25.

41 Ratzinger, "*In the Beginning*," 84.

way, reason discovered that its powers could be directed to the study of *nature as separated nature*. That is, instead of looking for God's presence within or "behind" nature, attentive to its symbolic and sacramental possibilities, we could explore nature as a self-contained system, a source of wisdom and a practical guide on its own terms. In this, we could start to imagine the ideal, "rational," and "natural" man with certain natural ends who could be quite happy and fulfilled as long as he conformed himself to nature. The Aristotelian creep in late scholasticism begins to find a systematic outlet here, notwithstanding the way medieval thinkers had recognized that any legitimate powers of man only find their proper fulfilment in God.

From this, as suggested earlier, the gift of grace to this natural man came to be seen as increasingly "extrinsic," that is, an add-on from the outside that does not really contribute much to my earthly existence here and now, but consoles me with the prospect of life after death. As the growing discoveries of science would increasingly yield the possibility of a comfortable, secure existence, the invocation of God becomes less frequent, less urgent. The insistent specter of death, the urgency of existence, the sense of our own limitations, the sense of a need to adapt all our behaviors to a transcendent, divine pattern all start to lose their sharp edge.

Reforming our way to secularity

By the time we arrive at the Protestant Reformation, much of the damage has therefore already been done. For those Catholics who might be tempted to think that all of our problems today are reducible to the Reformation, it is perhaps better to think of the Reformers' response as representing a massive rejection of what it keenly — and to a large extent *rightly* — perceived to be Catholic theology's idolatrous flirtation with various forms of abstractions and unhealthy side-shows and therefore the usurpation of a more original scriptural conception of faith. Whatever else it may indicate, the Reformers' rallying cry of *sola scriptura*, *sola fide*, and *sola gratia* also evocatively embody their sense of the betrayal and corruption of the deeper modes of faith by the Roman Church.

Of course, the Reformation did not so much solve the crises it rightly or wrongly identified as much as it would create "shadow" problems, problems that tended to be the reverse image of the original. The Reformers thus tend to further "liberate" faith from bondage to reason, grace from bondage to nature, but in doing so transformed faith into a separate world, a ghetto, and grace into a foreign invading force that does not really answer the yearning cry of the heart. Free from any intrinsic fulfilment in grace, nature and practical reason can end up, for all practical intents and purposes, left to their own devices. Rather than relocating nature and reason "inside" the person transformed by the baptismal relation, the effect instead is that nature and reason are set "free" from faith. Behold secularity.

While early reformers such as Martin Luther (1483–1546) and John Calvin (1509–1564) were clear that nature was still under God's ordinance, this view would in the long term increasingly foster the secularization of nature already well and truly begun in the extrinsicist conception of nature in Catholic theology. Weber attributed much of the stimulus of the "disenchantment" of the world to a nature freed by the Reformers (again, prepared for by the scholastics, we might add) and now able to be concerned with its own productive pursuits. In other words, the extent to which the "world" no longer symbolically bears witness to the divine and to which everyday social practices do not flow from a sacramental kind of framing is the extent to which the individual will increasingly live "as if" God did not exist, and accordingly seek to control and shape nature according to his own, now unconstrained, will.

"The point," says Schindler, "is that a reason and nature in relation to which love and grace have been conceived as extrinsic will likely, over time, learn to get along just fine *without* love and grace."[42] As we have seen in chapter one, the extent to which one lives *practically* "as if" God did not exist is the extent to which one will inch towards the despair and crisis of meaning unmasked by postmodernism.

The crisis provoked by the Reformation did not in the end stimulate a recapturing of a more original and pristine faith as much as it created new dead ends. With the benefit of hindsight, we could say that inasmuch as the more narrow immediate imperatives that occupied the response of the Catholic counter-Reformation came to be regarded as a universal style of theologizing in their own right, Catholic thought thereby effectively denied itself the kind of theological *ressourcement* that might have prompted a deeper return to its sacramental roots. Perhaps a greater sense of identity here might have given the Church new tools to fight more effectively against the creeping tide of secular politics and practices that

---

42 David L. Schindler, "Christological Aesthetics and *Evangelium Vitae*: Toward a Definition of Liberalism," in *Communio* 22 (1995), 210.

begin to change the landscape of early modernity as the modern nation-state began to flex its muscles.

As it turned out, philosophical and theological thinking, fixed in more functionalist and rationalistic modes, could do little to stem the creeping tide of secular categories that would break out in all their glory in the Enlightenment. Against this new "enlightened" consciousness and new modes of enquiry, Catholic thought tended to resort to its own version of epistemological rationalism in a trenchant attempt to out-rationalize the new opponents of Christianity, an effort concomitantly hooked up with dogmatic denunciation of the first principles of the Enlightenment. MacIntyre's point here is worth considering. He thinks that the priority given to securing clear epistemological foundations (a particular imper-ative of Enlightenment philosophy) "doomed Thomism to the fate of all philosophies which give priority to epistemological questions: the indefinite multiplication of disagreement."[43] Christian philosophizing and theologizing, insofar as it hooked itself up to this wagon, would therefore not be immune to Nietzsche's demolishment of the claim that truth could secure its own unshakable foundations.

Conciliar dreams, post-conciliar nightmares

To make a long story (very) short and (very) simplified, by the time we arrive at the Second Vatican Council (1962–1965) we reach breaking point. The whole rationalistic edifice comes crashing down. In its best aspects and from its best thinkers, the Council envisaged and hoped for a return to a more scriptural, Patristic, and liturgical kind of faith, a faith that would once more drink at the sources, which would begin first and foremost with the Mystery hidden before all ages and now revealed in Christ, and would be able to engage the world from the deepest point of its identity. The so-called *nouvelle théologie* movement in France and Germany in the early part of that century did important and seminal work in this regard, and remains a fundamental source of genuine inspiration and renewal, still waiting to be deeply re-tapped.[44]

However, what happened immediately after the Council, unfortunately (and what we are still dealing with today on many fronts), was merely

---

43 MacIntyre, *Three Rival Versions of Moral Enquiry*, 75.

44 Cf. Hans Boersma, *Nouvelle Théologie and Sacramental Ontology: A Return to Mystery* (Oxford: Oxford University Press, 2009).

the mirror image of what came before. If counter-Reformation theology (neo-scholasticism) gave us propositions and dogmas that began to mute the centrality of Christ, the "liberal" theology that asserted itself and enjoyed popularity in the first decades after the Council gave us a mushy, naive, ideological, and uncritical sentimentalism that would hand Christ over to secular powers and standards more or less completely. Here, in the name of *aggiornamento* ("getting up-to-date") and reading the "signs of the times," the Church now ceded many of its authentic modes of existence — already sublimated for so many centuries by its own rationalistic tendencies — to the culture of modernity, in hindsight wrongly judged as a neutral or even benign phenomenon.

The so-called "liberal" Christ worshiped by large segments of the Church after the Council is the Christ who does not really care what I do so long as I am "happy" and let other people do what they want, and do not offend their feelings. This Christ is not the suffering Son who has entered into the depth of my alienation from the Father and who offers me the gift of adoption, who in his person opens me to a living relationship with divinity, situating the call to conversion, holiness, and fidelity within a relationship to a person. The God of liberal theology is a weak God, an absent or incompetent Father who refuses to show his children the path of life, to distinguish good from evil. Perhaps this God would counsel Satan himself, not to repent and be saved, but to "discern" his concrete situation, and to celebrate any good found therein.

But such a theology and such a God can do little more than provide a half-way house between belief and nihilism. As a *theological* paradigm, liberal theology is and always will be in a perpetual state of death, even if today, sadly, it seems to be recrudescing in tawdry new forms in the Church. Having rejected Christ, it appears to the younger generation as little more than dressed-up hypocrisy, defeatism, infidelity, with an embarrassing and in many cases downright idolatrous liturgical sensibility. In a word, liberal theology is always little more than poorly masked nihilism, the way of accommodation and despair, made all the more insidious the more it parades as something it is not. At least nihilism proper — in its postmodern forms — does not mask the death of God but tries to honestly confront it and the despair that it provokes.

The silver lining, of course, is that the post-Conciliar period was also blessed by two popes who carved a rich theological path through the malaise of their generation and who, just as importantly, also offered their own personal witness of holiness. Pope St. John Paul II and Pope Benedict XVI charted a theological, anthropological, moral, and liturgical path through the turbulence of the age, bequeathing a fruitful inheritance to future generations, even as our immediate situation seems to darken.

Nevertheless, a frank assessment of the cultural and ecclesial situation today should remind us that there are no short-term guarantees in history, even for those with faith. What the next chapter holds, no one can say.

Culpable failure, new opportunities

And so, where does this all-in-all rather somber, gloomy story leave us? If we look to the world around us, if we look to our own experience, we should be able to see that love, worship, and beauty are the three things that the world (and perhaps most of the institutional Church today) universally does not understand and can find no place for. The sexual revolution illustrates the crisis of love; the absence of God and the "worship" of technology, freedom, choice, progress, rights, tolerance, and *ourselves* illustrates the crisis of worship; that we no longer have the eyes to see a deeper meaning in anything outside of "scientific," instrumental, and pragmatic truth illustrates the crisis of beauty.

Of course, you might sometimes hear it claimed that the problem we are facing today is a crisis of *truth*, a crisis of *reason*. We do not know how to think, how to be rational, and if we once again just thought and reasoned properly, then we could get ourselves out of this mess. But in response, again, I would say that it is in fact *a certain conception of "truth" that is to blame for getting us into this mess in the first place*. That is, the extent to which theology tried to be "true" apart from faithful witness — true apart from the intrinsic love, worship, and beauty that are the marks of the joyful self-disclosure of and participation in the "truth" of Christ's Person — is the extent to which it had already lost faith in the only "reasons" worth both living and dying for.

In coming chapters, I will attempt to provide indications of what theological thinking might look like when it again takes seriously its vocation to love, worship, and beauty. Note again that it cannot simply be about "going back" *en masse* to some previous synthesis or system. One cannot go back from the death of God except by being more radically conformed to Christ. Better metaphysical systems and sharper principles and qualifications in the end cannot save us. My contention is that only by re-conceiving the *entire* shape of human existence in more radically baptismal terms can we hope to present a viable answer to a cultural consciousness and imagination held captive to the death of God. This theme will be developed in particular in chapter five.

At its heart, I will suggest, theology must be pursued from within the baptismal "wounding" of the creature in Christ. That is, theology can speak only from within the ambit of the Cross, the descent into death with Christ and the rising up with him into the new life of baptismal adoption. It is here — *and only here* — that theology can speak and give "reasons." Today, anything less than a properly baptismal theology will merely perpetuate the swing from one false alternative to another.

But far from giving up on reason and truth, the baptismal alternative that I will propose is instead their fullest ground of assurance. In fact, this is a radically "postmodern" position. The small "story" that we tell from within the radically particular account given by faith cannot rest on anything outside of itself. It cannot be definitively "proved" or made universal on any other basis. But of course, we who have been touched by faith know that it is not just *a* story; it is *the* Story. The paradox, however, is that the universal, all-encompassing truth of the Story can only be discovered by our entering *into* it and discovering our roles within it.

But first, we need to consider further the extent to which our allegiance is held captive by social and cultural forces of our immediate situation that reject the full baptismal "immersion" of the person into love, worship, and beauty. This we pursue in our next chapter.

THREE
Narratives of Secularization

I will not walk with your progressive apes,
erect and sapient. Before them gapes
the dark abyss to which their progress tends —
if by God's mercy progress ever ends,
and does not ceaselessly revolve the same
unfruitful course with changing of a name.
I will not tread your dusty path and flat,
denoting this and that by this and that,
your world immutable wherein no part
the little maker has with maker's art.
I bow not yet before the Iron Crown,
nor cast my own small golden sceptre down.

J. R. R. Tolkien, "Mythopoeia"

IN OUR LAST CHAPTER WE EXPLORED SOME OF the historical sources and causes of today's crisis of meaning. I suggested that part of the reason for this crisis can be traced back to the loss of a perspective more natively grounded in love, worship, and beauty. My cumulative point was that this loss has had a dramatic and negative effect both on the self-understanding of faith and on the history of ideas and our cultural and social world today. And so in this chapter I want to continue fleshing out some (certainly not even close to all) of the more practical social implications of forgetting and sidelining love, worship, and beauty within our modern liberal secular culture.

By speaking of "practical social implications," the reader should note that I do not intend to begin by focusing on some of the more obvious negative manifestations of this forgetting in liberal societies that might first come to mind for the believer; for example, things like abortion, euthanasia, assisted reproductive technologies, pornography, gender fluidity, same-sex marriage, etc., and the increasing threats to religious freedom mediated by refusals to submit to this liberal canon of sacred cows. Clearly, these are grave existential threats, morally, socially, legally and most of all in their capacity to colonize and destroy the sacramental structure of Christian faith.[1]

I do not think that it should be considered controversial to make the claim, as does Rod Dreher in regards to his own American context, that the *Obergefell* decision of the U.S. Supreme Court enshrining a constitutional right to same-sex marriage "was the moment that the Sexual Revolution triumphed decisively, and the culture war, as we have known it since the 1960s, came to an end. In the wake of *Obergefell*, Christian beliefs about the sexual complementarity of marriage are considered to be abominable prejudice—and in a number of cases, punishable."[2] More ominously, but no less truly as far I can see, Dreher concludes that "the public square has been lost."

Yet what I am most interested in here is exposing the rationale for these practical consequences at its deepest level. My efforts are thus designed to bring out a logic that is *prior* to—though certainly not distinct from—the actual "pelvic liturgies," if you will, that exert such a powerful force in our present "neoliberal" social and cultural configuration. For at their deepest level, the sexual beliefs and practices of the dominant secular narrative began as the effects rather than the causes of a perversion of love, worship,

---

1 A number of thinkers have identified the same-sex marriage issue as a recent game-changer in its effect on the ability of Christians to publicly practice (and certainly *preach*) basic tenets of their anthropological convictions. See for example, Ryan T. Anderson, *Truth Overruled: The Future of Marriage and Religious Freedom* (New Jersey: Regnery, 2015); Rod Dreher, "Sex after Christianity," in *The American Conservative* (April 9, 2013), at http://www.theamericanconservative.com/articles/sex-after-christianity/; David S. Crawford, "Liberal Androgyny: 'Gay Marriage' and the Meaning of Sexuality in Our Time," in *Communio* 33 (2006); David S. Crawford, "Gay Marriage, Public Reason, and the Common Good," in *Communio* 41 (2014); David S. Crawford, "Public Reason and the Anthropology of Orientation: How the Debate Over 'Gay Marriage' Has Been Shaped," in *Communio* 43 (2016); Douglas Farrow, "Why Fight Same-Sex Marriage?," in *Touchstone Magazine* 25 (2012), at http://www.touchstonemag.com/archives/issue.php?id=166; Michael Hanby, "The Brave New World of Same-Sex Marriage," in *The Federalist* (Feb 9, 2014), at http://thefederalist.com/2014/02/19/the-brave-new-world-of-same-sex-marriage/; John Milbank, "Gay Marriage and the Future of Sexuality," in *ABC Religion & Ethics* (March 13, 2012), at http://www.abc.net.au/religion/articles/2012/03/13/3452229; John Milbank, "The Impossibility of Gay Marriage and the Threat of Biopolitical Control," in *ABC Religion & Ethics* (April 23, 2013), at http://www.abc.net.au/religion/articles/2013/04/23/3743531.htm.

2 Rod Dreher, *The Benedict Option: A Strategy for Christians in a Post-Christian Nation* (New York: Sentinel, 2017), 9.

and beauty that is already to be found deep within the core metaphysical, anthropological, and "religious" convictions of liberalism in its story of freedom and liberation.

In what follows, therefore, I will accent the more primitive origins and core convictions of classical liberalism as its theorists began to consummate and extend those secularizing trends that in our previous chapter we argued were already gestating in the womb of pre-Enlightenment philosophical and theological discourse. Here, it is liberalism's primary stories of enlightenment and emancipation, the full fruits of which only become visible in the sexual revolution of the 1960s and in today's ever-more vigorous forms of progressive identity politics, that we are most interested. In particular, I will focus on liberalism's narrative about itself as a peace and freedom-bringing force for good that a supposedly "secular" society is thought to be the product of and agent for. And I will link this historical claim up with today's near-unshakable belief that we, with our benign secularity, are far more civilized and enlightened than our superstitious religious forbears. I will ask if this story is in fact true, or if it instead masks a more basic but unacknowledged set of beliefs and practices that in fact perpetuates and valorizes new and varied kinds of violence. Only once I have sought to tell this more foundational story will I make a few observations about how the pelvic liturgies of today's liberalism extend and consummate this story.

Without assuming that this is the *only* way to approach the fundamental logic of modernity, I will in this chapter read the secular grammar of liberalism as a paradigm of violent relations that represents the logical social and cultural completion of the rejection of love, worship, and beauty that first began within theology itself.

A secular age?

Today, we live in an age that is often called "secular." Charles Taylor has written a book called *A Secular Age*. On his account, "secularism," "secularization," or "secularity" can be described in a number of different ways. He identifies three of the most common of these descriptions.

First, it is often thought of in purely political terms. As he puts it, "in our 'secular' societies you can engage fully in politics without every encountering God, that is, [without] coming to a point where the crucial importance of the God of Abraham for this whole enterprise [politics] is brought home forcefully and unmistakably."[3] So "secular" here refers to a situation where God has no stake in the political operations of secular democracies.

Second, secularity is often thought of "in terms of public spaces."[4] Here, religious rituals, festivals, and language, as well as all references to the divine or eternal, have been eliminated from public expression and discourse. As Taylor explains, "these [public spaces] have been emptied of God, or of any reference to ultimate reality." In other words, as we observed in our first chapter, the majority of the things we do in everyday, ordinary life no longer bear any reference to a deity or even a religious idea or ideal that might condition and qualify the way we exercise our freedom and talk about what is true or meaningful.

Ratzinger has suggested that both the political and social sides of secularization represent a drastic overturning of the religious traditions of the West. As he puts it, "in Europe a culture has developed that constitutes the absolutely most radical contradiction not only of Christianity, but of the religious and moral traditions of humanity."[5]

Finally, Taylor describes his preferred understanding of the secular, which is simply an empirical and neutral description of a general situation or condition wherein faith, once a cultural given, is now simply one option among others. Secularity marks the factual transition "from a society in which it was virtually impossible not to believe in God, to one in which faith, even for the staunchest believer, is one human possibility among others."[6] That is, in this assessment, it is not so much that secularity is *positively atheistic* or hostile to Christianity in the Nietzschean sense that "God is dead and we have killed him" as that secularity is perceived in more neutral terms as simply a backdrop condition that permits a diverse range of "life" options (including religion) that individuals are now free to pursue on their own terms. Though some negative results are to be expected within this horizon (at least from the point of traditional religious faith and practice), Taylor in this book is far more hopeful that in the main secularity represents genuinely humanizing possibilities for cultures and societies.

In a similarly more optimistic reading, Dutch Catholic theologian Lieven Boeve prefers to speak of "de-traditionalization" and "pluralism" rather than "secularism," noting that the purging of God from the center

---

3 Charles Taylor, *A Secular Age* (Cambridge, MA: Belknap Press, 2007), 1.
4 Ibid., 2.
5 Joseph Ratzinger, "Europe in the Crisis of Cultures," in *Communio* 32 (2005), 348.
6 Taylor, *A Secular Age*, 3.

of social and political life does not mean that He disappears or "dies" completely or that it is no longer possible to practice one's faith in such a society.[7] Rather, it just means that God takes up occupancy in spaces other than the public and the shared. And in this, it is not *necessarily* the case that secularity will be a wholly negative phenomenon. On this reading, it is more that it is a "different" situation, with different challenges, but not necessarily an existential crisis of meaning per se.

Obviously, the judgment we make on what secularism is has everything to do with the extent to which we think the world we live in and the faith we practice are in fact in crisis. My position should not be surprising: In chapter one I called both modernity (including in its postmodern form) and liberal theology forms of nihilism, and in this, my suggestion is that the harder that one tries to retain meaning while at the same time pushing God ever further to the irrelevant margins, the lower one sinks into the pit of nihilistic despair and meaninglessness. In this sense, the extent to which secularity and secular practices embody therapeutic strategies that help to dull the radical spiritual edge of existence is the extent to which they will be dallying with nihilism.

Thus, how we define and understand secularism — how we assess its level of toxicity or harmlessness — determines the antidote that we might prescribe for it. Crucially, then, how we define and understand secularism will have everything to do with how we define evangelization. If we think that it does not really matter if we live six and half days of the week as if God did not exist, or if we think that God probably does not really care about most of my thoughts or actions so long as my motivations are sincere or I think that I am following my conscience, then conversion and evangelization will likely not be much of a priority.

But here is my teaser: the baptized person — the one who has been called to a radical spiritual childhood of "adopted" sonship in God, through the Son — can *never* live as if God did not exist or if faith were only an "option." This person — the person who has experienced the love of the Father, through the Son, in the Spirit — should chafe at the thought of having to ever quarantine this love, of having to act as if this love were not at the center of all meaning and existence. Baptism must bleed into every single area of my life.

---

7 Cf. Lieven Boeve, *God Interrupts History: Theology in a Time of Upheaval* (London: Continuum, 2007).

This does not mean that everything must then become "sacred," i.e., that there is no longer some kind of legitimate distinction between a divine and human reality, between divine pursuits and worldly pursuits. Rather, it means that any legitimate distinction between "nature" and "grace" or "faith" and "reason" is never the warrant for their "practical" divorce, or for turning the human dimension into its own hermetically sealed reality where no divine horizon is permitted to shape one's human pursuits. For as we have suggested, as soon as one tries to "practically" separate the two "worlds" of faith and reason, one ends up separating them *absolutely*.

In chapter five, I will propose that baptism is the connecting link, the new "world" that provides the locus and the grammar for the proper prudential distinction and integration of likeness and unlikeness to divinity, of "sacred" and "profane" activities. For the world itself changes for the person who is baptized. It means that the baptized person goes back to the world, appropriates it in a new, *sacramental* way, and in this subverts any and every attempt to "secularize" the world.

For now, let us continue to figure out what secularism means.

Diagnosing secularity

What does it actually mean to say that today's social context is "secular"? What are the practices of secularism? Is secularity an insidious subversion of faith or a harmless — indeed perhaps *helpful* — neutrality that helps people get along free of the allegedly divisive and violent effects of religion?

If I am correct in reading the passage to modernity as a theological transition from an understanding that prizes love, worship, and beauty to one that prizes instrumental reason, freedom *from* having to worship a deity, the "choice" to idolize whatever one wants, and inability to perceive the radiant depth of existence understood as love, then you can be absolutely sure that the "secular" world that we live in will somehow signify or embody this fact at a deep level and in practical ways that are *not* harmless and *not* helpful.

So the first thing to assert is that any practices belonging to secularism *will not be neutral*. For they are the fruit of — and they will dispose us to — certain allegiances and commitments, certain ways of looking at the world, a certain canon of values, "doctrines" even. Indeed, *any* practice, any idea, any belief is always committed to some grounding and organizing philosophical or religious presupposition, some ultimate account about how the world works, even if it is simply that "we cannot know what reality is" or "there is no need to know what reality is."

Make no mistake: a refusal to take up a formal position on ultimate questions (e.g., "we cannot know if God exists") generates just as many social implications (totalitarian ones too) as a positive claim to meaning ("God exists"). Indeed, a purported agnostic neutrality can nurture much more coercive, insidious, and hidden forms of social imperatives and mappings, inasmuch as its outward neutrality masks its just-as-resolute commitment to imagining the social world in a particular way. What we must do, then, is gauge the concrete effects of adopting a purported negative or agnostic position in regard to the question of ultimate meaning.

The metaphysics of liberalism

Most of us likely have some experience of how *intolerant* the supposedly "tolerant" liberal individual can be when our beliefs conflict with his. "Liberalism" — which we can here define simply as a marker of the social and political philosophies (and the associated social configurations) that derive from, support, and embody the Enlightenment ideals of liberty and equality — purports to provide a neutral basis upon which a plurality of beliefs can be practiced and tolerated, and through which individuals can be prevented from coming into conflict because of their belief differences. At least on the surface, the liberal's list of virtues compels him to respect your rights, freedom, and opinion, and indeed may even seem to protect and guarantee them. Today, however, you are more likely to be shouted down in a public forum by a liberal than by a fundamentalist Christian.

According to American Catholic theologian David L. Schindler, this phenomenon can be explained only on the understanding that liberalism is itself from the first and to its core a positive, *practical* — that is, socially *productive* — and dogmatic form of atheism: not only does it *imagine* or think about the world in atheist fashion (i.e., as if God does not exist), but in absolute terms it actively *creates* and *organizes* the world in an atheist fashion as well, thus circumscribing in advance the place and appearance of any properly theistic claims and beliefs that might be made by some of the citizens of a liberal state.[8] In other words, the "secularism" proposed

---

8 Cf. David L. Schindler, "Grace and the Form of Nature and Culture," in *Catholicism and Secularization in America: Essays on Nature, Grace, and Culture*, ed. David L. Schindler (Notre Dame, IN: Communio, 1990).

by liberalism is as much its own *positive* account of how the world works as it is a *negative* critique of a religious account of how the world works. Its claim to embody a negative, agnostic, or neutral point of view that does not pass judgment on claims that go beyond practical reason is in the end far too modest for its own intentions.

So if you and I in our hubris attempt today to offer some fundamental critique of or disagreement with the liberal canon of values from the perspective of our "faith" — our irrational, superstitious, narrow, ideological, fundamentalist, bigoted, anti-woman, and homophobic faith — then woe to us! What this should tell us, then, is that the liberal canon of values (and vices) is itself governed by a deeper "metaphysical" commitment (i.e., an ultimate account of existence and reality), one that organizes and frames reality according to its own deepest logic, and which forbids deviation from this logic.

Within this arena, as long as we theists play according to the mapping and rules it sets up — practicing our religion "privately" and respecting the liberal dogmas of abortion rights and same-sex marriage, for example — then we will be free to hold to our own (personal) beliefs. But as soon as we dare to challenge these sacred cows of liberalism and the presuppositions that support them — perhaps on the strength of a claim that they bear little resemblance to tenets of a public rationality that all people, whether of faith or otherwise, could be expected to be able to agree on — we discover that our opinion is not tolerated at all. Indeed, we discover that we may in fact be sanctioned and ostracized for our beliefs.

To our surprise, we discover that we are having a fundamental "truth" conflict with liberalism: we are arguing about ultimate values and claims, precisely the kind of arguments that liberalism was supposed to have purged from the public square. And we discover that liberals' support of abortion and same-sex marriage has a distinctly "religious" feel to it: they seem *absolutely* committed to these as dogmas or doctrines and they now want everyone else to submit to them as well.

So, as a preliminary diagnosis, we can say that the values and practices of liberal secularism are perhaps not as benign or neutral — or universally accepted — as they were once thought to be. To understand the deeper allegiance that grounds them, and to come to grips with the extent to which we too are held captive by them, we need to explore the phenomenon further. What we find may shock us, but also hopefully liberate us.

Secularity as "religion"

At the origin of the logic of liberal secularism is a cultural and social narrative:

In the beginning was religion, and only religion.

Now religion was irrational, absolutist, and divisive, and so chaos was on the face of the earth. Religion drove kings mad. Because of religion, because religion was all, Catholics killed Protestants, Protestants killed Catholics, and both Protestants and Catholics killed pagans across the seas. And darkness covered the face of the earth.

And from the darkness, far in the West, came the Liberal State, and the Liberal State said, Let there be light. And there was light. And the darkness was afraid.

And in the Liberal State there was no religion. And the Liberal State calls itself Secular. And it was so.

And the Liberal State said, Let us divide religion from life, and, lest the darkness return, let us place between religion and life a firmament that cannot be crossed. Let us bury religion deep in the heart of man, where it can do some small good but no harm. And let us make religion innocuous and rational.

And the magicians and sorcerers and court prophets shouted and said, All you have commanded, so shall we do.

And it was so. And the Liberal State saw that it was good.

And peace dripped like honey from the rock and flowed like wine from the mountains. Lions supped with lambs. All nations rejoiced in the Liberal State, for its mercy endures forever.[9]

This story, recounted here in Presbyterian theologian Peter J. Leithart's review of a book by Catholic theologian William T. Cavanaugh,[10] cleverly highlights the view that classic liberalism has of itself as a purifying, liberating, and rationalizing force in Western history. It promulgates the view that before the discovery of "pure" or "secular" Enlightenment reason, there was only darkness, irrationality, and violence. It is commonly said that we were

9 Peter J. Leithart, "Myth of Religious Violence," in *First Things* (July 2012), at https://www.firstthings.com/blogs/leithart/2012/08/myth-of-religious-violence. See also Hart's account of modernity's "enchanting tale" about itself in *Atheist Delusions: The Christian Revolution and Its Fashionable Enemies* (New Haven: Yale University Press, 2009), 33–4.

10 William T. Cavanaugh, *The Myth of Religious Violence: Secular Ideology and the Roots of Modern Conflict* (Oxford: Oxford University Press, 2009).

"saved" from the so-called "Wars of Religion" in Europe in the 16th and 17th centuries by a peace-loving and rationally enlightened secular liberal state.

In order to restore peace among the bickersome and bloody religious disputes of Catholics and Protestants, the Peace of Augsburg (1555) declared that the religion of any given state would now be decided by its ruler (*cuius regio, eius religio*). Cavanaugh suggests that this is a crucial moment that marks a formal ceding of ultimate authority from ecclesiastical to secular civil powers: that is to say, the beginning of *an absolute divide* between the secular and the Sacred, a new mapping of space and time wherein "religion" would soon refer to an interior, privatized sphere of the individual and "secular reason," sanctioned and enforced by the state, would become the new universal language of the real. The Church was allowed to exist within this new arrangement, but it was forced to limit itself to the administering of religion as a purely private reality for individuals. For their part, individuals could not, *as Christians*, participate in the politics of the newly secular state; participation in said politics was premised on a self divested in practice from its particular allegiances and commitments.

The "secular" is here *imagined* as an autonomous, self-sufficient social category conceived entirely outside of the jurisdiction of any religious claims. While we may be happy that now the Church could get out of the corrupting business of nation-building and temporal politics that has at times proved so devastating for its spiritual credibility throughout the centuries, we also need to recognize that there is something much more subversive going on here at a deeper level. For the new secular/sacred split is not simply a practical, prudential separation where both still "play on the same team" (that is to say, God's "team"), as it was in the medieval order. No, the authority of the secular ruler will now soon come to operate in near-complete abstraction from any theoretical or practical reference to divine order and authority, direct or derivative, visible or invisible.

Today, we see this in the tendency to invoke the "separation of Church and State," not for the protection of religious freedom, but as an absolute distinction that *forbids anything but a secular perspective* from informing the political, social, and ethical discussion of issues in society. The secular, so conceived, needs nothing beyond itself to justify itself, and forbids any measure beyond the principles of constitutional law, popular opinion, and democratic processes conceived in exclusively positivist terms, and thus fundamentally susceptible to the mechanisms of power and increasingly progressive mutations.

In order to have a voice in social and political issues in this arena, Christians must therefore sublimate or mask the faith-based reasons for their commitment to this or that position on any given issue. They find themselves compelled, as noted by Catholic theologian Matthew Tan, to translate their message into the idioms and standards set by secular discourse and institutions.[11] But in reducing their argument to the rules of liberal discourse, Christians must therefore participate in that discourse's hidden commitment to the death of God.

To this day most Christians think that to stand up for some truth in society means to make a case for that truth on "secular" grounds without fundamentally challenging liberal first principles. We may intend only to do this "tactically," as a way to try to articulate something of our own position (which of course actually rests on very different first principles) without rocking the liberal boat too much.

But if it is true that the playing conditions of liberalism are already "loaded" against Christian conclusions, then perhaps our attempts to present arguments for conclusions that flow from our Christian worldview should more consciously subvert and question those very conditions. Otherwise we may find ourselves advocating or even believing and being duped by the denuded accounts of elements of our faith that we have surgically removed from their animating sources — take the example of defenses of "natural" marriage in the face of same-sex marriage legislation — that are neither faithful to Christ nor even appealing to the liberal, whose entire disposition and appetite is geared to the very antithesis of "nature": positivistic and autonomous freedom and choice outside of the horizon of a notion of creation.

What is also significant here is that far from being a reflection on the true nature of things, the brand-new categories of the "secular" and of "secular reason" are themselves judgments that belong to a contingent, historical set of events, and because of this are just as particular and situated as the categories generated by religion or tradition. That is, it is not that they are deduced or proven from the nature of reality itself according to some pure universal measure, but rather that they too rely on particular historical judgments and motivations and on a contextually generated set of rational presuppositions, all of which have proved impossible to rationally substantiate;[12] hence the "postmodern condition" that subconsciously haunts the most assured claim of the modern liberal. Belief in the secular is, in other words, "impure." It depends on a certain fundamental way of looking at the world and reality that is itself prior to and not provable by some universal measure of reason.

And so Anglican theologian John Milbank suggests that "Once, there was no 'secular'.... The secular as a domain had to be instituted or *imagined*, both in theory and in practice."[13] In other words, the secular itself has the kind of beginning for which it attacked religion: a historical, temporal, and contingent beginning — a beginning grounded in persons and places — rather than a truly universal one. And its mode of justification is grounded in these contingent and contextual conditions of its beginning.

Or as MacIntyre expresses it, it turns out that liberalism is simply another tradition. That is, though its aim was to transcend tradition by appeal to truly universal principles, it could not in fact (cf. Nietzsche's critique) end up as anything but "an historically developed and developing set of social institutions and forms of activity, that is, as the voice of tradition."[14] MacIntyre concludes: "Like other traditions, liberalism has internal to it its own standards of rational justification. Like other traditions, liberalism has its set of authoritative texts and its disputes over their interpretation. Like other traditions, liberalism expresses itself socially through a particular kind of hierarchy."

This, then, is the paradox: the culture of liberal secularism has a "religious" foundation and character. It is just that its "religion" is premised on a fundamental agnosticism about the world beyond the senses and the lab, the effects of which we will look at more deeply in a moment.

If this is true, then the Christian's willingness to conceive of and debate issues according to the criteria of the conditions of this alternative religion represents a tacit acceptance of fundamental principles that are in fact the direct antithesis of fundamental Christian convictions. We should not therefore be surprised when, scratching below the surface, we discover that most Christians are in fact just as secular as liberals in many of their basic operational presuppositions and practices. One cannot live and

---

12 Cf. MacIntyre, *After Virtue*, chapters 4 and 5.

13 John Milbank, *Theology and Social Theory: Beyond Secular Reason* (Oxford: Blackwell, 2006), 9.

14 Alasdair MacIntyre, *Whose Justice? Which Rationality?* (London: Duckworth, 1988), 345.

operate "as if" God were dead, even merely tactically, without this having some deleterious effect on one's own heart and mind.

Further, we should not be surprised when the procedural arguments in which we have cloaked our broadly Christian or pre-modern conclusions increasingly have little or no effect in social discourse within liberal societies, or indeed prompt intolerance and vitriol. If the "neutrality" of liberalism is in fact a "religious" claim already weighted towards the antithesis of a Christian worldview, then most people formed by the social and cultural air of liberalism will already be committed to a properly secular horizon of belief. No merely procedural form of argument can thus be effective in what is an essentially religious conflict, a clash of civilizations, a competition between worldviews.

Language games

The claim that the practices of liberalism are framed by fundamental metaphysical and religious presuppositions is not simply lazy, rhetorical, or ideological, even if "religious" in this context is being used in a somewhat different sense than we are perhaps used to. If we look even more deeply into the self-understanding and features of liberalism and the liberal state, we see suspiciously religious terminology, imagery, and commitments at every turn, all of which call into question liberalism's claims to indisputable secular enlightenment. In this, we can observe that its *modus operandi* does not consist in a complete separation from the terms and ideas that represent the Christian heritage it wishes to overturn. Rather, as some commentators have pointed out, its fundamental tenets are best understood as derivative "mutations" of earlier designated meanings of terms. "The achievement of liberalism," says Catholic political scientist Patrick J. Deneen, "was not simply a wholesale rejection of its precedents, but in many cases attained its ends by redefining shared words and concepts and, through that redefinition, colonizing existing institutions with fundamentally different anthropological assumptions."[15]

For example, Iain T. Benson notes that the word "secular" (*saecularis*) is itself not original to liberalism.[16] Within medieval Christendom the term denoted a distinction made between temporal or worldly time and

---

15 Patrick Deneen, *Why Liberalism Failed* (New Haven and London: Yale University Press, 2018), 23.

16 Cf. Iain T. Benson, "That False Struggle between Believers and Non-believers," in *Oasis* 12 (2010).

eternal time. For the medieval mind, both times still refer to *God's time*, exist within His providence, and are to be offered back to Him in gratitude and praise. This is the origin of the traditional distinction between "secular" and "religious" clergy: secular clergy are your typical parish priests, ministering to the lay faithful who live their vocations in the world; religious clergy are those who dedicate themselves fully to the coming Kingdom in the monastery or cloister.

But as Benson points out, in its modern sense the word "secular" mutates to represent a distinct this-worldly realm independent from eternal or divine meaning. It is important not to miss the significance of this. For while on the surface it is the same word, in each instance it refers to a different reality. Liberals today use "secular" as a marker for the radical autonomy of the world and (human) rationality, while Christians originally used it as a temporal-eschatological distinction within a world and rationality that remains God's through and through.

If you do not catch sight of the deeper differences, then you might not realize that what liberalism actually facilitates are the conditions for *a complete understanding of the world and existence without God*. Its use of language serves this imagining. This becomes very important when we consider that while many of the "dogmas" of liberalism (such as rights, tolerance, freedom, and equality) may appear on the surface as roughly compatible with Christian concepts, they are already filled from the outset with a particular meaning generated by the broader presupposition that God does not exist in any socially or culturally meaningful sense. These terms, then, are not neutral, but are themselves mutations of earlier theological ideas that now have a different function within a liberal framework.

David L. Schindler notes that this is why it is so difficult to win an argument with a liberal over the ethical status of issues like abortion.[17] Whereas we might launch a (liberal) defense of the value of the life of the unborn child on the grounds of that child's "right to life" played off against the alleged right of the mother to "choose," the liberal will launch a counter-defense based on a valorization of the woman's "right to choose" what she does with her body over against any alleged right of the "fetus."

We may of course retort that, *clearly*, the fundamental right to *life* of the child ought to trump whatever right the woman invokes on the basis of certain challenges associated with a pregnancy. But the liberal will be

17 Cf. Schindler, "Grace and the Form of Nature and Culture," 17–18.

equally insistent that, *clearly*, the quality of life of a person already in the world trumps that of one not yet in the world, and one whose presence was perhaps never desired in the first place. We will likely shake our head in amazement at what to us might appear as indefensible semantic gymnastics, but at this point we may need to consider that while our perspective is informed by belief in a loving God who has shared the gift of love and life with us and called us to discipline and harmonize our acts with this gift, there is no such fundamental backdrop informing the worldview of the liberal who defends abortion as a right of freedom and self-determination.

Schindler points out that this "logic which makes the self, that is, in its constitutive or ontological separateness from the other, the center of action and thereby the center of obligation, leaves vulnerable precisely those selves who are least able to act for themselves and thus to make demands for themselves. An unborn human being is a self who is vulnerable in just this way."[18] And so, outside of deeper reflection and conversation about the source and foundations of any supposed right — a deep "worldview" conversation — "pro-life" and "pro-choice" debates can only be a shrill and combative surface jousting.

All of this is to say that the liberal use of the word "secular" itself already signifies a whole range of ultimate commitments; that is, fundamental presuppositions about what is real and what is important, and therefore also a certain hierarchy of values formed from these presuppositions. Not to recognize this deep layer of "belief" that informs the liberal worldview is to remain ineffective in our engagement and risk falling victim ourselves to the denuded terminology in which liberals frame the debate. Liberals themselves have their list of virtues and vices, their dogmas and creeds, and they are committed to them as absolutely as we ourselves might be committed to our Christian faith. And all of this suggests a much deeper subterranean theological conflict that can never be overcome within the constraints of liberal discourse.

A new salvation

Continuing to explore liberalism's reliance upon mutations of earlier Christian concepts, we can next draw attention to the mythology of the State as savior. The liberal state, as we saw in Leithart's review of Cavanaugh's book, presents itself as the savior of all from religious violence.

---

18 Ibid., 18.

And in this, the state compels our allegiance and deference, doing so by practices and rituals — or "liturgies," as both Cavanaugh and American Reformed theologian James K. A. Smith put it — designed to encode and provoke loyalty to and fervor for the state's soteriological narrative, *viz.* its story of salvation. Smith suggests that when it comes to things such as patriotism or consumer culture, "we need to recognize that these practices are not neutral or benign, but rather intentionally loaded to form us into certain kinds of people — to unwittingly make us disciples of rival kings and patriotic citizens of rival kingdoms."[19]

As savior, the state replaces the Church as a moral guide that seeks to tell us who we are and how we are to behave. Its soteriology is also a story of redemption, what we need to do to be "saved." Obey, and we will keep you safe. Do this, but do not do that, and you will be happy. Liberalism also tells a creation story and presents us with an eschatology. It tells us who the person is in his or her most original, primitive state, what constitutes the "good life" for that person, and what "ultimate values" that person should strive after. And liberalism thereby preaches *an anthropology*: it tells us within strict parameters who we are and what our destiny is.

We can thus say that liberalism is a religion in the sense that it does not merely promote a "live and let live" philosophy that is agnostic on questions of truth and meaning — indeed, a theory that proposes an account of social life could never be authentically agnostic. Its mantras of choice, freedom, and agnosticism regarding an ultimate human end and good are supported in and masked by its commitment to a set of purely immanent ends and goods. This commitment is encoded and propagandized by a particular set of social practices or "liturgies" which function to promote allegiance to the fundamental values of liberalism. And today, the extent to which one can criticize or opt out of these values is ever-narrowing.

Alien invasion

What this should tell us is that liberalism lives off of the residual capital of the Christian imagination while gutting it of its heart and feeding off its flesh, much like the alien life-forms in the *Alien* movie franchise live off their human hosts before sloughing them off when they have reached maturity. Liberalism imagines and presents itself within the persisting

---

19 James K. A. Smith, *Desiring the Kingdom: Worship, Worldview, and Cultural Formation* (Grand Rapids: Baker, 2009), 90–91.

thought-forms and lingering energy of a Christian worldview, parasitically using its remaining forms as a way to our hearts and our allegiance while subtly mutating its truths. But I would say that we are now perhaps witnessing the historical moment when the liberal alien comes fully to life, when it is finally prepared to kill off the Christian host that has given it its life, thus accelerating the long defeat already begun.

Be that as it may, the fact remains that the quintessentially modern lifeblood that courses through the veins of liberalism derives from the spiritual energy of Christianity, such that the extent to which it kills the host is the extent to which it must take increasingly dark and totalitarian postmodern forms as it consciously distances itself from the Christian patrimony that now seems more and more repulsive to the liberated liberal mind.

As I suggested in the first chapter, this is what is important about the "postmodern" recognition of the inner nihilism of so-called "modern" existence. The person who discovers the actual emptiness, irrationality, and failure of the modern world as understood by liberal theories will — if not duped by its therapies — recognize that the world so created by liberalism is a sham; that it promises a pale and groundless alternative to the Christian story that fails to deliver, fails to satisfy, and fails to rouse and inspire because it is too shallow and empty to do so.

As a consequence, some turn to passive forms of self-medicating (such as shopping). Others, like Nietzsche, refuse to acquiesce, adopting instead a principled, almost eschatological interior resistance to liberalism's liturgies. Yet for every submissive capitulation and principled resistance, the insecurity and loss of meaning and identity provoked by the postmodern condition also manifest more crudely and violently in the aggressive assertions of things like identity politics, which today seem to be coalescing around issues of race, poverty, inequality, class, and gender. Given these destabilizing trends, appeals to classical liberalism's vaunted conception of universal humanity, rights, freedom, tolerance, and the like over against the particular claims that issue from new forms of neo-liberal identity are increasingly ineffective.

In order to fully come to grips with the impotence and emptiness of this liberal world and, indeed, the extent to which it actually *causes* much of the violence it claims to save us from, we need to look more closely at its grotesque subversions and parodies of authentic Christian practices, particularly from the perspective of more of its secular "liturgies."

A liturgy of violence

Does liberalism really save us from violence as it claims? Cavanaugh retorts that the violence that liberalism supposedly saved us from was in fact in many respects *already a secular violence*. In other words, the early modern history of Europe, coming as it did on the heels of the crumbling medieval order, was as much a jostling for earthly rule as it was a jostling for this or that abstruse theological doctrine. As he puts it, "the 'Wars of Religion' were not the events that necessitated the birth of the modern state; they were in fact themselves the birthpangs of the state."[20] Or as Hart argues, the so-called Wars of Religion "ought really to be remembered as the first wars of the modern nation-state, whose principal purpose was to establish the supremacy of secular state authority over every rival power, most especially the power of the church."[21]

In fact, what we see here is the very creation of what we now understand as "religion." To return to Leithart's account of Cavanaugh's narrative, we see him voice Cavanaugh's retort to the liberal state's claim that religion causes violence.

> And he [Cavanaugh] answered them and said, You profit! Your naming of religion is useful to you. By it, you allow people to do some things in public, things you name "secular." And by it, you do not allow people to do other things in public, things you name "religious." By it, you pretend that you are protecting us from violent "religion" so that we will love you. By it you stir up patriotic zeal that looks just like "religion" but which you name "secular." By it, you demand that young men offer their lives as sacrifices to you, while telling us that other young men who offer their lives as sacrifices to God are nutty. By it, you encourage large crowds to wave flags at fighter jets, but do not allow small crowds of children to pray at school. By it, you prove that the West is superior to the rest. By it, you excuse yourself for dropping bombs on all the rest who have not learned about the firmament established between religion and life, all who are not as you are.

Cavanaugh argues that liberalism first cooked up the notion that traditional religion — previously understood as a socially enacted,

---

20 William T. Cavanaugh, *Theo-Political Imagination: Discovering the Liturgy as a Political Act in an Age of Global Consumerism* (London: Bloomsbury, 2002), 2.
21 Hart, *Atheist Delusions*, 88.

all-encompassing reality—was *the* cause of violence as a way of propos-
ing the liberal state as the savior. Rather than attempt to eradicate religion
totally—this would have been unrealistic at that time—liberal theorists
did something far cleverer. They simply recreated "religion" in such a way
as to make it "fit" within the supervision of the State as its benign and
submissive vassal. If "religion" is simply an interior affair of the individual, then it can be sealed off from the business of state power and public
discourse, and thus be effectively controlled.

Moreover, when religion does flare up in fundamentalist violence from
time to time, this can nicely reinforce the cult of the state as savior. For
example, terrorist attacks (which are today at least partly a consequence
not only of religious violence but of *secular* violence as well) provoke
fear, which makes people more readily hand over more and more of
their freedom to the state, and allows Christians to unblushingly support state-sanctioned violence, such as torture, assassinations, and the
bombing of foreign villages. Terrorism also provokes nationalist rituals
of patriotism, which serves as the ritual glue that unites us enlightened,
progressive Westerners against the "others," those backwards religious
and ethnic fundamentalists.

Cavanaugh argues that all of this only masks the *true sources of violence*,
and the violence that we ourselves in the West perpetuate and justify. For
example, while we are rightfully shocked and horrified by atrocities committed by groups such as the "Islamic State," the West nevertheless quite
happily presides over its own insidious genocidal practices daily, sacrificing
its smallest lives to the idols of "choice" and "lifestyle." While groups like
the Islamic State openly celebrate their cult of violence, we self-righteously
justify and dissemble our own. Thus we acclimatize ourselves ever more
unblushingly in a dissimulated, hidden, hypocritical, and as such more
irredeemable and corrosive violence (and despair).

Perhaps we as Christians even tacitly join in the logic of accommodation
to evil, by for instance reducing the evil of abortion to merely one issue
in a suite of social justice causes. While Christians should speak against
injustices wherever they appear, pleas for a "consistent life ethic" often
mask a tacit acceptance or even loss of consciousness of the distinctively
grave horror and violence of abortion.

So, the contemporary cult of liberalism does not "solve" the problem
of violence; it merely redeploys it to more insidious and covert sites. As
summarized by Cavanaugh, "The rise of the modern nation state is a

historically contingent event that has produced more, not less, violence. It has done so not by secularizing politics, but by supplanting the imagination of the body of Christ with a heretical theology of salvation through the state."[22] Hart claims that "for the sheer scale of its violences, the modern period is quite unsurpassed":

> [by] midway through the twentieth century, Western society had become so inured to the idea of war as a total conflict between one entire people and another that even liberal democracies did not scruple to bomb open cities from the air, or to use incendiary or nuclear devices to incinerate tens of thousands of civilians, sometimes only for the vaguest of military objectives.[23]

Hart thus questions the Enlightenment's grand narrative about overcoming intolerance and violence:

> if it were really true that the emergence of the secular state rescued Western humanity from the rule of religious intolerance, then what we should find on looking back over the course of Western European history is a seamless, if inverted, arc: a decline from the golden days of Roman imperial order, when the violence of religion was moderated by the prudent hand of the state, into a prolonged period of fanaticism, cruelty, persecution, and religious strife, and then—as the church was gradually subdued—a slow reemergence from the miserable brutality of the "age of faith" into a progressively more rational, more humane, less violent social arrangement. This, though, is precisely what we do not find.[24]

22 Cavanaugh, *Theo-Political Imagination*, 5.
23 Hart, *Atheist Delusions*, 97.
24 Ibid., 86. Instead, Hart continues, we have witnessed "a new age of territorial and (ultimately) ideological wars, nationalist and (then) imperialist wars, wars prompted by commerce, politics, colonial interests, blood and soil, and (at the last) visions of the future of Europe and even of humanity: England's wars with the Netherlands, Spain, Portugal, and France, Sweden's wars with Poland, Russia, and Denmark, France's wars with Spain, the Netherlands, and the League of Augsburg; the war of the Spanish succession, the war of the Polish succession, the two Silesian wars of Austrian succession, the third Silesian war; revolutionary France's wars with Britain, Holland, and Spain, the wars of the First, Second, and Third Coalitions, and all the Napoleonic wars; the wars of Italian unification, the wars of German unification, the Franco-Prussian War; the first and second Balkan wars, the First World War, the Second World War … (to name just the most obvious examples).

Genealogies of violence

Why is it that this Enlightenment story is in fact more fiction than fact? One of the main reasons that liberalism is unable to actually save us from violence and rather increases it exponentially is its "creation story," upon which is built its basic anthropological assumptions, its basic vision of who the human person is. Within the vision articulated here, there is good reason why liberal theorists think that we need the state to save us. Where Christianity places emphasis on the person's capacity for sociality and self-governance as a being created for relationship, guided by virtue, and open to the radical transformation afforded by redeeming and sanctifying grace, the liberal has no such grounds for confidence in the motivations that might guide any individual.

Early liberal theorists such as Thomas Hobbes (1588–1679) and John Locke (1632–1704) presupposed a more or less brutal "state of nature" or "original violence" as the original lodestone of human identity. That is, they bracket out any possibility that the person could be guided and inspired by anything more than his own selfish interest (anything that the Christian would say to the contrary deriving from the echoes of the capacities native to our original state of Paradisal perfection[25]), focusing instead on the "real" historical condition of fallen man *as fallen man.* This, interestingly, suggests a recognition that even for the liberal theorist, violence is not religious *per se*, but is as much a feature of man himself as anything else. We will take up this point in the next chapter.

As Schindler has pointed out, outside of a creation story that stresses an "original unity" or a fundamental condition of being from, with, and for the other, liberal theorists opted for an extreme secularized view of the person, defined first as an atomistic individual for whom relation to others is added only after the fact, optionally or merely nominally. Outside of an original defining relationship to others, the first good of the individual is egoistic: one's own survival or gratification. Any responsibility I have to others only holds if it does not conflict with the first, my own good, which must be regarded as distinct from the moment of relationship. And therefore any act of selflessness or philanthropy appears, not as something native

---

Never in European history had there been so many standing armies, or large armies on campaign, or so many men endowed with the power to send other men to kill and die."

25   John Paul II refers to the "echoes" of original innocence that man still carries in his heart despite the effects of the Fall. See John Paul II, *Man and Woman He Created Them: A Theology of the Body*, trans. Michael Waldstein (Boston: Pauline, 2006), 202, 347.

to the identity of the person, but rather as an out-of-the-ordinary act of generosity or heroic gesture of good will; or at the very least, something naturally owed only to one's "tribe."

All of this presupposes a primitive state of conflict or competition between persons who essentially wield their rights against one another in a Darwinian battle of the survival of the fittest. It is simply assumed that people will come into conflict with one another as a function of the natural order, indeed of their "human nature" properly speaking. More importantly, it is also assumed that there is little possibility of a genuinely redemptive moment in which the person might discover a deeper law of identity and relating to the other that might offer a radical spiritual transformation of any egocentric orientation.

Schindler therefore argues that all of this constitutes anything but a neutral account of the person and reality: liberalism "advances a definite metaphysics … whose central burden is to displace the person's natural community with God and others, and with truth and goodness" with a community "made up of formal-independent, logically self-centered individuals."[26]

The state as savior from violence

Now, to this primitive state of conflict and violence between individuals comes the state, offering its mediating salvation. All the individual has to do is sign a "social contract" with the state, agreeing to its terms and conditions, and letting it mediate the violent squabbles endemic to a world of subjective rights-holders and superstitious religious foment. The state says: "Give your violence to us, and let us both *protect* you from it and *practice* it for you in a legally sanctioned way. We can manage everything through a legal framework backed by the threat of force."

What is unique here is that the liberal state places little or no emphasis on the need for individuals to seek a more basic personal excellence or virtue. That is, while the classical and Christian social orders placed a high premium on a self-governance grounded in broader metaphysical and religious presuppositions, liberalism consciously undermined this approach, instead embracing a freedom founded in self-interest.[27] In this way, handing yourself over to the *liberal* state allows you to shirk your

---

26 David L. Schindler, "The Repressive Logic of Liberal Rights: Religious Freedom, Contraceptives, and the 'Phony' Argument of the *New York Times*," in *Communio* 38 (2011), 533.

27 Cf. Deneen, *Why Liberalism Failed*, 21–31.

own responsibility to seek genuine, personal redemption. That is, without calling you to personal account, the state will both *enable* your violence and *manage* it for you.

First, as long as you do not break the law, you are not obligated to confront or stamp out the disorders within your own heart. As long as you are not breaking the (socially constructed) law, you are free to pursue whichever activities you like — liberalism passes no judgment on lifestyle choices as long as they meet the bare (and ambiguous) minimum of not causing harm. As Hart puts it, "the liberties that permit one to purchase lavender bed clothes, to gaze fervently at pornography, to become a Unitarian, to market popular celebrations of brutal violence, or to destroy one's unborn child are all equally intrinsically 'good' because all are expressions of an inalienable freedom of choice."[28] Further, the state will act as a "legally" sanctioned proxy for your violence, carrying it out in your name within the constraints of the "law," thereby insulating you from its effects and preventing you from having to get your own hands dirty.

Second, through its laws, the state compels you on pain of punishment not to give into a personal violence that might cause harm and unrest. By the same token, however, the state also comes down hard and inflexibly on you if you fail to keep your violence within the law's prescribed bounds. It is no coincidence that a society with a crumbling personal morality and ethics is also one with rapidly proliferating and encroaching laws, bureaucracies, surveillance, and prison populations.

Further, employing the unique insights of Catholic anthropologist René Girard (1923–2015) (whom we will see more of in the next chapter), philosopher Robert Doran notes the paradox that while certain types of violence have obviously been overcome in modern society, others have replaced them:

> the mastery of violence on one level (the end of personal violence — revenge killings, duels, blood feuds, etc. — as an acceptable outlet for grievances, i.e., the monopolization of violence by the state) coincides with the exponential increase of violence on another: war between states or factions within states, and now, international terrorism such as the attacks of September 11, 2001.[29]

28 Hart, "God or Nothingness," 56.
29 Robert Doran, "René Girard's Apocalyptic Modernity," in *Comunicação & Cultura*

Doran then muses that "it is as if we have been moving forward and backward simultaneously. We feel more secure within our respective communities[30] and yet worry that the world will explode." In all of these ways, then, you could say that the liberal state perpetuates and redeploys violence rather than in fact solving and overcoming it.

The point is not that other systems of justice will themselves lack judicial and penal processes with similar drawbacks and deficiencies that relate to managing violence in the name of basic social living. It is rather that liberal premises about the individual in fact *deny him any genuine possibility of redemption by default*. Liberalism recognizes and promulgates no pre-juridical or pre-political source and order for him to draw on beyond its own self-referential and purely positivist legal imagination. Liberalism, in thrall to its own fiction of neutrality in regard to questions of ultimate meaning, thus serves to exacerbate and intensify violence by offering nothing positive — attempting no genuinely non-political account of the self — to address the real violence and despair at the heart of the human condition.

Freedom for manipulation and exploitation

As a consequence, the human person is reduced to the proportions of an individual ego with no intrinsic relation to others and no defined end beyond the subjective exercise of his own freedom; he is left a "hollow man," a person with no rudder, no determinate object or good to orient him, no appetite for heroic virtue or aspirations to the eternal. This is a person easy to manipulate, not out of fear, but by stoking and conditioning desire and emotion. The person without an identity needs to have someone else give him one.

It is no coincidence that capitalist practices are the grammar of liberalism, that the person is above all else an economic variable, a consumer. At the heart of said practices is a kind of managed violence, in the softer sense of coercion and manipulation: the consumer is a blank slate waiting to have his desires written *for* him. With no reference to a good or goods transcending the subjective ego, the consumer is inherently vulnerable to being manipulated by the interests of ideology and wealth accumulation.

---

11 (2011), 42.

30 At least some of us might. It could be argued that increasingly there are no guarantees here either any more. A lot has happened since 2011, the year Doran's article was published.

Various social forces within liberalism have become masters at stoking our desire. Cavanaugh has suggested that simply describing ourselves as materialistic misses the point. Rather, what a liberal consumerist society consumes is not so much things but *desire itself.* Advertising is most effective when it keeps you coming back time and time again for the next new thing, even if the "new" thing is simply an iPhone of a different color or with some trivial extra gimmick. The practices of advertising can thus be thought of as a kind of drug-dealing. The goal is to keep users in a perpetual state of unfulfilled desire so that they will keep coming back for the next fix. Precisely *what* we consume is irrelevant. *That* we consume, and often, is what matters.

Liberalism thus creates any number of predatory social and economic practices that reinforce patterns of exploitation, greed, waste, and environmental degradation. On top of that, we export our violence to foreign shores, perpetuating economic forms of slavery so that we can continue to feed our desires with an endless supply of affordable, disposable goods.

Against the argument that our consumption at least provides *some* means of income for those in situations of poverty in the so-called Third World, Cavanaugh observes that this kind of offshore strategy is better understood as essentially a crassly opportunistic exploitation. In a bid to keep production costs as low as possible, corporations deliberately take advantage of people who will work for subsistence wages because this is the only income they may have access to. The "better this than nothing" argument thus masks and tacitly legitimizes a moral and ethical failure to promote within such communities positive economic practices that might actually *lift* people from poverty. Subsistence wages, long hours, no job security, threat and intimidation, dangerous working conditions — the Third World is the globalized economy's *Oliver Twist.*

Meanwhile, we should not be blind to how a global economy and the sovereign interests of capital therein can displace and alienate our own communities by taking business overseas and thereby subjecting the domestic working class to mass unemployment and a myriad of consequent social problems. One could say among other things that liberal capitalist economics, particularly in its globalized form, destroys local sources of production and the communities that both serve and benefit from it. Both foreign and domestic labor figure only inasmuch as they can serve the ends of capital. Big businesses feel little filial responsibility to the local communities in which they operate, and in the name of economic imperative are quite happy to relocate to where the costs of production can be kept as low as possible. Large-scale corporate ownership and stakeholders (rather than local ones) ensure that any attempt to quantify the value of a company to the local community in terms of its personal and social capital carries no weight. And so it seems almost impossible to reconcile a global economy with the Catholic social teachings of the need for a priority of labor over capital and the principle of subsidiarity.

Pelvic homages to the death of God

To return to the discussion of pelvic liturgies that opened this chapter, the same predatory, calculative, and consumerist impulses that belong to the grammar of the individual who wields a purely empty freedom also extend to patterns of violence over one's own body and the bodies of others. It was only a matter of time until this logic would burn off the final residue of a Christian vision of sexual norms and practices (already in decline at the time of Nietzsche's madman's declaration of the death of God), replacing them with the instrumentalized and commodified notions of body, sex, and gender driven by the imperatives of a self freed from any kind of objective restraint, natural or sacramental, that characterizes today's increasingly post- or trans-human consummation of the sexual revolution.

When this happens, self and body are bifurcated, dissolved of any symbiotic relation to each other. "Identity" or "orientation" floats freely above the body, the latter now stripped of any indication of or capacity for a transcendence beyond choice and desire. The body that for John Paul II symbolizes a primordial, sacramental order of love and gift beyond mere freedom and nature,[31] one that carries the "anticipatory signs, the expression and the promise of the gift of self, in conformity with the wise plan of the Creator" (*Veritatis splendor* 48), is "neutered" (both ontologically and physically) by a liberal notion of the self as constituted only by the individual's desire, a self who operates in the horizon of a nature no longer shaped or constrained by the wisdom of the Creator.

From the point of view of ontological identity, this means that the being of the self is made sexless or androgynous. Maleness or femaleness and fatherhood or motherhood, then, are like inessential or optional additions to one's deepest identity. Catholic theologian David S. Crawford has made

---

31 Cf. John Paul II, *Man and Woman He Created Them*. We will consider the foundation of this claim in more detail in chapter five.

the devastating observation that the moment you make the basic frame of sexual identity androgynous or "gay" (and so subordinate the biological givenness of sexual difference wholly to the determinations of the will understood as choice or "orientation"), you effectively make *every* form of sexual identity — including heterosexuality — gay. That is, the given structure of sexual difference is made an ontologically and morally irrelevant factor when it comes to determining what it means to be a person. Sexual identity is thus reducible to a choice or preference.

Thus, to "identify" as heterosexual in this framework will be merely the product of a subjective judgment of the will, on par with the judgment of someone who identifies as homosexual or transgender. "To conceive sexuality, and consequently marriage and family, according to the logic of 'orientation,'" Crawford argues, "is already to have conceived of them in gay terms, it is to have grafted their meaning onto the underlying and controlling concept of the gay movement. They become, in a word, only a variant within the logic of 'orientation.'"[32] The more "gay" or "trans" become normal, the more defenses of "straight" as grounded in a more basic ontological order beyond the will become intolerable.

It is this move that has made the notion of a gender identity wholly beyond sex conceivable. That is, it is now becoming acceptable for one's preferred gender "identity" to bear no necessary relation to one's given biological sex. And it is also this move that is making it socially and legally impossible to advance the argument that the norm of sexual identity is that which manifests in the union between a man and woman in marriage. In many places it is now considered intolerant or even a form of "hate speech" to suggest that marriage understood as a union between a man and a woman — one that includes children as the fruit of sexual congress understood as rightly and always containing that possibility — is the norm of an ontological order which the state should recognize as having a privileged and sacrosanct status that must be respected and safeguarded as such.

Whether or not pleas for "marriage equality" are driven by a legitimate concern for rights and equality, however misguided, the practical effect of a legal understanding of marriage as between abstractly conceived "persons" rather than between a man and a woman is that its basically androgynous or gay anthropology fundamentally undercuts and relativizes any moral or ontological principle beyond politics and positive law that

32 Crawford, "Gay Marriage, Public Reason, and the Common Good," 421.

might secure a more robust understanding of the person as more than a subjective bearer of certain constructed and therefore arbitrary legal rights. When this happens, legal relationships replace natural or ontological ones, displacing any notion of human identity or selfhood beyond the vagaries of freedom and choice or beyond the democratic and political processes that encode and police that freedom and choice.

The drastic consequence of displacing the normative power of our primordial sources of identity is that the state in effect becomes your father. That is, the ties that bind one to spouse and children are now more than anything else the legal artifices of the state. As theologian Douglas Farrow has pointed out, according to Canadian law as of 2005, a mother and father are no longer the "natural parents" of their child or linked to him by a "blood relationship," but instead are defined as "legal parents" and linked by a "legal relationship."[33] The ties that bind, therefore, are merely "legal fictions," as Farrow puts it, and therefore inherently vulnerable to more "progressive" permutations. As legal fictions of a purely positivistic and therefore arbitrary concept of law, they are inherently susceptible to further ideological manipulation and distortion in the name of "equality," "rights," and "fairness," or negatively, "discrimination," "hate," "prejudice," and the like.

All of this is ominous precisely because it dissolves the primary frame and reality of the relationships which the state and citizen alike ought to defer to and protect. The liberal state becomes the author of marriage, which is then shaped by the same nominalist, positivist, and individualist premises that belong to liberalism's deepest metaphysical and religious commitments. What we are witnessing now in the moves to redefine marriage is simply the more radical and progressive side of these premises and commitments.

Hence, says Farrow, "same-sex marriage does away with the very institution — the only institution we have — that exists precisely in order to support the natural family and to affirm its independence from the state. In doing so, it effectively makes every citizen a ward of the state, by turning his or her most fundamental human connections into legal constructs at the state's gift and disposal." Even more ominously, Milbank argues that at heart the drive for same-sex marriage is a "strategic move in the modern state's drive to assume direct control over the reproduction of the population,

33   Farrow, "Why Fight Same-Sex Marriage?"

bypassing our interpersonal encounters. This is not about natural justice, but the desire on the part of biopolitical tyranny to destroy marriage and the family as the most fundamental mediating social institution."[34]

Technology as the queen of the sciences

If these are the kind of first ontological and then social and legal possibilities introduced by the liberal embrace of an essentially androgynous anthropology that neuters the body, what of the more practical bio-technological possibilities?

From the point of view of freedom as will, couple these new existential imaginings with technological possibility and you have the ingredients needed for a reengineering of the human itself via bio-technology. Today, "gender reassignment surgery" allows you to deliberately destroy the sex you were born with, a truly staggering (and only very recently both morally and practically unthinkable) kind of violence. Increasingly, our capacity to imagine a self immune from any claim of bodiliness is by means of advanced technology made reality, albeit a kind of perverse Frankensteinian reality. And this capacity serves as more cannon fodder to undermine the notion that one should attach *any* normative significance to any ontological consideration regarding the relationship between selfhood and embodiment that posits something beyond the will or legal fiction.

This is the logic that makes things like abortion, euthanasia, contraception, assisted reproductive technologies (embryonic stem cell research, surrogacy, three-parent in vitro fertilization), and gender reassignment surgery not only socially and morally *acceptable*, but also perverse forms of moral *imperative*. At any given point I may (or even must) have these options if I am to fully realize a perceived freedom beyond the claims of a moral order that might precede, have priority over, and therefore restrict my subjective choice.

For example, if I am in a same-sex relationship or in no relationship at all, if I so desire it I can now "make" a child through assisted reproductive technologies. By a combination of the disincarnate premises of gay anthropology and advanced technological means, procreation now becomes an artifice, entirely at the disposal of our will, both to make and to destroy, no longer bound to an order of relation and gift that precedes and shapes the freedom of the individual. Procreation is thereby now made *formally*

---

34 Milbank, "The Impossibility of Gay Marriage and the Threat of Biopolitical Control."

and *legally* extrinsic to the sexual act, and thus a matter of pure choice. In my freedom I can both destroy and make a "fetus" at my leisure.

Thus the gay anthropology that legally and institutionally underwrites same-sex marriage now by technology fully consummates a non-pro-creative understanding of sexual intercourse that, as British philosopher Elizabeth Anscombe recognized with such acuity back in 1958, was even then already encoded *de facto* in the cultural embrace of contraception.[35] In sum, the pelvic liturgies of liberalism thus all correspond to that free-dom-as-will of the individual who today demands to go beyond the limits imposed by nature, reason, or faith, and by technology is now more and more permitted to do so.

However, as I have already suggested, the problem with an account of freedom as pure will, with no real object in an order beyond law, politics, and technology, is that it remains fundamentally vulnerable to coercion and manipulation. The moment you reify the arbitrary will, disconnecting it from the true sources of love, worship, and beauty, you render yourself vulnerable to an order of forces and wills — blind and otherwise — beyond rational control. A blank slate is far easier to write on than a full one.

As John Paul II was fond of pointing out, a freedom not tied to some prior and constitutive measure of truth is very easily dragged into a war of the strong against the weak, made all the more insidious when this war is dressed up in the language of democracy and law. He spoke of a "tyrant state which arrogates to itself the right to dispose of the life of the weakest and most defenseless members, from the unborn child to the elderly, in the name of a public interest which is really nothing but the interest of one part" (*Evangelium vitae*, 20).

This is why in the end liberalism fosters a new form of slavery, a new bondage of the will to increasingly inhuman forms of violence, all the while seemingly unable to provide any real restraints on what it has unleashed. Hanby has spoken compellingly of how in the absence of any order beyond the will of the self, it is technological possibility that comes to be the ulti-mate principle that shapes our freedom. "As technological products extend their reach and their effects accumulate," he suggests, "this perpetual war on the limits of possibility takes on a life of its own, making servants of its would-be masters and determining the conditions of human thought

---

35 Cf. G. E. M. Anscombe, "Modern Moral Philosophy," in *Philosophy* 33 (1958).

and action."[36] Hanby thus refers to technology "as a kind of fate," a logic that in the end consumes everything else in its wake.

Heidegger said something similar: "Everywhere we remain unfree and chained to technology whether we passionately affirm or deny it."[37] He too spoke of technology as a kind of fate, as an almost inexorable material unfolding of a deeper spiritual failure to see things according to categories other than cause and effect, force, calculation, and utility. The danger of technology, for Heidegger, is that it obscures the possibility and call of what he describes as "a more primal truth."[38] Today, under the name of "science" breathlessly uttered as if of a god, it has become a kind of first philosophy, a worldview.

While we might think that technology is driven by and under the control of the will, Hanby suggests that actually the opposite is more true. Even if technology is originally the product of the will's imagination and desire, it very quickly outstrips the will, becoming its master, shaping the desires of the will in the image of its endless possibility.

Hanby suggests that the essence of the sexual revolution is technological. "Sexual freedom" could not really become a practical possibility until the invention of the Pill. "Same-sex marriage would have remained permanently unthinkable were it not for the technological conquest of procreation"; further, "it would be impossible to imagine that a man might 'really' be a woman if we did not also imagine it were technologically possible to transform him into one."[39]

Technology thus both cultivates the imagination and the will and furnishes them with real objects and possibilities. It is only then that politics, understood as collectivized will, can, in service to its new master, set itself to the task of more comprehensively discrediting and overturning the social norms and mores that might prevent the possibilities of technology from being implemented. Though we think that we are free and that our desires are our own, it is rather the case that both freedom and desire are now being produced by our machines. We are already being annihilated by Skynet.[40]

36 Hanby, "A More Perfect Absolutism," in *First Things* (October 2016), at https://www.firstthings.com/article/2016/10/a-more-perfect-absolutism.

37 Martin Heidegger, "The Question Concerning Technology," in Martin Heidegger, *Basic Writings*, ed. David Farrell Krell (London: HarperPerrenial, 2008), 311.

38 Ibid., 333.

39 Hanby, "A More Perfect Absolutism."

40 Parts of this section were presented in a paper at the annual meeting of the Australian Confraternity of Catholic Clergy in Adelaide on July 11, 2017, entitled "Bioethics

Economics as the logic of technology

If both individual and collectivized will become one unwitting hand-maiden of technology, economics is another. While from collectivized will — here, the "identity politics" of the social and political Left — issue the new moral imperatives of freedom, justice, fairness, rights, equality, representation, and the like, from economics issues the cold and inexorable imperative of profit and bottom line, something now usually held in equal measure by political Left and Right. An economics bound to technology-as-worldview will view things and persons as resources to maximize and perfect the technology that fosters (perceived) freedom and real wealth. That is, to view nature instrumentally, as a means to maximize freedom, is to reduce it to a means-end calculus. This leads to treating nature in the abstract, as "energy" (Heidegger speaks here of a "standing reserve"), a neutral source of raw power to fulfill the formless manifold desires of freedom.[41]

From this flow industries devoted not simply to providing the basic necessities of life and legitimately raising the standard of living for all, but to fulfilling the intertwined destinies of will and technology. Industry joins this destiny willingly, for it presents ever more opportunities for unbounded wealth. And since the source of this wealth is linked to the vanities and insecurities of freedom and the endless possibilities inherent in an understanding of the earth's gifts as mere energy, no one should be surprised at the violence and exploitation committed in the name of the pursuit of profit, suitably masked of course by euphemisms such as "fiscal responsibility," "streamlining," "restructuring," and the like, not to mention corporations' public relations virtue-signaling exercises designed to show us how socially progressive and environmentally responsible they are.[42]

It is all of this that makes it that much more imaginable to treat human persons themselves as, on the one hand, "raw materials," sources of technological progress and profit maximization (as in embryo experimentation), and on the other, "useless eaters" or economic deadweight that must be cut off in the name of the prosperity and security of the proverbial "many" (as in euthanasia). What makes economics on this model so chilling is how effectively the imperatives of technology, will,

in a Post-Human Age."
    41 Cf. Heidegger, "The Question Concerning Technology," 322.
    42 Cf. Paul Tyson and Matthew John Paul Tan, "Ecological Disaster and Jacques Ellul's Theological Vision," in *Solidarity* 2 (2012).

and profits are reduced to the coldly logical and dispassionate language of economic calculus.

The banality and moral tone-deafness of purely economic calculus is captured well by a 2017 episode of the long-running UK science-fiction series *Doctor Who*. In it, the Doctor and his companions respond to a distress signal from a deep-space mining operation. Here they encounter a situation where apparently malfunctioning space suits are killing the crew who wear them, turning them into zombies. The Doctor eventually deduces that this phenomenon, rather than being caused by a glitch, is in fact the result of the algorithm of the mining company, which has determined that unthinking and non-breathing zombies are more cost-efficient than a thinking and breathing crew. This is not exactly malice on the part of the crew's employer, just the cold, hard, unyielding logic of the bottom line, something effectively illustrated by the Doctor's words at the climax of the story: "The end point of capitalism. A bottom line where human life has no value at all. We're fighting an algorithm. A spreadsheet" (Season 10, episode 5).

Overcoming secular violence

Thus, what began in the elevated and exulted narratives of freedom and emancipation told by liberalism in the 18th century ends in what Hannah Arendt described as the "banality of evil."[43] It ends in a kind of numb religious bondage to the impersonal and deterministic imperatives of technological possibility, in narratives of necessity (the idea of a profit margin) and even perverse responsibility ("mercy killing"). It ends in escalating violence that we seem increasingly unable to control, either ethically or practically. Whether it is the violence of modern warfare, terrorism, individualism, racial and class conflict, consumerism, advertising, globalization, "pelvic liturgies," politics, technology, or capitalist economics, in each case we are dealing with the same basic mutation of an account of the person that might offer something beyond the flat and coercive ideological horizons of secularity that are ever more rapidly radicalizing and tribalizing the discourse within its frame.

As I see it, the long and short of liberal secularism is that it mutilates an authentic Christian heritage that lives and breathes fully within the

---

43 Cf. Hannah Arendt, *Eichmann in Jerusalem: A Report on the Banality of Evil* (New York: Penguin, 2006).

modes of love, worship, and beauty. It promotes and rewards all the worst things that can happen when you try to think and act as if God did not exist; as if He were not Love, as if He were not worthy of worship, as if He were not the faithful Beloved and caring Father worth abandoning all for.

Catholic theologian Tracey Rowland remarked that "the myth of a purely secular rationality not only 'lied' but it failed to liberate and incite to love."[44] Liberalism takes us into a slow but inexorable decline that ends quite logically in postmodern despair and violence. Liberalism is the logical completion of the inner nihilism that crept into the Christian tradition once it forgot that love, worship, and beauty were its first nature. And we Christians are often uncomfortably aligned with and complicit in its violent practices.

There is a lot more that could be said, with much finer distinction and nuance. None of this is to deny the presence in liberal societies of individuals whose lives embody deeper values and a commitment to the good that subvert the secular logic of liberalism. It is worth conceding at some level Taylor's suggestion that "in modern, secularist culture there are mingled together both authentic developments of the gospel ... and also a closing off to God that negates the gospel."[45] You might say this is empirically true to some extent. As I said before, I am not myopic about Christianity's historic complicity in various forms of violence, nor do I think that there is any ideal Christian utopia of a past age or indeed the future (save our *heavenly* kingdom) that we should longingly pine for and place our hope in.

However, a question that Taylor seems to sidestep is whether any of the so-called legitimate "developments" of the Gospel that he sees in modernity do not themselves more properly belong to a more original, more faithful form of Christianity. If it took an alternative tradition to dig them out, then maybe we need to look more deeply at what we have in fact considered "Christian." If it is true that the decline of Christianity has something to do with the fact that it shot itself in the foot, so to speak, when it began to weaken and abandon its proper mode of love, worship, and beauty, then liberalism's effort to try something new was perhaps at least partly warranted (even if the alternative liberalism proposed is a less

---

44 Tracey Rowland, *Benedict XVI: A Guide for the Perplexed* (London: T&T Clark, 2010), 160.

45 Charles Taylor, "A Catholic Modernity?" in *A Catholic Modernity? Charles Taylor's Marianist Award Lecture*, ed. James L. Heft (Oxford: Oxford University Press, 1999), 170.

than adequate antidote). So, while I have proposed a robust critique of liberal secularism, I also acknowledge the ways in which historic Christianity has, in reneging on its proper mission and identity, helped to create the very conditions in which that secularism could appear, and in many cases found itself to be complicit in it.

At the same time, no one should underestimate or downplay the depravity and bankruptcy that we have shown to belong to the foundations and practices of liberal modernity. Hart grants that individuals within modernity may still possess and embody elements of "natural virtue," "innate nobility," and "congenital charity." And yet he also insists that "it would be a willful and culpable blindness for us to refuse to recognize how aesthetically arid, culturally worthless, and spiritually depraved our society has become."[46] The only way forward is the radical rejection and redemption of the violence that perpetually lurks in the human heart, whether it is manifested in a "religious" or a "secular" manner. Only a god can save us now.

In the next two chapters, I will begin to formulate my answer to the problems presented in the first three chapters. I will attempt to chart a path beyond both a Christian faith held captive to various forms of despair and violence and a secular alternative that only more radically perpetuates despair and violence.

---

46 Hart, "God or Nothingness," 71–72, note 9.

FOUR

The Redemptive Folly
of the Peace of Christ

"Despair, or folly?" said Gandalf. "It is not despair, for despair is only for those who see the end beyond all doubt. We do not. It is wisdom to recognize necessity, when all other courses have been weighed, though as folly it may appear to those who cling to false hope. Well, let folly be our cloak, a veil before the eyes of the Enemy! For he is very wise, and weighs all things to a nicety in the scales of his malice. But the only measure that he knows is desire, desire for power; and so he judges all hearts. Into his heart the thought will not enter that any will refuse it, that having the Ring we may seek to destroy it. If we seek this, we shall put him out of reckoning."

J. R. R. Tolkien, *The Fellowship of the Ring*

IN THE PREVIOUS CHAPTER, I SUGGESTED THAT violence sums up the metaphysical and "religious" essence of the ethos and practices of secular liberal modernity. But we must admit the great indignation that such a claim will provoke. For today we face a cultural narrative of nearly overwhelming proportions that insists that religion — especially Christian faith — is the single greatest cause of violence, of almost every social ill, injustice, and prejudice. To claim otherwise is to challenge a whole history and theater of interpretation. Such a provocative claim in this context, therefore, requires further explication.

To this end, I will begin where we left off in chapter 3, and move to an attempt to better source the violence which I claimed has in secular liberalism begun to move more rapidly to its nihilistic zenith. I think it goes without saying that under the pressure of the prevailing Enlightenment mythology propagated by secular culture, many (if not most) Christians secretly fear or assume that Christianity has no greater claim to truth than any other worldview or interpretation: that despite its claims to the highest transcendent truth, it too is at heart merely another human play for power and control, and that its institutional side in particular is just as corrupted as any other.

On the face of it, there may often be good grounds for such suppositions, particularly the concerns about institutional depravity. Hart does not mince words: "The enfranchised church has never been more than half Christian even at the best of times; often enough, it has been much less than that."[1] I fear that today we are far from the best of times.

We need to look deeper to see if what I have called Christianity's proper mode of being — that is, in love, worship, and beauty — belong more deeply to its identity than any of its violent failings, and whether it is in fact still possible today to again catch sight of its spiritual essence.

More than violence?

We have just seen that the practices of liberalism are grounded in an "ontology" of violence. Yet these practices have also been seen to have deeper roots in certain missteps made in Christian theology itself, in the infrastructural loss of the primacy of love, worship, and beauty. Most of us are aware of the claim of the so-called "new atheists" and the ubiquitous "com-box" expert who argue that religion — especially the *Christian* religion — causes violence.

To a certain degree, perhaps oddly, I agree with them. That is, I think it is true that there is some kind of a real "causal" connection between on the one hand a certain historical self-understanding of Christian faith that did indeed facilitate the slowly gathering forces of secularization and the attendant betrayal of love, worship, and beauty, and on the other hand the desiccated, violent rationalism of a liberal culture representing the logical completion of this movement towards nihilism.

From another angle, I also think that there is great truth to the claim that Christianity, *precisely when it is most true to itself*, indeed *intensifies* or *becomes the occasion* for violence inasmuch as it exposes and sharpens the dramatic struggle between good and evil, provoking and intensifying the urgency of evil by the revelation of the ultimate counterpoint to it in the face of Jesus Christ.

---

1 Hart, *Atheist Delusions*, 171.

Postmodern commentators, of course, broaden the notion that religion causes violence by claiming that *truth itself causes violence*. They argue that *all* "truth" — whether religious, political, or social — inasmuch as it is understood to be radically limited by perspective and desire rests on little more than relative and unsupportable claims driven by the will to power. Of course, a postmodernist would agree with the new atheists that historically speaking, Christianity has been acutely involved with various forms of historical violence. Again, all you have to do is spend some time in internet com-boxes to get a sense of the near-universal social consensus on this point.

Clearly, large swathes of modern and postmodern critique of Christian faith are based on a certain Enlightenment mythology whose goal was and is to discredit Christianity writ large so as to overcome it.[2] Nevertheless, our genealogy has suggested that Christianity's flirtations with the paths of violence and despair have more often than not taken far more subtle and pervasive forms. If this is so, Christianity has inadvertently helped to lay the groundwork for its own demise by not staying true to its own sacramental and liturgical confession.

It is primarily at this deep level — and of course when the cancer infects the concrete sphere of action — that the Church's complicity in violence must be confronted. The power of Christianity to be "a light for the nations" (Is 49:6) in the deepest sense is at stake, particularly in a world where the temptations of Left and Right have never been more threatening.

To this end, let us now descend more critically into the issues raised thus far to consider anew whether there is something unique to the Christian claim capable of restoring our blurred vision.

Sacred violence

As I have already mentioned, René Girard argued that Christianity is both the *subversion* and *intensification* of violence. Even if you agree with Cavanaugh that liberalism is at its core a religion of violence, and even if you posit that by contrast Christianity embodies the possibility of authentic unity and peace, it cannot be denied that short of radical ongoing conversion to Christ, the principles of Christianity do indeed contain the possibility of a sharpened and more devastating violent

---

2 Cf. Rodney Stark, *Bearing False Witness: Debunking Centuries of Anti-Catholic History* (West Conshohocken: Templeton Press, 2016); Hart, *Atheist Delusions*.

conflict between good and evil.[3] If Christianity represents the unmasking of the sources and mechanisms of violence (as Girard claims it does), then the stage is set for a new kind of violent confrontation and struggle when this threatens the ways of a world that resists its own redemption at all cost.

To begin, Girard submits that the religious impulse unique to human beings has archaic origins in a need to deal with the destructive social effects of violence.[4] Unlike Locke and Hobbes, Girard does not maintain that the state of violence is *original* to the human race. Nor does he believe that there is no real redemption offered for this condition.[5] But he does think that the violence that characterizes human relations is a powerful, determinative, and culture-shaping consequence of our fallen condition. Girard argues that religion arrives on the human scene, not from some starry-eyed contemplation of the heavens, but first as a practical strategy to deal with a fundamental disorder in the human soul, one that tends to provoke a deadly, competitive violence among persons.

In anthropological terms, Girard explains the origin of this violent competition in the phenomenon of what he calls "mimetic rivalry." On his account, at the heart of basic human behavior is not just desire for an object in the abstract, but desire for an object as mediated by someone else's possession of and desire for it. That is, what makes something valuable to us is that someone else has it; we desire something not simply because of any intrinsic or instrumental good that might be associated with the thing itself, but more fundamentally on the basis of whether *someone else* desires it. What I think of as *my* desire, then, is in fact shaped and mediated by someone else's desire. This phenomenon he calls "mimesis," or imitation. We might also think of mimetic rivalry in more classical terms as the vice of envy.

---

3 Cf. René Girard, *Battling to the End: Conversations with Benoît Chantres*, trans. Mary Baker (East Lansing: Michigan State University Press, 2010).

4 For the core of Girard's thesis see René Girard, *Things Hidden Since the Foundation of the World*, trans. Stephen Bann and Michael Metteer (Stanford: Stanford University Press, 1987); René Girard, *I See Satan Fall Like Lightning*, trans. James G. Williams (Maryknoll: Orbis, 2001).

5 See, for instance, Girard's comments in a 1993 interview in which he clarifies that he is "not trying to do away with the beginning of Genesis," but rather seeking to interpret human existence according to the empirical shape it takes after the "founding murder" of Cain. "Violence, Difference, Sacrifice: A Conversation with René Girard," interview conducted by Rebecca Adams, in *Religion and Literature* 25 (1993), 20.

Girard thus describes desire as a "triangular" phenomenon: there is your desire, there is the thing desired, and there is the other who models desire. The most concentrated paradigm of mimetic rivalry and triangular desire that might easily come to mind is sibling rivalry. No mother or father needs to have it explained how when one child gets a toy, the other child seems to inexplicably desire it at that precise moment. Almost inevitably, there will be conflict when the child without the toy tries to claim it for himself.

Girard proposes that this mimetic rivalry is what is going on at a macro-level when there is violence in a community. In order for a community to dispel the violence caused by the various forms of mimetic rivalry in its midst, it must find a way to quell the engine which produces it. On the basis of his study of sacrifice in primitive communities and in ancient mythology, Girard argues that in order to do this, the community finds a "scapegoat" on which to pin their collective guilt. That is, the community unites against a single victim who is saddled with all of the violence and guilt that exists within each individual's heart, and put to death. By this, the community — now a mob — has been able to dissipate its competitive violence by proxy, thus resolving the conflicts generated by mimetic rivalry, at least until the next crisis come along and a new sacrificial victim is needed. In coming together against a common threat, Girard speaks of a "cathartic" effect being generated in the community. One need only think of the single will of a mob, or the perverted forms of social cohesion that develop among those gossiping about a particular someone else.

The long and short of this for Girard is that because the scapegoat helped bring peace to the community, it is a logical next step for the community to venerate that individual, turning him into a god. For if peace was brought to the community through the death of this individual, then it must be the case that he was more than human. And so a religious cult builds up around this figure. When the community realizes that violence still continues in the community despite the original sacrifice, they determine that it must be because their god (the original scapegoat) demands *more* sacrifice. And thus a ritualization of the single-victim (scapegoat) mechanism occurs, where repetitive cultic sacrifice reproduces the cathartic effect of the death of the first scapegoat, thus reinforcing the divine status of that scapegoat, and bringing renewed peace to the community.

Girard suggests that *this helps to explain the close association of religion with violence.* We can summarize his thinking in three points. First, "religion" arises because we are already violent. That is, violence originates in the disorder of our own hearts. So, contrary to what the new atheists claim, it is not religion *per se* that causes violence. "The violence we would love to transfer to religion," says Girard, "is really our own, and we must confront it directly. To turn religions into the scapegoats of our own violence can only backfire in the end."[6]

Second, religion bears a close relationship to violence. For by means of religion, violence is able to be contained in controlled, ritualized expression. Religion is able to manage human violence by directing and sanctioning it in ritualized (and therefore controlled and limited) form by the single-victim mechanism. This selective sanctioning of violence thus prevents violence on a mass scale, and thereby facilitates the restoration and preservation of social cohesion.

Third, religion thus in a certain sense "causes" violence, or better, indirectly helps to perpetuate and valorize it. It becomes a useful vehicle for its controlled transmission. In mitigating general violence, it simultaneously gives a stamp of divine approval to specialized sacred forms of violence.

Thus while religion in its archaic, "scapegoat" form helped to control and mitigate violence overall, it nevertheless could not get to the root of the problem; it never found *true* redemption and, coupled with the way that it *authoritatively legitimized violence* (i.e., in ritualized form) it thereby also became its formal authorization. Insofar as violence is thereby validated by the sacred, the risk is that things like "holy war," "jihad," or various forms of coercion in the name of faith become acceptable.

Christ's subversion of religion and violence

For Girard, what the *Christian* "religion" brings to this phenomenon is in fact both the radical *subversion* of religion and the only authentic *redemption* of violence. For in Christianity, the victim is unequivocally revealed as innocent and the finger is pointed back to the collective violence of the mob and the guilt of each human heart (a process that begins in the Old Testament with the Jewish rejection of human sacrifice). The Gospels leave no doubt that the victim (Christ) is supremely innocent, and that those (us) who cause his death are the guilty ones. In this, Christianity represents a massive deconstruction of the ancient sacrificial system.

---

6 René Girard, "Violence and Religion: Cause or Effect?" in *The Hedgehog Review* 6 (2004), at http://www.iasc-culture.org/THR/THR_article_2004_Spring_Girard.php.

Christian faith, then, pinpoints the *true* cause of violence within our disordered hearts; it is we ourselves who must be held accountable for our own violence. We must confront our own darkness. For Girard, this is why after Christ the power and energy of ancient religious sacrificial ritual drains away. Christianity demythologizes and unmasks the superstition and violence at work in ritual sacrifice, thus emptying its classic forms of their cathartic social power. Instead, in Christ we find the true sacrificial "Lamb of God who takes away the sins of the world" (Jn. 1:29), the one who redeems our violence, showing us a true catharsis in the way of love. Christianity radically undercuts the ways of the world through a God who Himself embodies the radical subversion of violence by dying on the Cross, in resisting of all forms of violence right to the bitter end.

It is precisely here that "weakness," in the person of the small, the lowly, the victim, the loser, reveals a paradoxical strength that destroys the paradigm of violence, the way of the world. To be a Christian is to be small. *To be a Christian is to be a son or a daughter, to be God's child, and in this, paradoxically, to be "big" and "strong."*

Girard suggests that this is why Nietzsche reacted so strongly against Christianity, calling it a "slave religion"[7] and a "religion of the herd."[8] What for Nietzsche was the *betrayal* of the strength and honor of the mythological vision of gods and men is for Girard the *subversion* of the violence of those myths, the subversion and unmasking of all religious violence and ideologies of domination. Both Nietzsche and Girard understand how profoundly Christianity changed the values of the world, how deeply it "transvalued" these values. Girard indeed considers that Nietzsche was prophetic because of this keen recognition, especially at a time when so many of Nietzsche's contemporaries were treating Christianity as just another religious mythology, thus missing its true originality and novelty.

But what makes Nietzsche's recognition so tragic, according to Girard, is that he could not see how the unique renunciation of violence in Christianity was in fact the ultimate — and *only* — way to transcend the "herd mentality": "He opposes, so he believes, the crowd mentality, but he does not recognize his Dionysian stance as the supreme expression of the

---

7 Cf. Friedrich Nietzsche, *Beyond Good and Evil*, trans. Walter Kaufmann (New York: Vintage Books, 1989), 204–8.

8 Cf. Friedrich Nietzsche, *The Will to Power*, trans. Walter Kaufmann and R. J. Hollingdale (New York: Vintage Books, 1968).

mob in its most brutal and its most stupid tendencies."[9] As Girard sees it, the true "herd" that Nietzsche *should* have hated is not Christianity, but rather the self-righteous mob that gathers to condemn the innocent victim. The mob does not confront its own darkness, but mindlessly and self-righteously perpetuates its destructive violence.

Nietzsche, then, inasmuch as he could not accept the overcoming and redemption of violence offered by Christ, thereby paradoxically consigned himself to the mob, to the herd whose mediocrity and groupthink he so desperately hated. Nietzsche's tortured ranting against Christianity betrays the supreme tension of a mixed marriage of genius and delusion in his thought—as does, perhaps, his own tortured, psychotic end.

While Girard believes that Christianity is the massive subversion of all violence, he nevertheless recognizes—presciently—that this does not simply or automatically mean the end of human violence writ large. For in draining the power of archaic religious sacrifice, Christianity alarmingly also drains the cathartic effect of the single-victim mechanism. If ancient religion allowed a socially cohesive, cathartic, and controlled release for our violence that did not require deep personal transformation, what happens when this outlet is taken away? What happens if individuals do not submit to the personal *ascesis* and conversion required for the Christian subversion of violence to bear fruit?

The extent to which we do not accept the demanding conditions of the redemption of our violence in Christ is the extent to which our violence, now deprived of the catharsis of the single-victim mechanism and heightened by our conscious rejection of the face of God, must find new outlets, more insidious and horrific. The heart and mind of the person who rejects Christ go dark; the natural goodness that they might otherwise have had grows cold in their heart. They become deadened to human virtue, to the beckoning echoes of the true, good, and the beautiful implanted in their hearts at their creation and fulfilled in Christ's redemptive sacrifice.

All of this helps to explain further the deepening violence of the secular horizons of liberal modernity. Because old "religion" no longer works, and because we have rejected Christ, we have to turn to new forms of ritualized catharsis to quell the violence in our hearts. We find new outlets, new scapegoats, new rituals, new excuses to avoid a confrontation with ourselves. The state takes up ownership of the primary religious impulse

9 Girard, *I See Satan Fall Like Lightning*, 173.

(in the Girardian sense), becoming the new administrator and guardian of sacred violence, as embodied in the violence of its primary practices and liturgies. There is nothing like an airstrike against a common enemy to bring a people together.

Meanwhile, organized religion must adapt to the fact that its rites and rituals no longer seem to have the same power they once possessed. Christ has stripped them of their power apart from him, while secular liturgies now claim the primary allegiance of their people. Short of redemption, transformation, and new life in Christ, a religion must seek new outlets or coping strategies for violence.

Religion may thus take a fundamentalist or politicized form. That is, it may seek to rehabilitate itself as the vital center of people's lives by engaging in new forms of "holy war" with liberal secularism in an attempt to gain back the influence and territory stolen from it.

Alternatively, religion may learn to accept a more neutered identity for itself. It may market itself as "inwardness" or "mindfulness"; as the purveyor of ethics or justice; a set of teachings on the good life; perhaps as a global force for promoting tolerance, diversity, and human rights. It may present itself as a form of transcendental meditation, an escape from violence through indifference to and detachment from the world.

But the extent to which religion cannot effectively offer and mediate genuine salvation and really deal with and redeem *our* violence and *our* sin, and the extent to which it can no longer claim to be a universal solution, is the extent to which it is no longer a credible bearer of good news. The rise of the option of outright atheism or various "new age" alternatives perhaps speaks to the dissatisfaction with the neutered and impotent options that mainstream religion now represents.

The bottom line in all of this is that the peace of Christ upsets the equilibrium of the world, paradoxically creating a kind of power vacuum where new kinds of subversion and violence can flourish, and ultimately setting human history on the course of its long defeat. Returning to Girard, in his later years, he became increasingly pessimistic about our ability to control the forces unleashed by Christ's unmasking of evil. He spoke of an "escalation to extremes," of a violence spiraling out of control towards the possibility of apocalypse, one caused by man's own self-destructive rejection of Christ. In this, while Girard finds Christianity's demystification of the violence of the single-victim mechanism to be "good in the absolute," it has nevertheless "proven bad in the relative, for we were not prepared to shoulder its consequences. We are not Christian enough."[10]

But rather than admitting this, we instead find ways of rubbing the sharp edges off the Gospel's apocalyptic elements, thereby avoiding the obvious import of their words: apocalyptic texts tells the grim story, not of God's vengeful wrath or punishment, but of the consequences of *our own* sinful failure to follow Christ: "Humanity is more than ever the author of its own fall because it has become able to destroy its world…. Therefore we have to awaken our sleeping consciences. To seek to comfort is always to contribute to the worst."[11]

To take all of this to heart heightens the need to confront our own violence. We should not try to dull the force of Christ's words when he says: "Do not think that I have come to bring peace upon the earth. I have come to bring not peace but the sword" (Mt. 10:34). Christianity is not the "religion of peace" in the benign way that it is often proposed it should be, as a force for social good. The peace that Christ brings is not the peace of tolerance, diversity, or increasingly progressive enlightenment. Christ comes first and foremost with the crushing imperative that I must do spiritual battle — *I* must confront the violence of *my* own heart, *I* must be *intolerant* of *my own* sin, *I* must reject the diverse temptations of *my own* disordered will.

To reject this ultimate healing is therefore to radically embrace and intensify our own violence, to legitimize our weakness and to try to shape the world around ourselves so that our violence and weakness might come to be affirmed as a virtue, that mercy might be the balm that merely absolves us of responsibility for our sins. The real sinner is the one who has seen the face of God and yet does not repent, who has consciously accepted and chosen violence.

The ever-present threat of violence

We should not be blind to the way that Christianity, in its worldly, institutional side, is susceptible to the very violence that its founder, Christ, has unmasked and offered redemption from. The Church too can give itself over to violence, more easily than we might like to think. While we may pat ourselves on the back for no longer directly participating in political or social violence, make no mistake, we still find more covert ways to be

---

10 Girard, "On War and Apocalypse," in *First Things* (February 2009), at https://www. firstthings.com/article/2009/08/on-war-and-apocalypse.

11 Ibid.

violent; whether it is the violence Christian believers and leaders do to the Gospel by reducing its message to a mere reading of the signs of the times; in Christian institutions' eager aping of the violent, impersonal, person-destroying modes of bureaucratic and corporate models of governance and operation; the Church's tacit legitimizing of and collaboration with the violence of the secular nation state, through tenuous and often imprudent alliances with political parties or regimes, often in the interests of a naive belief that some good may come of it, or, more insidiously, for social and political gain or security.

The perennial temptation for the Church is to adopt worldly strategies, to make dubious worldly alliances in the effort to propagate the faith, to maintain status, or simply to survive. Cavanaugh recognizes this: "The church's many sins have often been a direct result of the wielding of coercive power."[12] For Matthew Tan, if the Church is to have any truly *Christian* effect in the world, it must be characterized by the renunciation of violence and coercive power. The Church must instead become the embodiment of "a concrete alternative communal site," one that works to prevent the true message of faith "from being domesticated by the dominant cultural form."[13] In short, when the Church reduces the message of Christ to mediocre social and pastoral programs of false diversity, tolerance, or accommodation, when it uses that message to legitimize any kind of violence or falsehood, it implicitly participates in the violence of secular liturgies that celebrate the death of God and thus becomes a scandal and stumbling block to true faith.

I do not purport here to prescribe in detail how Christianity should relate to secular powers. The relationship with the "powers that be" will to a certain extent always be messy, confused, and regrettable. What I am most interested in is what I would call the proper mode and identity of the Church, which is to proclaim — even to its own death as an influential and privileged worldly institution — the prophetic radicality of the Gospel: precisely those elements of faith that can never be brought into any kind of prudential or conciliatory dialogue with the world. For it is here that the true power of the Gospel resides: in its proclamation and the power of that proclamation to change lives and convert hearts on no basis other

---

12 William T. Cavanaugh, *Migrations of the Holy: God, State, and the Political Meaning of the Church* (Grand Rapids: Eerdmans, 2011), 5.

13 Matthew Tan, *Justice, Unity, and the Hidden Christ*, 63.

than its givenness. This is the core that the individual Christian must hold onto at any and all cost. This is the "mere Christianity" that in its "mere-ness" or its smallness is precisely the radical way of the true power of love.

I wish to argue that, far from thereby condemning Christianity to some interior ghetto of the individual Christian soul, this is the originating point of a genuinely sacramental world, a set of genuinely sacramental practices, a genuinely sacramental "politics" with the power to subvert, out-narrate, and out-perform the secular powers of the world, not by force, not by tactics or strategy, not by process, but by the simple living of the hobbit.

Rediscovering faith on Mount Doom

We might now take stock of where all this leaves us. If we pick up the *Lord of the Rings* analogy that I employed in chapter 1, you could say that we have passed through Mordor and now stand at the crack of fire on Mount Doom, the Ring in hand, confronted with the choice between good and evil, between entrusting ourselves to love, worship, and beauty or "reasons," despair, and violence. We have journeyed through the twists and turns of Christian history where we have discovered the source of the main challenges for faith today.

I have suggested that there is no simple answer to the question of what evangelization might look like in a "postmodern" context where God is dead, because there is for many of us no simple answer to the question of *faith itself* in this context; the tentacles of the so-called "postmodern" condition extend far more deeply and uncomfortably into our hearts than most of us would like to admit. We *ourselves* conceive of faith outside of love, worship, and beauty more constitutively—and therefore practice a more nominal faith—than most of us would like to admit. We *ourselves* are participants by default in the violent secular practices that embody and transmit liberalism's celebration of the death of God to a far greater extent than most of us would like to admit.

For this reason, the moment of decision at the crack of Mount Doom is a critical one. What will our choice be?

At the risk of mixing our metaphors, consider a scenario from the 1999 film *The Matrix*, where the protagonist Neo finds himself forced to choose between a return to the false (but comfortable) existence of the simulated world (the Matrix) created by the machines, or the real (and harsh) world of the underground resistance to the machines. Morpheus, the leader of the resistance, presents this to him as a stark choice between a blue and a red pill:

This is your last chance. After this, there is no turning back. You take the blue pill—the story ends, you wake up in your bed and believe whatever you want to believe. You take the red pill—you stay in Wonderland, and I show you how deep the rabbit hole goes. Remember: all I'm offering is the truth. Nothing more.

My goal thus far has been to impress upon the reader the importance of provoking this existential choice. For whether we have consciously faced this choice or not, one way or another we are already living one of its possibilities. Either we are in therapy or we are in truth; in despair or in faith. This choice is always pressing, but I would suggest that it is even more so today given the kinds of challenges that face us in a postmodern condition of secular violence.

Given what we have seen so far, perhaps it is a foregone conclusion that most people will today choose therapy, despair, and violence. All of us have of course succumbed to such choices in our own lives. And to return to our hobbit motif, we can see in Frodo's failure to voluntarily throw the Ring into the fire a kind of archetypal representation of the inevitability of our own failure apart from some mysterious intervention. Like St. Peter (cf. Mk. 14:66–72), Frodo fails the test at the critical point. For the temptations and fears are too monumental; the forces of hope and goodness too depleted. And so instead of chucking the Ring in the fire, we keep it for ourselves, refusing a story beyond that which we can control and create for ourselves.

Perhaps at this moment we give up on faith altogether, embracing the power of darkness and despair. Perhaps we say that there is no genuine escape from violence, and that all we can do is attempt to get the most out of what little time we have.

Or maybe we attempt—like Boromir—to have the best of both worlds. We think we can make an existential choice for truth and faith, and yet employ the practical methods of the enemy to propagate and defend them. Yet this choice comes with great peril, for "you cannot serve God and mammon" (Mt. 6:24). To adopt the logic and methods of evil will in the end destroy all that is good that much more effectively. This choice thus carries with it the risk that our evangelical efforts will only perpetuate various forms of nihilism (forgetfulness of God, reason without God, false gods, meaninglessness, mediocrity, mission statements). Indeed, they may themselves sometimes be the fruit of a nervous energy born of our own insecurity, guilt, and nihilistic fears as much as of genuine faith. Either way, my point is that we all need to first confront *our actual understanding and practice of the faith itself* in much deeper, much more radical ways.

To this end, let us not make our momentous decision too hastily. On the journey that has brought us to this existential point — the journey of the historic "fellowship" of faith — we have had many companions. We have seen companions succumb to the power of the Ring and betray us. We have seen them fail the test of faith, succumbing to the temptation to give inappropriate "reasons" for faith. We have seen them give themselves over to a secular paradigm of force, power, and violence.

But in the fellowship of faith we have also had persistent, stubborn, "salt of the earth" companions who, despite their own doubts and inadequacies or the unfaithfulness and coercion of the powerful, always stood up hero- ically for what is right, willing to die rather than betray their friends and the pursuit of truth. We have had noble, saintly, prophetic companions who pointed the way when all hope seemed to be lost, who placed a gentle guiding hand on our freedom, who held our hand through it all. We have had loyal friends never willing to give up on us in moments of severe adversity, who were more willing to suffer and die themselves than to see us suffer or die.

Now is the moment, the either/or; the "choose your own adventure" part of the story. We must choose for ourselves the path that we will take. We must decide if we will entrust our heart to the moments and encounters in our life that have revealed — however faintly — love, worship, and beauty, or if we will choose the "wide gate" (Mt. 7:13), the path of least resistance, the way of "reasons," the way of despair and violence. We must give ourselves completely to a cause. We can no longer stand on the sidelines. At this point, we can no longer rely on the advice of our friends. None of them can make this decision for us. We must confront it ourselves.

But here, on the brink, at the existential moment of decision, something remarkable can happen if we find the capacity to open ourselves to the authentic experiences of good in our life, to entrust ourselves in hope to these experiences, to hold out for something more despite the pain, disillusionment, and fear. For someone else intervenes at this moment, a "person," but not one of our companions. We realize that in fact we are *not* alone. We realize, in fact, that without this person we could never hope to make the right decision; that on our own, we would always choose the path of despair. We discover a person who has walked with us always; who has preceded us, who has been speaking to us all along through our companions, our history, and our experiences. We discover that if we allow this person to lay claim to us, if we give ourselves over completely to this person, he, without taking away our freedom, will come to live in us, and in this will radically exceed the doubts, uncertainties, and darkness of our heart and the false witnesses who have betrayed us along the way.

I am convinced that at the heart of any crisis of faith, any "crisis of legitimation," any moment of indecision, any experience of betrayal or loss, there is always a greater presence — a person — working on our heart, arriving before us, preparing the way, offering healing, intervening for us, perhaps in the most unexpected kind of way, as in Frodo's unanticipated deliverance from his fatal decision by the teeth of Gollum. Thus, the response from this person always exceeds the limits of our own efforts. There is a claim on us greater than our own claim on ourselves.

For the baptized Christian, this call and claim are already especially strong. God named you and loved you before you were born, but by baptism the Father's love has become an "existential," historical, "real" part of you; it pervades *your* being, becomes the air that *you* breathe, the food that *you* eat, even if more often than not our freedom forces it to lie dormant. Nevertheless, it is always there, issuing a perpetual call and summons to you to return to the fullness, to hurl the Ring of power, despair, and violence into the fire, to let Christ live in you.

None of this is automatic or "magical": it is always an ongoing dramatic engagement, an existential and cosmic struggle. But the true power resides on the side of grace given in baptism that never stops "working on you." It is precisely through renouncing the Stoic or Pelagian "go it alone" solitary struggle for justification and "proof," and by entrusting oneself instead to the "smile" of the other, that one can discover the deeper transformation that comes with accepting oneself as chosen and named by Christ for filial adoption.

This is the first answer that Christianity must give to the soul searching for meaning in the postmodern condition. It must offer them a horizon, a context, a world in which the call of Christ can resound in all its originality and vitality. Our salvation comes as the most radical and unexpected of gifts, a gift that outstrips both our greatest achievements and discoveries and our lowest points and worst depravities. Only in the person of Christ, the One in whom the gift of adoption into the Father is given, can be found true deliverance from despair, violence, and captivity to false surrogates of belief. This is to say that ultimately, faith cannot rest on anything other than love — the radical call of love given in the historical encounter with the Son who reveals the Father. Faith, properly speaking, in this first movement of God's love cannot be earned, it cannot be won, it cannot be learned, it cannot be trained, it cannot be proved or deduced; it can only be *received* as the gift of love and allowed to grow and be nourished within love.[14]

Balthasar argued that love alone is credible.[15] Nothing other than the love of Christ poured out for us — a love given definitive shape in and through baptismal and liturgical participation in the sacraments, as we will begin to argue in the next chapter — can be a criterion or justification for Christian faith and belief.

This of course is to reiterate bits and pieces of what I suggested in the introduction of this book: that the "big" questions in life can only be resolved by "small" answers; that truth can only be rightly apprehended in relationship; that the small answers of the mother's smile and of baptism lie at the heart of sacramental conversion and transformation.

It is here — in the small, the humble, the honest; in the manger at Bethlehem; in the humiliation of the Cross — that the person can be changed. It is here that the world can be transformed, that human action can take on truly prophetic and effective shape. It is here that it becomes really and truly possible to have an encounter with faith, to toss the Ring of despair and violence into the fire. For faith — nothing more, nothing less — can move mountains (cf. Mt. 17:20).

In the following chapter, I will take the next step into the possibilities of the redemptive folly of the peace of Christ. We need to flesh out the fuller shape of this peace if we are to successfully negotiate the temptations of the Ring. To do this, we will more systematically consider how the peace of Christ — and the means to successfully conform ourselves to it — is given to us in baptismal shape, and how our successful overcoming of the postmodern condition can only truly be found here.

---

14 It is worth listening to Catholic philosopher Maurice Blondel here: "the truth of Catholicism is not demonstrated simply by the miracle of an institution's surviving so many disasters, nor by the beauty of its achievement; it has within it a power of self-justification which is independent of historical proofs or moral probabilities; and it is important not to reduce that internal criterion to an extrinsic and accessory argument." Maurice Blondel, "History and Dogma," in *The Letter on Apologetics & History and Dogma*, trans. Alexander Dru and Illtyd Trethowan (Grand Rapids: Eerdmans, 1994), 269.

15 Cf. Balthasar, *Love Alone Is Credible*.

FIVE

How Baptism Defeats the
Postmodern Condition

*There, peeping among the cloud-wrack above a dark tor high up in
the mountains, Sam saw a white star twinkle for a while. The beauty
of it smote his heart, as he looked up out of the forsaken land, and
hope returned to him. For like a shaft, clear and cold, the thought
pierced him that in the end the Shadow was only a small and passing
thing: there was light and high beauty for ever beyond its reach.*

J. R. R. Tolkien, *The Return of the King*

OUR PREVIOUS CHAPTER PROPOSED THAT JESUS
Christ remains the only real alternative to violent practices; those
practices which lurk embryonically inside the human heart,
those which are valorized and sanctioned by religion, and those which
are embodied in the religion of liberalism. What faith in the Christ who
in his person is both human and divine offers is an encounter and a world
where the hobbit can receive the transformation necessary to negotiate
and overcome these violent temptations of the Ring.

In this way, Christ has in his divine and human person given us the only
thing that can outwit and conquer our captivity to violence and despair.
Faith — the faith that grants access to the kingdom of heaven — in this sense
is not a ring, but the scriptural "pearl of great price" (cf. Mt. 13:45–46).
There is nothing wrong with the pearl itself, only what we do with it.

Some give it away. Some take our "postmodern condition" as warrant
for rejecting an understanding of Christ as "the way, the truth, and the
life" (Jn. 14:6), however subtly this may be construed. For example,
Lieven Boeve suggests that Christianity should become little more than
an "open narrative," the site of a "tense conversation" between narratives, a
conversation in which truth and meaning give way to vapid dialogue and

a benign, tolerant getting-along. He thereby seems to "recontextualize" Christianity (and Christ himself) out of existence.[1]

But the pearl is much more valuable than that. Moreover, the attempt to avoid ultimate questions of truth and falsity in the interests of getting along or making things easier only opens the door to more insidious hidden forms of violence, power, and compromise. Rather than simply assuming that the pearl is useless, far better to use the so-called postmodern condition as an inspiration to return to the primordial sources and font of faith, to the small and the particular, to its fundamental practices.

In what follows, I will propose a more developed baptismal framing of and solution to our crisis of faith on Mount Doom. I will try to illustrate that the gift of baptism is the first gift of the kingdom of heaven to the person, the in-breaking of that kingdom into the experience of the person as a fundamental call, summons, and world. It is the gift that will allow a completely and utterly transformed relation to reality and to God for the person. It is the gift that breaks our bondage to sin, that issues the first and definitive challenge to the debilitating conditions of the postmodern condition and the violence of liberalism. It is the gift that becomes the fundamental reference point for our love, our desire, our reason, our nature, for our fundamental search for meaning, and ultimately, for evangelization — first for ourselves, and only then for others.

Accordingly, I hope that it will again become possible to find existential contact with something that transcends the artificial boundaries and restrictions imposed by the postmodern horizon of violence and despair. I hope it will become possible to envision a systematic perspective within which to better engage the secular narratives that we have been exploring, both those that continue to be active as corrosive solvents within the horizon of faith and those which are fully consummated in the secular liturgies of modernity and postmodernity.

My goal in this chapter is thus to present baptism as the absolute answer to our existential crisis of meaning, our various crises of legitimation. While I do not purport to come close to a definitive or complete resolution of the many threads of crisis that haunt faith today, I hope to at least begin to show how a more robust and courageous baptismal logic can begin to restore at least an *imaginative* vision of faith again capable of revealing the true radicality of God's offer of adoption through the gift of his Son.

---

1 Cf. Boeve, *God Interrupts History.*

The baptismal gift of faith

The pearl of the kingdom is first given in baptism: "What do you ask of the Church of God?" asks the priest. "Faith," replies the catechumen. Baptism is the gift—the *saving* gift—of *faith* that offers life everlasting. Baptism is the pearl of faith, the new relation by which the world's violent claim on you is revoked.[2]

In its negative function, baptism revokes bondage to original sin, the stain that makes us choose violence over love, the stain that makes us try to "think" the truth outside of the concrete practices of love, worship, and beauty that are born from Christ's sacrifice and allow access to the love of the Father. In the rite of baptism, the catechumen descends with Christ into the dark waters of death to confront what some ancient descriptions called the "sea monster"[3] of our own darkness and violence, our own alienation from God through sin. In the crucified Christ, the spotless victim, "the Lamb of God who takes away the sins of the world" (Jn. 1:29), the power of violence and death is vanquished, and the catechumen rises with Christ from the waters of death that have now become the waters of life. He emerges with Christ, in Christ, into the new light of faith, a radiant baptismal person, a child who now shares in Christ's own relation to the Father as beloved Son.

In its positive reality, then, the faith given in baptism is thus not simply the revocation of sin so that one can rise again to live merely as a cleaned-up "natural" individual. That is, baptism does not only represent the regeneration of our moral abilities so that we can live with a greater degree of human perfection and virtue, and from this achieve eternal salvation and avoid eternal damnation. Baptism is not simply a moral veneer laid over a still natural identity. Recalling the debates about grace we encountered in chapter two, its grace is not simply "medicinal."

Baptism accomplishes something far more radical than this. Not only does it shatter bondage to the interior disorder in the human soul, but in its positive dimension it "dramatizes" the whole being of the individual,

---

2 Speaking of the renunciation of Satan in the baptismal rite, St. Cyril of Jerusalem (313–386) tells his baptismal candidates that "when you renounce Satan, you trample underfoot your entire covenant with him, and abrogate your former treaty with Hell." St. Cyril of Jerusalem, *Mystagogical Catechesis* I, in *Documents of the Baptismal Liturgy*, ed. E. C. Whitaker and Maxwell E. Johnson (Collegeville: Liturgical Press, 2003), 31.

3 Cf. Jean Daniélou, *From Shadows to Reality: Studies in the Biblical Typology of the Fathers*, trans. Wulstan Hibberd (London: Burns & Oates, 1960), 73.

re-placing him in the world as a radiant sacramental person who now lives "by every word that comes from the mouth of God" (Mt. 4:4). The death and rebirth of baptism is real and total, in the sense that it uproots the individual from the fictions of an existence capable of being defined in abstraction from the living relation to the Father in Christ through the Spirit. Because baptism immerses the person in an immediate personal relation to the Father, it makes any definition of the person conceived outside of this new relation at best a pale substitute, a kind of half-life, or at worst an idolatrous claim to an existence that subsists outside of the trinitarian relations.

It can therefore never be enough for the Christian to allow merely structural or naturalistic understandings of the person (as in the Boethian definition as an "individual substance of a rational nature") to set the terms for or foundation of what Christ might then merely "add" to it. For by baptism a *new starting point* and *fundamental frame* has been revealed, one that purifies and perfects nature, but not simply in a way that "adds" to it. The Christian must begin in the Son.

And let us be honest: should this be that surprising or controversial if we take the words of Scripture and their accomplishment in the liturgical and sacramental rites seriously? If it is, it is perhaps a sign of how far our imaginations have fallen from belief in a faith that can truly enter the deepest fiber of our existential condition, which can overtake us with the mystical fire of love. The Christian must begin from the experience of being named, called, and chosen, a sacramental reality that now pervades his existence and presses down on his being with insistence and urgency.

I am not suggesting that natures, substances, and reason will have nothing to do with it. There will still be a place for a conception of what it means to be human based on natural and metaphysical grounds. Nor am I saying that baptism offers a pure vision of total knowledge that makes all others obsolete, or that it erases the tension and drama of the individual soul's particular and historical confrontation with meaning.

Rather, I am saying that from the point of view of what is given in Christ *to me*, in and through *my baptism*, I am now effectively unable without being dishonest to conceive of my own existence outside of the light of adoption. I cannot unknow it. I cannot return to the artificial limits of a conception of truth that imagines that a purely formal and non-eventful pursuit of the meaning of structures and essences belongs to the height of the intellect's capability. It becomes unimaginable to regard a natural, metaphysical, or scientific rationale for human existence as the really real.

Such must always be recognized as partial, provisional, perhaps, and a continuing source of reflection, but nonetheless incomplete, and, from the perspective of the limitations of our natural capacity to conform ourselves to it, inherently prone to the violent incursions of the sinful will's desire to recreate reality in its own image.

For by baptismal immersion, nature, substance, and reason are themselves crucified and reborn, placed "inside" the filial relation of love. And from this vantage point, in terms of what we bring to the world by virtue of our baptism, our evangelical mission must thus be to reveal a vision of the incorporation of every self and every natural capacity of that self into baptismal adoption. We will see more of this last point in our final chapter.

And so, by baptism, your reality becomes the reality of participation in the Father's gift of Himself to the Church in Christ and the Spirit, a gift which immerses you in the definitive relation of Christ's relation to the Father as Son. "But when the fullness of time had come," says St. Paul, "God sent his Son, born of a woman, under the law, to ransom those under the law, so that we might receive adoption. As proof that you are children, God sent the spirit of his Son into our hearts, crying out 'Abba, Father!' So you are no longer a slave but a child, and if a child then also an heir, through God" (Gal. 4:4–7).

In this, your new reality no longer has the same reference points as the old. You are not a slave, but a child, a son or a daughter. You are an heir. You are no longer bound deterministically to the law of sin. Your reality is now structured completely by the perspective of your adoption in Christ as a child of God the Father himself.

To think through baptism radically in its positive dimension — that is, to think of it as something much more than just the erasure of bondage to the concupiscent watermark of sin — is to stress that it is not just one particular part of your existence that is baptized, but rather *the totality of your existence*, including its basic structures and frames. And this is thus to say *all* of your thinking, your reasoning, your loving, and your acting now take place in a radically new theological space. You have become a theological person, with a new theological history and genealogy. This is your new fundamental reference point, the place from which you now measure and assess your relation to reality. You ask questions and find answers in a different way now. Faith is no longer a postulate, an idea, a shot in the dark, as it were. It has, through your adopted sonship, broken into your existential "subjectivity." It has, in fact, *become* your subjectivity.

The pursuit of meaning within baptism

If it is true that baptismal adoption is not just a veneer or something that simply "hovers" over the person, then we can offer the preliminary suggestion that by this, baptism provides the fundamental means to "out-narrate" the postmodern condition inasmuch as one is prepared to entertain its offer, to throw oneself into its possibility. That is, baptism upsets the premises that feed into the pathologies of this condition by changing the terms of the game. It thus displaces the person's deterministic captivity to the artificial limits of this condition, to its refusal to countenance an event capable of shattering bondage to a closed existence.

Baptism is thus the event *par excellence* that upsets the flatness, mediocrity, and closed conditions of the staging and the script of the liberal imagination, all those conditions which fuel violence and provoke existential crises of despair. It does so in its provocative claim to give the baptized person *a new relation*, a supreme point of contact with divinity itself that transcends both objective nature and subjective will.

For the Christian, it does not therefore have to be about trying to struggle upward on one's own or about searching for an ultimate criterion for truth outside of baptism. It need never be about trying to throw the Ring into the fire by oneself. It must never be about trying to construct or generate meaning under conditions other than recognition of the loving assurances of the mother's smile and, by adoption, the full measure of the Father's love. Rather, the place within which the existential question takes place is fundamentally the place of that sacramental smile, of a historical and interpersonal exchange of love that challenges all closed accounts of what it means to be human. It is the place where any question that is asked is a question *already asked* by an adopted son or daughter in the loving presence of the Father.

This is not to say that non-baptized or non-Christian persons are not already loved by God or that they too are not in some way recipients of the mysterious invitation of God's grace. We must, by what we know of our own baptism, recognize that each person bears the hope of adoption in his flesh, that the Father already desires and offers full adoption to each and every person. It is rather to say that the baptized Christian is now actually placed within the Spirit-filled space of redemption, sanctification, and adoption. He has already been *personally* called by name, he *really* inhabits the sacramental time and space of this call, and he receives the real graces of this new state. The call and claim on this person's being is thus that much stronger, constitutive, and ultimately demanding.

And so the existential question asked *here* is in a particularly fundamental sense always preceded and informed by one's election and adoption, and thus primed by the possibility of the deepest and fullest encounter with a genuine *answer* that stretches beyond all human limits. Because of baptism, the search for meaning always presupposes the intimate presence of an Other fundamentally basic to the constitution of my own self. It presupposes that I am in the debt of the Other, that my consciousness has been shaped and formed by the Other, that my reason is thus "impure" in the best possible sense; it is contingent, it is relational, it relies on the Other absolutely, and this is precisely its *raison d'être*.

It is not that knowledge or meaning is not possible strictly speaking outside of baptismal conditions, but that the only knowledge that *really and truly matters and to which we must as sons and daughters give witness* — the knowledge given in the horizon of election and adoption, the knowledge without which persons cannot know themselves, the knowledge of *love* — is precisely that which thinking subjects cannot generate on their own within the finite conditions that outside of baptismal adoption remain closed to the infinite. Baptism, by contrast, is a path which *can* offer a way out of the postmodern condition. All it demands is that we refuse to dull and downgrade its truly subversive character.

The pursuit of meaning without baptism

But just how important is the baptismal framing of the pursuit of meaning? Let us not move too quickly. We know of course that this new, *baptismal* discovery of oneself as given from the other is in fact not totally unfamiliar to the human condition. For to be generated by the other, to be constituted by the other, to be nurtured and cared for by the other, to be in the debt of the other, to be formed, shaped, and influenced by the other, belongs to the basic conditions of finite and temporal being. None of us are self-generated. Our being is porous, open to others. We rely on others for our basic survival and flourishing. We live in and are nothing without the community that surrounds us. We are all children of the mother's smile.

More importantly, the universal experience of love seems to suggest that this condition of vulnerability is in fact something to be *desired*, as a necessary ingredient of human happiness, even if the tendency of metaphysical thinking in the West, broadly speaking, has been to downgrade receptivity and contingency as inferior modes of existence. Love takes what might otherwise be a source of resentment and bondage and transforms it into the greatest joy and liberation. The true lover does not feel constricted by his beloved, but regards the loss of self in mutual self-gift as an infinite gain.

The question is how much weight we give to this quintessentially *human* experience, and to what extent this experience within our finite and temporal horizon can not only illuminate but actually *resolve* the question of ultimate meaning for the human subject. Perhaps the Beatles were right to say that "all you need is [human] love."

It should first be noted that today the whole thrust of rationalistic and technological thinking is premised on overcoming the limits of bodily existence and effacing the person's need for and reliance on the other — effacing the mother's smile. The effect is to create the illusion that you are sovereign in your choices and that your relation to others is contingent on your free granting of consent to and qualification of the other's claim on you.

In this, secular liberal paradigms tend to destroy or minimize the possibility that one could, over the din of secularist practices, even *hear* or *catch sight* of the deep meaningfulness of the vulnerability and dependency experienced in love as a perfection, and thus ever perceive any great significance in such an experience. All of this is to say that even if there is a deep meaning to be attached to a human experience such as love, the practices of secularism have made it almost impossible to perceive and make something of that meaning in any deep way.

Moreover, throughout this book I have argued that it is not only contemporary secularism that has truncated our capacity for a deeper mode of thinking that might subvert closed horizons of all kind. As our genealogy in chapter two demonstrated, we had been busy setting up roadblocks for ourselves long before the death of God became an imaginable possibility and social reality. By constricting the modes of love, worship, and beauty made flesh in Christ and given in love to the creature — all those elements given and perceived within the pure relation of the person to God's adoptive love — we fostered the conditions for a return to closed and static notions of nature, reason, and morality. That is, by seeking too directly to "ground" the event of Christ in the structures of being (in order to make it more credible or "provable"), we uprooted these structures from their personal self-revealing source. We gave them a kind of semi-autonomous identity in abstraction from that which in Christ became visible as the personal radiance of elective and adoptive love.

In this, we effectively took a step backwards. We tried to return to an earlier, more undeveloped stage, a stage prior to that definitive living relation to the personal source that alone gives all structures their proper meaning. And in the process, we thereby began to make idols of nature, reason, and morality, distorting what truly liberating message they could give us when placed within the evangelical perspective of the event and person of Christ, into a desiccated naturalism, rationalism, and moralism.[4]

And by this, we denied ourselves the capacity to approach the question of meaning from a more dynamic, existential, and personal point of view, from the point of view of the person who begins from *within* the eventful experience of love rather than the cold structures of systems and logic. If we take the mother's smile as emblematic of a capacity for personhood beyond mere individuality (for it is not an individual instantiation of the species that a mother loves, but *this* unique person, *this* fruit of a unique relationship), we can draw attention to the limitations of the "kind of being" definition of the person, as in the Boethian definition.

An explanation of what it means to be human in Christ that does not from the first allow Christ's "real presence" to speak to us from its sacramental, ecclesial, and liturgical originality, risks never feeling the full weight of the novelty, indeed, the *absurdity* of what the triune God has offered to humanity. If God has truly offered what we say he has, then in this offering is the most remarkable answer to the existential cry of the self.

From this angle, St. Paul's hymn to love in 1 Corinthians — today often victim to saccharine interpretations — can take on a somewhat different significance. "If I speak in human and angelic tongues," he says, "but do not have love, I am a resounding gong or a clashing cymbal. And if I have the gift of prophecy, and comprehend all mysteries and all knowledge; if I have all faith so as to move mountains, but do not have love, I am nothing. If I give away everything that I own, and if I hand over my body so that I may boast, but do not have love, I gain nothing" (13:1–3). Without love, without the relation given to us as pure gift, it matters not what I do nor where I look. I am lost. I am nothing.

---

4 For a helpful account of moralism, that is to say morality divorced from love — a consequence of departing from love, worship, and beauty that we have not really developed in this book — see Livio Melina, "The Fullness of Christian Action: Beyond Moralism and Antimoralism," in *Logos* 8 (2005). See also Melina, *Sharing in Christ's Virtues: For a Renewal of Moral Theology in Light of* Veritatis Splendor (Washington, D.C.: CUA Press, 2001) and David L. Schindler, "Is Truth Ugly? Moralism and the Convertibility of Being and Love," in *Communio* 27 (2000).

Nevertheless, for the sake of argument, let us presume for a moment that (even over the current din of secularism and despite captivity to deformations in the understanding of faith) a person does in fact arrive at some profound intuition that to receive one's existence as gift and to be in the debt of the other according to love in fact carries the deepest existential weight and significance. For it is true that the experience of the mother's smile (at least when it is not effaced by the pelvic liturgies of liberalism) carries within itself the capacity to promise and grant a foretaste of some horizon of infinite love beyond itself.

So assume that this person comes to the empirical conclusion that in the end it is love and not mere thought or structures that is most real and most credible: that a smile has more meaning than an idea. Perhaps he perceives that the truly momentous locus of human meaning is not to be found in the stable patterns of natural ends, structures, and "substantial" definitions, not in the most abstruse and elevated cosmic speculation, not in the ubiquitous "human spirit," not in the closed technological practices of liberalism, but rather in the pure light that shines from the mother's smile. Does this person need anything more? Is this love already salvation and grace?

Balthasar answered this question by saying that even the most sublime experience of human love cannot grant the *absolute and eternal* affirmation needed to guarantee the meaning and identity sought by the creature. It cannot tell me that I — *this* person — have a value and dignity that transcend the limits of space and time and that make me something more than one anonymous member of a particularly sophisticated species. It cannot tell me that I am a *person*. It cannot tell me that there is anything particularly significant about the fact that *this* person, in *this* circumstance, is having an existential crisis of meaning and seeking an answer to his being. It cannot actually give *me* an infinite meaning. It cannot conquer *my* inevitable death. It cannot overcome the existential angst, enervating anxiety, or therapeutic numbness that accompany the failure to resolve the riddle of *my* death.

No matter how much you love and how much another loves in return, no matter how sublime or intense the experience of love, in the end, any human guarantee of love is one both granted and received by a finite, temporal being, and is ultimately defeated by death. Finite beings cannot promise or attain infinite love. Even the mother's smile — that paradigm to which we have been granting so much significance — cannot in the end guarantee or deliver an ultimate and eternal meaning, for "the mother's affirmation [of her child] could be withdrawn."[5] "Ultimately not even a fellow human being can tell another who the latter really is in himself," Balthasar continues. "The most emphatic affirmation can only tell him who he is for the one who values him or loves him."

And so there is a trace of nihilism even in the smile of the mother. That is, even the pursuit of meaning that is inspired and framed by the most profound human experiences cannot in the end on its own grant a way out of the postmodern condition, and may even risk perpetuating it, inasmuch as it instills a hope for something it cannot deliver on its own. You may be able to *speculatively* posit a meaning beyond the finite and the temporal, but until that posited meaning actually breaks into the finite and the temporal—into your horizon of experience—it remains a theoretical and impersonal postulate constructed from below that cannot actually enter into your horizon. Posited meaning remains merely an abstract idea or therapeutic hope unless it truly enters into the fabric of space, time, and experience.

All of this means that the human condition is essentially a tragedy, and that it is this that ultimately feeds all existential crises, as Nietzsche recognized so acutely. We *sense* that eternity and infinity are what we are made for, but we lack the ability to escape the closed conditions of temporality and finitude, and so we distract and delude ourselves with idolatrous coping strategies that never truly cut it, and that in fact draw us ever farther away from the human love that ought to be a nurturing pedagogy for eternal love. The deepest experiences of our existence, particularly the experience of love, scream for eternal validation and fulfillment, for something more than any of us can give them. And so this validation and fulfillment, short of the in-breaking of transcendence, remain unavailable to us, such that we always sit on a knife's edge between the most elevated hopes and capacities and the most disappointed, tragic, degraded, violent, and suicidal possibilities. The love of which the Beatles sang ends in the mud of Woodstock.

It is this condition of constitutive tension which led both Ratzinger and Balthasar to assert in particularly strong terms that to be a person and to

---

5 Hans Urs von Balthasar, *Theo-Drama: Theological Dramatic Theory*, vol. 3, *The Dramatis Personae: The Person in Christ*, trans. Graham Harrison (San Francisco: Ignatius Press, 1991), 205.

find meaning, properly speaking — that is, to be one called, named, and granted eternal sonship, and thus to have the closed conditions of existence shattered — is only possible with Christ.[6] No amount of speculation, imagination, or transcendental contemplation — no solution short of the radical shattering of the very footings of existence — can break the tragic conditions of a human existence existentially separated from God by sin.

Once the veil has been lifted, once we have seen the vision of everything that could be in Christ, and, even more significantly, once we have seen the horrors that await when Christ is definitively rejected, it really is *Christ or nothing*. "The gospel of a God found in broken flesh, humility, and measureless charity," says Hart, "has defeated all the old lies, rendered the ancient order visibly insufficient and even slightly absurd, and instilled in us a longing for transcendent love so deep that — if once yielded to — it will never grant us rest anywhere but in Christ."[7]

Without Christ, we can only produce pale approximations of ultimate meaning and unsatisfying forms of therapy. We may place our hope in philosophical speculations or transcendental meditation or spirituality as a way to feed our infinite hunger. We may live with stoic resignation, even a stance of contemplative waiting for an event that we hope *might* break through finitude, but never in fact does (Heidegger's tragic choice). We may place our hope in relationships, in the experience of love, or in a poetic embrace of meaning satisfied with endlessly deferring the riddle of an infinite desire with no realizable terminus. And all of this may, in short bursts, give us some sense of fullness or some hope for eternity.

But in the end, these strategies to cope with nihilism never in fact solve the problem, much less confront or vanquish it.[8] And as such, they are all stalked by the unsettling whispers of a despair that tell us that none of this is what we truly want or can ultimately be happy with. Moreover, death in the end remains the specter that haunts all attempts to find meaning within finitude and temporality. And after Christ's arrival on the world stage (regardless of whether his claims are true or not), no strategy of

---

6 Cf. Hans Urs von Balthasar, "On the Concept of Person," in *Communio* 13 (1986); Ratzinger, "Concerning the Notion of Person."

7 Hart, "God or Nothingness," 74.

8 Balthasar criticized Heidegger for having "no adequate answer to the question of existence he raises. A philosophy which will not firmly answer the question of God one way or the other lacks intellectual courage, and a pragmatic and realistic humanity will pass it by and get on with daily living." Balthasar, *Glory of the Lord*, vol. 4, 450.

human coping could ever hope to live up to the promise or dream of a God who walks among His children, who loves them, who forgives and redeems them, who offers Himself as the sacrifice that subverts and overcomes their violence, who calls them to new life with Him through adoption. To reject the possibility presented in Christ is thus to render all coping strategies hollow and empty, leaving only one serious alternative possibility to pursue: evil.[9]

An infinite horizon

This rather long discourse on the impossibility of deep meaning outside of baptism helps us begin to confirm just what it is that baptismal faith in its full glory offers us in our present condition. The first thing we can reaffirm is that inasmuch as baptism shares the Christ-event *literally* with the baptized person through the mediation of the Holy Spirit and the Church, it shatters the closed conditions of a human search for meaning that remains within the limits of temporality. "He who passes through the font," says St. Ambrose of Milan (340–397), "that is from earthly to heavenly things—for this is the *transitus*, that is the Passover, a passing from sin to life, from guilt to grace—… does not die, but rises again."[10]

It may not be the case that the person automatically perceives and internalizes the gift that has been given in baptism, but whether perceived or unperceived this adoption is now a new divine horizon in his life. The person is now inside the dramatic stage of salvation history. A hope and possibility beyond bondage to violence and despair is now in play. It is possible for truth to be more than an ascending postulate, faint hope, or therapeutic solace.

What remains to be done is to flesh out the beginnings of a more *systematic* articulation of the full measure of this baptismal horizon, one constructed on the intuition that to become a new creation in Christ, to be caught up in the Son's own relation to the Father, represents not a mere addition that "tops up" our definition of what it means to be human, but something that might offer the possibility of a more comprehensive

---

9 Envisioning a world without beauty—a world without a relationship to truth animated by something greater than the mere truthfulness of something in the abstract—Balthasar suggests that "man stands before the good and asks himself why it must be done and not its alternative, evil. For this too, is a possibility, and even the more exciting one: Why not investigate Satan's depths?" Balthasar, *The Glory of the Lord*, vol. 1, 19.

10 St. Ambrose of Milan, *De Sacramentis* I, 4, 12, quoted in Daniélou, *From Shadows to Reality*, 181.

response to the kinds of challenges to faith we saw in chapters two and three. These challenges are many, and my contention is that they can be effectively remedied only if we have the courage to respond to them from a point deep within the givenness of the sacramental form of adoption.

In what follows, then, I will start to edge a little closer and somewhat more systematically to this givenness, mindful not to move too quickly, however, or to suggest that more than the barest of sketches can be presented here. The reader is warned that the following sections will be a little more challenging.

Full immersion in the Mystery

The vision I propose can in very broad terms be understood as a kind of baptismal intensification for our own time of certain main ideas and emphases of some of the greatest theological minds of the twentieth century, as they began to formulate their own responses to the tensions and self-secularizing trends in the understanding of faith. These trends, after gestating for many centuries, were by the 1960s maturing or mutating into the secular aspirations of liberalism in all its variants, and in the first couple of decades after the Second Vatican Council were welcomed by large swathes of the academic and ecclesial intelligentsia with open arms.

By 1968, de Lubac was already speaking of "a total 'secularization' that would expel God not only from social life, but from culture and even from the relationships of private life."[11] If de Lubac spoke then of a secularism only "*trying* to invade the consciousness of Christians themselves,"[12] how much more might he speak today of one that has successfully colonized that consciousness.

Of the last century's theological minds, Balthasar, de Lubac, Wojtyla (John Paul II), and Ratzinger (Benedict XVI) might be foremost in the Western Church. Each in his own way contributed to a renewed and at times profoundly original understanding of the person as emerging from and ordered to an order of fulfillment that begins and is inscribed, not merely in "nature" or in some deferred eschatological future, and certainly *not* in secular counterfeits, but in the here and now of liturgical and sacramental

---

11 Henri de Lubac, "The Total Meaning of Man and the World," in *Communio* 35 (2008), 621–22.

12 Ibid., 621. Emphasis added.

life in the *communio* of the Church. It is the historical, the ecclesial, the sacramental, the Christological, the pneumatological, the trinitarian, and the eschatological given *together* in the anthropological fullness of life in Christ and the Spirit that constitutes the primary frame and reference point for a *theological* notion of the person capable of overcoming the dualisms and distortions of both ends of the ideological spectrum.

At one level, it is of course odd that we should think of this as constituting anything particularly novel or ground-breaking. Taking as paradigmatic the baptismal theology of St. Paul, for example, it is impossible to evade the fact that the text of Scriptures and their embodiment in the liturgical rites of the Church everywhere speak of the dramatic encounter of the person with a God who is alive and who calls us into His presence in a manner that is total, one that involves a real death for *the* real life. Evading this is possible only if one is willing to take the existential richness of Pauline theology and either consciously "demythologize" or "Jesuiticize" it by rote or else make it methodologically secondary to a more "substantial" baseline notion of person to which this theology is only "added."

In this, my judgment is that both theological liberalism and theological conservatism or traditionalism have failed (albeit in different ways and to different extents) to conform to the truly baptismal theological standard that I would argue is native to the New Testament and the spirit of the Fathers of the Church. Judging from our current situation in the Church, our evasion of the immersive structure of faith everywhere presupposed in the New Testament has been more complete and borne more fruit than we have perhaps imagined.

As a consequence, when I say that we need to now baptismally intensify the respective visions of Balthasar, de Lubac, Wojtyla, and Ratzinger, it means that I think we have reached a cultural point where an even more sacramental and mystical account of Christian existence is warranted. We need a more synthetic and organic first-person perspective within which all of the diverse elements that make up faith can be more effectively unified and encountered as such. A theology that springs from a point already inside the baptized person's filial relation to the Father in Christ will represent not only the defeat of the postmodern condition as a threat external to faith, but also a challenge issued to *internal* conditions that persist in shielding us from total immersion in the faith.

There are key elements in each of our thinkers which provide important points of departure for a baptismal deepening. As hinted, a common theme that unites their theological reflections is an articulation of the person from a point of view already deep inside the drama of the event of Christ and salvation history, a point of view for which I use "baptismal" as an organic marker. For example, consider Balthasar's claim that the pursuit of personal identity and truth can only be discovered within an aesthetic and dramatic context. As he puts it, "if we want to ask about man's 'essence,' we can do so only in the midst of his dramatic performance of existence. There is no other anthropology but the dramatic."[13] Baptismally intensified, this would be to say that there is no other anthropology but the *baptismal*, one that begins in the very flesh of one who has received adoption as gift.

Further, note de Lubac's conviction that the event of grace in Christ is such that the pursuit of the meaning of nature after Christ must presuppose at the heart of every being's natural desire an insatiable longing for an eternal end that no temporal end can satisfy.[14] I would say that in the light of *what we come to know in Christ*, we can speak more urgently not only of a "natural desire for God" implanted in human souls, but a natural desire for *baptismal adoption*, for the relation that shatters all abstractions and reductions.

John Paul II's articulation of the perspective of "the acting person"[15] and his development of a "theology of the body"[16] remain definitive accounts of the way in which the discovery of oneself as a person and a body emerges from and belongs to participation in a deeply sacramental and ecclesial existence, one that has deep roots in the experience and bodiliness of masculinity and femininity. I would now speak more urgently of the imperative of a theology of the *baptized* body, one that begins even more radically inside the dramatic forms of Christ's spousal union with the Church.

Finally, we can refer to Ratzinger's conviction that being a Christian cannot be reduced to abstractions, but is rather born from "the encounter with an event, a person" (*Deus caritas est* 1). This could be shaped as a more explicitly *baptismal* encounter with an event, with a person — an encounter

13 Hans Urs von Balthasar, *Theo-Drama: Theological Dramatic Theory*, vol. 2, *The Dramatis Personae: Man in God*, trans. Graham Harrison (San Francisco: Ignatius Press, 1990), 335.

14 Cf. Henri de Lubac, *Surnatural: Études Historiques: nouvelle edition* (Paris: Desclée de Brouwer, 1991). Cf. also Maurice Blondel, *Action (1893): Essay on a Critique of Life and a Science of Practice*, trans. Oliva Blanchette (Notre Dame, IN: University of Notre Dame Press, 1984).

15 Cf. Karol Wojtyla, *The Acting Person*, trans. Andrzej Potocki (Boston: D. Reidel, 1979).

16 Cf. John Paul II, *Man and Woman He Created Them*.

that takes shape from the theology of the baptismal and Eucharistic liturgies.

To attempt to think through these horizons of thought in a more unified manner is to approach them neither from "above" nor "below" but rather from *within* the existential "here" and "now" of the sacramental world within which the baptized person is situated as a participant. This is to say that salvation history as a historical reality "out there" or "back then" is in fact *already* existentially present to me in my baptized being. By baptism, one is enabled to read faith from the inside, by a kind of feeling, touching, tasting relation to a Presence that has already made me a part of itself.

All of this I have been already been hinting at throughout, particularly in chapter two. You will recall that there I began to seriously argue that the absolute starting point for reflection on truth and meaning cannot be other than the perspective of the person whose contact with truth and meaning is *already* mediated by a prior relation and encounter without which any other descriptive strategy must remain stunted. A baptismal relation to the Father in the Son represents the epitome of this anthropological law. Baptismal adoption represents the pinnacle of a presence or givenness that cannot rest on anything other than itself, but which opens the person to the fullness of Christ's divine sonship, sharing a blinding excess of meaning that radically reshapes the existence of the person prepared to enter into the labor required to accept and live this gift in its totality.

Now, after the West's great experiment of the possibility of meaning after the death of God, we have arrived at either a new dusk or a new dawn. My contention is that a new dawn will require a greater willingness to entrust ourselves anew to what is absolutely unique to Christian faith.

Adoption from the sacramental middle

To put more sacramental flesh on this proposal, then, will be to immerse ourselves more deeply in the fundamental grammar of Christian existence. The baptismal rite's dramatic immersion of the person into the events of salvation history, into participation in the death and resurrection of Christ, is itself already the product of a drama of *other*, much more eminent persons' responses to the loving initiative of the Father. Your baptismal rebirth already presupposes the Son's *yes* to the Father's plan of salvation, and is "born" from and shaped by the maternal mediation of the Bride, the Church, who in Mary offers her perfect and unconditional *yes* to the Bridegroom and who by this *yes* opens the door to the adoption of the entire world, giving to me the possibility of my own *yes*.

This is to say that baptismal adoption does not take place in a vacuum. That it can take place at all depends upon a *yes* to the Father that we ourselves could never have given. It depends, primarily, upon the Son's *yes* to the Father—"not my will, but yours" (Lk. 22:42)—but then upon Mary's *yes* to the Father—"Let it be done to me according to your word" (Lk. 1:38). By the obedience of the Son, the Word is offered, and by the consent of Mary to the Holy Spirit, the Word is made incarnate.

It is the perfect filial consent of each which then makes possible the perfect "marriage" between the Word and the mystical body of Christ, the Church. It is the Church that, under the continued mediation of Mary's perfect consent, accepts and receives the salvific fruitfulness of the Bridegroom. In the Church, the Father's will that "everyone be saved and come to the knowledge of the truth" (1 Tim. 24) is literally begun in the sons and daughters "born again" (Jn. 3:3) from Christ's spousal union with the Church.

Note again that salvation is not therefore merely a power, a force, or a process without a context. It does not materialize magically out of thin air as it were, by a sovereign unilateral divine act or proclamation, neither requiring nor desiring our response or any intermediary setting. Instead, the Father's desire to save mankind originates in the real relation and dialogue of love already present among the trinitarian Persons, which is then shared with the world in and through the assent of the Marian Church, and which is enacted and re-enacted in historical time and space through an embodied network of new sacramental relationships and identities in the Church.

In other words, salvation is accomplished and communicated in and through what we might simply call the "sacramental middle": the existential ground of relation wherein humanity and divinity are sealed together in a new relationship. By the Father's initiative in the Son, through the Marian, Spirit-animated Church, the fundamental reference points for what it means to be human have changed. The existence and identity of the baptized self rests in a pure relation to the Father, in the Son, through the Holy Spirit, one that originates and is established, sealed, and fructified in the maternal mediation of the Marian Church who gives birth to, guards, and treasures what has begun in her by the Bridegroom (cf. Lk. 2:19). It is from this sovereign vantage point that we can then recognize other selves as already called to and fulfilled only by this new birth of adoption.

Again, it will be "inside" this historical relation of excessive, perfect love — inside a relation to a historical person — that all meaning will now be received and framed. In Christ, truth and meaning are dramatic: discovered and received in their fullness in the sanctified time and space of the history of the Son given to the Church.

Becoming a baptismal person in the Son

To accent the sacramental middle as the new ground of the believer's relation to the mystery of existence is to recognize that the baptismal person who occupies this middle is now the pure creation, neither of nature nor of grace understood as an abstract "below" and "above," but of the unique union of the two in space and time in the Son. The baptized person is, as St. Paul puts it, a "new creation" (2 Cor. 5:17), one for whom a new ground of identity has been established. Sacramental existence is a "hybrid" existence, neither human (i.e., as it was from the beginning) nor divine (man does not become God). Rather, human existence is in a new way both generated and sustained by the possibilities inherent in Christ's "hypostatic" personhood; that is, in the personhood of the one who is both fully God and fully man.

In *Christ's* personhood — that in which we come to share by baptism — we see the measure of humanity and divinity held in perfect balance in one person, in whose existence the human and divine are perfectly synthe-sized or embodied in a way that is neither "naturally" human (below) nor "supernaturally" divine (above). Instead, in Christ a *new* form of existence is revealed in which "the property of both natures [human and divine] is preserved and comes together into a single person and a single subsistent being," as the Council of Chalcedon (451) succinctly expressed it.[17]

The tradition has in the past been hesitant, for a number of reasons, to extend this obviously unique and exclusive Christological personhood to the human person. As we have already suggested, the preferred choice was to retain a more basic structural definition of the human person that remained within the limits of a natural horizon, or as Ratzinger put it, "entirely on the level of substance."[18] While this might appear as a way to make sure that the being of God and man are never confused — the two have

---

17 Dogmatic Definition of the Council of Chalcedon, at https://www.ewtn.com/faith/teachings/incac2.htm.

18 Ratzinger, "Concerning the Notion of Person," 448.

a qualitatively different kind of existence — there are certain risks associated with it. It leaves the definition of the person vulnerable to a naturalistic reduction wherein grace is only seen as "adding." This may then lead to what Ratzinger describes as the "narrowing" of an "I and you" formulation of existence, where the "you" is understood as essential to the existence of the "I."[19] The consequence of this is to risk a loss of the "we" dimension where identity is found by being in relation or communion with the other. And eventually, when pushed to the extreme, the "I" may determine that it no longer needs either the "you" or the "we" for its constitution. For all practical intents and purposes, then, man himself becomes God: he assumes the position of sovereign totality, answering to no one but himself.

My point is that clear distinctions can become full dualisms. The bottom line is that if the relationship between Creator and creature is not held in the correct tension, the structure of our simultaneous likeness and unlikeness to God risks either eclipsing the creature (everything is God) or eclipsing the Creator (everything is man). There have been many different historical permutations of each distortion, but what all of them share is an inability to fully accept the paradox of a relation wherein the greatest freedom and expansion of the self comes with the deepest self-emptying of the same self, and in its refusal to grasp after a meaning not given as gift rather than a vision only given and made possible in Christ.

My contention is that grounding questions of likeness and unlikeness more firmly in the hypostatic mode of Christ's personhood, given baptismally to creatures in their transformation into children of God the Father in the Son and mediated by the sacramental forms of the Church, provides the only truly effective context within which to faithfully negotiate this question and properly frame subsequent use of reason and pursuit of truth. This is because by baptism the first movement of the relation of likeness and unlikeness *has already been accomplished* in the baptized flesh of the person. Put as simply as possible, the one who rises triumphant with Christ out of the font as a child of the Father, is in Christ a new person, possessing a new form of existence grounded in the Son's unique hypostatic identity. The baptized person is reducible neither to nature nor grace, but rather possesses each in a new way, from a new point. It is here, I suggest, that the relation and difference between God and man can be best appreciated and safeguarded.

19   Ibid., 454.

What baptism allows us to see is that even before the intellect tries to figure out what belongs to man and what belongs to God, as it were, and what might be the ultimate meaning of existence, one's very existence is by baptismal adoption *already* a living, pre-cognitive embodiment of and participant in the historical event and flesh of *the* Person who forever united—with "no confusion, no change, no division, no separation"[20]—the human and divine nature into its definitive form. You yourself, in your person and in your flesh, after baptism, *in Christ*, are a living "hinge," a new union of nature and grace.

Before we drown in all of this, let me now try to restate and clarify the implications of what I have just said. My claim is that before we can for the sake of necessary precision or clarification partition the mystery of faith into human and divine spheres (faith and reason, nature and grace, etc.), we must begin by looking more seriously at the crucified and risen flesh of Jesus Christ. We must look upon the person of Christ as bearing in himself, in his perfect unity of human and divine nature, and in the expression of this unity in his life, his passion, his death, and his resurrection, the complete form and archetype of what it means "to be."

Now, it would be one thing if the Son simply came to earth, put on a good show, impressing us in a merely exemplary way with his superhuman ability to be both God and man in his person, and then went back to where he came from, leaving us with our own skins intact, as it were. Instead, the Son's entire hypostatic drama is performed *pro nobis*, for us: "For God so loved the world…" (Jn. 3:16). It is driven by the Father's love, by His desire to save us from sin and death, to make us a new creation, to make us His children, not just in some remote future or at the level of the mind, but rather here and now in the full drama of our historical existence. It is because our redemption is premised on and achieved by the *yes* of the Son and the *yes* of Mary which together allow divinity to enter the horizon of history and set up shop, so to speak, that the gift of the Word and the efficacy of its message are not merely exemplary or moral realities extrinsic to us. They are not mere ideals to aspire to or imitate.

Rather, in what I have called the "sacramental middle" is communicated a Word and a reality that have truly entered and truly inhabit time and space. What is most real is the Love that has drawn and is drawing us into itself, which redeems and reorganizes every true and good created reality,

20 Dogmatic Definition of the Council of Chalcedon.

placing it inside the *sacramental* time and space of the Church. It is a Love that extends the unthinkable form and archetype of the Son's personhood *to us*, a Love whose goal is to make us full sons in the Son, to share the incredible riches of the trinitarian life itself with us.

Christ's unique personhood, then, is *pro nobis*. It is fully aimed at us as its full realization. It is not an "ontological exception,"[21] exclusive only to him as an ideal merely to be imitated, but by baptism it is for us the fulfillment of what it means to be human. To become a son or daughter, then, is to stand on and be a part of the holy ground of the Son's relation to the Father.

Relating God and man baptismally

This section heading recalls a nearly identical heading in chapter two, where we considered the various ways in which questions of Creator and created, nature and grace, faith and reason, and the like have been construed in the tradition. We are now positioned to articulate a *baptismal* accounting of the fundamental relation between God and man.

If baptismal adoption is in fact the actualization of God's desire that all be saved, that all come to know him as Father—if it truly baptizes us into Christ's death so that "we too might live in the newness of life" (cf. Rom. 6:3–4), if it indeed makes us "joint heirs with Christ" (Rom. 8:17)—then what is demanded of us, as His children, is that we receive this inestimable gift according to the same measure by which it is given. To be faithful to the glory, majesty, and power of God—to the supreme radicality of His kenotic gift of Himself revealed in the perfect humanity and divinity of the Son—requires that we treat the gift of adoption as a reconstitution of our being that does more than "add." Anything less is an insult and affront to the one who has given the gift. Any attempt to cling to an identity that is less than that of a son in the Son, where election and adoption only "hover" over the bedrock of a personhood generated from some other point, shortchanges the humiliation and glorification of the Son for our sake.

This is to say that the best way to protect that essential distinction between God and man that must yet remain between an infinite Creator and a finite creation is to *increase the right kind of relation*; it is *not* to seek to protect the gratuity of grace by retreating from the historical reality of

---

21 Cf. Ratzinger, "Concerning the Notion of Person," 448.

the union of divinity and humanity in Christ to a purely formal accounting of that which belongs to nature and that which belongs to man, as the neo-scholastics did. It is not to retreat to a point beyond what Christ has *in fact* created in the person and what the liturgy and the sacraments will dramatize and recapitulate over and over again (more on which later).

My contention is that the relation of inestimable intimacy and closeness in baptismal adoption is itself already simultaneously a logic of the proper distinction between God and man that must yet remain. For as *child* — even more so as a child of *God* — my identity *remains and can only ever be an absolute gift*, no matter what ennobling grace is given to it. I am still absolutely given. Even as I participate in the greatest realization of what it means to be human, I remain under the same anthropological law fundamental to being human, wherein existence is wholly derived, contingent, dependent, and relative to others. In becoming "like God" in Christ, then, I do not become less human. I am still the same being for whom the other is essential, the same being for whom a smile is of the essence. Thus, as Balthasar puts it, baptismal adoption cannot be taken to imply that "the believer becomes Christ substantially." It cannot mean "a direct participation in the hypostatic union" or a "progressive pantheism."[22]

As suggested, this anthropological law of contingency and dependency is not overturned in Christ but given its ultimate inscription. My existence still belongs to the same law of contingency, dependency, derivativeness, and relativity that typifies basic anthropological existence, only now this is a law given by the infinite and absolute as the gift of sonship. What an infinite and absolute law of relation overcomes is not the truth that *to be* is *to be in relation and remain dependent on the other*, but rather the limitation that being related to other merely finite and temporal beings inevitably carries. Baptismal adoption therefore gives us the *eternal* contingency, dependence, derivativeness, and relativity that truly redeems, saves, and deifies, that lasts forever, and that incorporates every true finite relationship into itself.

As such, my baptismal existence is nothing without the one who gave it. It rests completely, in an ontological sense, inside the hypostatic personhood of Christ. Take away or reduce *his* personhood, and mine disappears or is diminished. The baptismal person cannot truly "know thyself" except by

---

22 Hans Urs von Balthasar, *Explorations in Theology II: Spouse of the Word*, trans. A.V. Littledale and Alexander Dru (San Francisco: Ignatius, 1991), 171.

reference to the existential condition of being a child. Outside of Christ, there is only the abyss.

In this, the baptismal relation remains the ultimate safeguard against the sin of presuming a selfhood that categorically does not need or only *relatively* needs the other, that is free to form and shape its freedom, that can demand from God its salvation on its own terms, or that can forego the labor of conforming heart, mind, and freedom to the immense gift already given.

This is the proper sense of *distance* or *difference* that arises for the one who correctly perceives himself *as a child*, who recognizes in and through the experience of receiving his self as a gift that salvation, like existence, is entirely due to the free, loving initiative of the Father, and that short of existential subsistence in this gift there can be no hope of aligning the varied tasks of my freedom faithfully with it.

And yet, along with the recognition of difference, baptismal adoption also brings with it the legitimate assurance that despite the contingency and relativity of my existence, there is nevertheless a kind of necessity to the Father's elective love. This is not the assurance of a necessity that begins and ends in the sin of presumption, but one co-extensive with *having actually received and experienced* the radiance of the Father's love, a love that is steadfast and faithful, a filial love that truly desires *my* salvation and adoption and is actually accomplishing it in me.

Having concretely experienced this love, the baptismal person can now quite normally and healthily "presume" that yes, God truly is love! Yes, God *has* elected and adopted me because it belongs to the deepest essence of His trinitarian self to love and to give. Though I know that I am not worthy, that I am a sinner, I can nevertheless depend on a love that is contingent only on my free response and faithfulness to his loving initiative.

Faith and reason inside baptism after the death of God

With all this, I hope to have shown how it might be possible to renegotiate an approach to the existential question after the death of God. Such a baptismal approach holds open the possibility of both a genuinely contemplative or doxological *and* an intellectual pursuit of the mystery hidden in God from all eternity (cf. Eph. 3:9; Col. 1:26) but revealed "to his holy ones, to whom God chose to make known the riches of the mystery…" (Col. 1:27). By conceiving of the tasks of faith and reason from *inside* the baptismal relation impressed on our flesh and our consciousness, it will become possible to pursue meaning and truth without the pretension "to know" absolutely or solely according to the measure of one's falsely sovereign selfhood.

At the same time, I do not mean to imply that a legitimate distinction between the pursuits of faith and reason no longer exists. All that I claim is that for us, as baptized persons, any more technical, instrumental, procedural, philosophical, artistic, social, or cultural kinds of rationality in other fields are, for all their "legitimate autonomy" (*Gaudium et spes* 59), nevertheless still pursued by one who bears the mystery of election and adoption in his flesh and in his mind. For baptized persons, distinctions between modes of knowing are made from a point already *inside* the baptismal relation. My point is that baptismal adoption cannot be sloughed off as irrelevant. It *will* impact how one sees the world and how one conducts oneself, whether positively or negatively. If we cannot see this, it means that we are persisting in the tendency to think of baptismal adoption in only moral or exemplary terms, as only a qualification or ideal that has not yet reached into the insides of our horizon. And if so, then we are closer to the despair and violence of the modern/postmodern condition than we know.

Much more can and should be said here, but let this suffice for now: for the Christian, *after and in the face of the social and cultural death of God*, the battle for truth and meaning cannot prescind from deeper consideration of the new horizon that has been gifted to us by our adoption. What this might mean more practically we will see in our final chapter.

Adoption as liturgy, liturgy as adoption

Thus far we have focused on a vision of baptism in light of the full possibility granted the person who subsists inside the relation of the Son to the Father. We have also noted how the person is "born" into this relation via the "sacramental middle," the forms of which express and mediate this paradigmatic relation. And I have suggested that the baptismal logic that belongs to this middle serves to offer a more primordial way of relating God and man and a new ground for the ancillary pursuits of reason.

Now, it is precisely this "middle" and the way that it *concretely* feeds this baptismal relation to the Father that needs further explication. For without such explication, our relation to the Father in the Son — no matter how real this gift is in terms of how it changes our basic identity and frame — will remain formal and abstract — undramatic — and as such will be corroded by the world's continuing violent claim on the self.

This is to recognize that baptismal adoption does not yet take us out of the embodied theater of worldly time, the condition of what John Paul II called "historical man" or the "man of concupiscence."[23] Though we are children of God, and though we occupy the new embodied time of the sacramental middle, our freedom does not yet rest in the peace of the beatific vision. We are still subject to temptation and sin. An ongoing labor of conversion to baptismal adoption is therefore needed in order to conform our freedom more perfectly to the full measure of the Father's gift of divine sonship.

In this (difficult) labor, however, we are not left to our own devices. The Father does not adopt us in his Son and then leave us orphans (cf. Jn. 14:18). Instead, as Christ assures us, he gives us "another Advocate to be with [us] always" (Jn. 14:15). This Advocate, the Holy Spirit given to the Church at Pentecost (cf. Acts 2:1–4) as promised by Christ, is more than a personal guide or a generic moral power who intervenes from time to time in our lives with inspiration or suggestions. Nor is the Spirit an agent of rupture and disturbance who flits about restlessly looking for dubious and novel causes to champion — this is more akin to how Satan operates (cf. Gen. 1:15, Job 1:6–12, Mt. 4:1–11, Eph. 6:11, 1 Pet. 5:8).

No, the Spirit "*of adoption*" (Rom. 8:15)[24] and the "Spirit of truth" (Jn. 16:3) is instead to be found at the center of the Church, faithfully actuating the mandate given to him by the Father and the Son of deepening and completing the work of salvation and conversion begun in us by the Son, speaking not on his own authority or initiative, but on that of the Father and the Son (cf. Jn. 16:12–15).

Indeed, the entire sacramental middle is itself already the work of the Spirit present from the first in the saving historical work of the Father and the Son. It is the Spirit who animates the Church, who enables her to conceive and bear the Word given to her by Jesus Christ (cf. Lk. 1:35). Without the gift of the interceding Spirit, the event of Christ and the offer of our salvation and adoption would be inaccessible to us. It would remain trapped on the other side of the broad ditch of history. Christ's return to the Father (cf. Jn. 16:28) would have been the end of his historical work. All that could have been left would have been the memory or perhaps the "idea" of what he accomplished. Faith could only be a transcendental

---

23 Cf. John Paul II, *Man and Woman He Created Them*, 234–35.
24 Emphasis added.

interiority. It could only consist of a stoic effort to conform ourselves to an ideal not present to us in the flesh.

But the Spirit changes everything. Present in a hidden manner from the very first moment of Christ's ministry, the Spirit is present *now* in the ecclesial forms that mediate the presence of Christ, a presence that because of the Spirit is alive; the Son is alive and present to us sacramentally in the mediation of the Church, even though he is not with us in his historical flesh.

So, if we say that Christ is really present in the Blessed Sacrament, it is only because the *Spirit* was already and is now present, animating and fructifying the Body of Christ, sealing and communicating Christ's sacrifice, making it a living sacrifice for us here, now. If it is the "Eucharist [that] makes the Church," as de Lubac rightly put it,[25] it is only because the Eucharist, as the mystical reality of Christ's self-gift to the Church in history, has already been given by the intercession of the Spirit. That is, the *historical* event of Christ — his sacrificial offering of himself that is the historical origin of the Church in her identity as Bride and Mother — is by the Spirit's faithful carrying-through of Christ's mission made a *sacramental* event, a sacrificial offering truly "present" to us and for us, one that continues to "make" the Church, adding more members to Christ's mystical Body, more branches to his Vine (cf. Jn. 15:5).

Because of the Spirit, then, we find a living, efficacious network of sacramental encounters and mediations in the Church. We are the recipients of Spirit-filled forms of personal communication that are both our origin and the continuing air that we breathe and food that we eat. To say that my baptismal existence rests completely in Christ is thus to say it also rests completely in the living forms that mediate his historical presence to me. Without these forms and the intercession of the Spirit who vivifies and seals them, my baptismal existence would simply hang suspended outside of my historical occupation of the world.

---

25 "Now, the Eucharist is the mystical principle, permanently at work at the heart of Christian society, which gives concrete form to this miracle [the Church]. It is the universal bond, it is the ever-springing source of life. Nourished by the body and blood of the Saviour, his faithful people thus all 'drink of the one Spirit,' who truly makes them into one single body. Literally speaking, therefore, the Eucharist makes the Church." Henri de Lubac, *Corpus Mysticum: The Eucharist and the Church in the Middle Ages*, trans. Gemma Simmonds (Notre Dame, IN: University of Notre Dame Press, 2006), 88.

Liturgy and sacraments as the grammar of baptismal adoption

This means a couple of important things. First, it means that if we seek to truly understand what it means to be an adopted son, we must search the sacramental grammar of our relation to the Father. This means that the liturgy and sacraments must be recognized as the lifeblood and grammar of baptismal existence, for they are the places where the Spirit is most active. We must look for our baptismal selves inside the Son's relation to the Father, yes, but we can only do this by inserting ourselves into the living, Spirit-filled, sacramental time and space of the Son's gift of himself to the Church. We must be attentive to the signs and symbols of this world, treating them as reality *par excellence*, as the concrete language of our relation to the Father in the Son. They are the new "smiles" that radiate and nurture adopted existence, that respond to and engage the full range of the existential condition of being human.

Second, if this is true, I suggest that it means there is something in the liturgy and sacraments that is not quite captured by conventional approaches or, especially, the approaches typical in the context of the liturgy wars of the post-Conciliar period, where reflection has been torn and fractured by the more basic theological and anthropological conflict about who God is, who man is, and what their relation might be after and in the face of the social and cultural horizon of the death of God. However, rather than approach this problematic context head-on from the standard dialectic of liturgical "traditionalism" versus "progressivism," I propose that a possibly fruitful theological and anthropological approach — a kind of baptismal "phenomenology" — is one that begins from *what we already know* about the person from the perspective of election and adoption as we have articulated it up to this point. For the one already called, chosen, and named by the Father there can be no such thing as liturgical worship and sacramental grace except as the existential consummation and faithful deepening of a relation already made a reality in his flesh.

For such a person, the Eucharistic liturgy is not only an encounter with Christ from whom salutary moral benefit or devotional inspiration may be derived, but with the same ecclesial and spousal event of Christ and the Church that made us sons of God the Father. Before it is anything else, the Eucharistic liturgy is encountered as the *return* of the child to the very font of life that generated or "made" him or her. It is an immersion back into and a reliving of the gift of the Bridegroom to the Bride, of the

Son's gift on the Cross, of the pierced side of the Lamb from which flowed the blood and water of our redemption and adoption.

The Eucharistic liturgy is thus only properly understood when it is conceived as a baptismal and ecclesial event that remembers, actuates, and restores the filial bond established between the Father and his children in the priestly ministry of Christ, the spousal Mediator of the Father's covenant with us. By it we are immersed back into the mainstream of the eternal and temporal flow of salvation history, into the mystery of the love of the Father and the Son, into the gift of the Son from the Father, into the sacrifice of the Son for the Church, into the gifts of election and adoption born from the Spirit's fruitful mediation of the Father's gift of the Son to the Church.

Through the Eucharistic liturgy, then, our baptismal relation to the Father in the Son becomes and remains *concrete and actual*. The liturgy thus constitutes and feeds this relation. It is the concrete place where the gift of baptismal adoption came from and where it is sustained and purified. By it, baptismal adoption becomes more than a comforting idea or static state of existence. Rather, it becomes a living relational exchange of existences, human and divine; a concrete practice and discipline of love; a web of sanctifying relations that now forms the living heart and existential horizon of one's entire existence. This, then, is the liturgical heart of the sacramental middle.

One baptismal and Eucharistic font

From this liturgical source of adoption, it becomes possible to better recognize the logic and character of *all* the sacraments as concrete, expressive mediations of the Eucharistic liturgy that grounds and mediates our baptismal relation to the Father in Christ. Each sacrament originates in the event of salvation communicated by and made real in the Eucharistic liturgy. Each sacrament therefore originates in and belongs to the Eucharistic microcosm of the total drama of adopted existence and the existential exchange of love between God and man.

Nevertheless, as already suggested, if it is true that the Eucharist is the "source and summit of the Christian life" (*Lumen gentium* 11), it is baptism that is its sign and "hermeneutic." That is, there can be no meaningful approach to the Eucharistic liturgy that is not first a *baptismal* approach. Only by baptism, my rebirth from the salvific fruitfulness of Christ's union with the Church, can I perceive what it is that the Eucharist in fact poured and is pouring out *for me* in the Eucharistic sacrifice.[26]

Without baptism, the Eucharist must only appear as the claim of an "objective" presence extrinsic to me that might inspire devotional fervor. Or sometimes it might be used as a kind of inspirational or pedagogical template that illustrates the ideal logic of gift-giving for human sociality, the moral or ethical benefits of which may be at least partially explicable outside the horizon of baptismal belonging to the Father in Christ. But unless the distance between my presence and Christ's "real presence" is bridged by an event that redimensions space and time, that "hypostatically" unites human and divine nature in one divine Person and adopts *me* into this union, there can be no Eucharist as a *genuine mystical union of the person with God* in its truest reality, as a spousal event that connects the person to his filial origins. In precisely the "hypostatic" context given in baptism, however, the Eucharist can appear as an exchange of loves in which we ourselves are also present. It can appear as an event that takes place "inside" our baptismal relation to the Father in the Son. Baptism and the Eucharist are therefore two central pillars of what we have been broadly calling the baptismal or sacramental identity of the person.

Second baptisms

But no account of a liturgical and sacramental existence is complete without recognition of what is so often the transient and imperfect character of our inhabitation of this adoptive, Eucharistic existence. For, as already suggested at the beginning of our reflections on baptismal adoption and the liturgy, baptism is not a fail-safe that guarantees a serene resting in the Son's relation to the Father. The baptized are still subject to sin; salvation is still a serious struggle, a lifelong labor of conversion (cf. Phil. 2:12). None of us can as a consequence presume to ever perfectly inhabit the Son's relation to the Father. We are constantly at risk of distorting the Father's claim on us and separating ourselves from the communion of Christ and the Church that mediates our relation to the Father.

But from this point of view, the gift of the fullness of baptismal life received in the liturgy and the sacraments is mediated by the same rhythm of death-to-life played out in the font. Here, the sacrament of penance appears as a kind of re-immersion of the self who has failed to live up to

---

26 In this, when I speak of baptism, I speak also implicitly of the sacrament of confirmation, which belongs to and completes the grace of baptism in the anointing of the Holy Spirit.

its baptismal promises into the "font" of Christ's sacrificial and redemptive love here communicated in the confessional. By the encounter with the Father of mercies here, the sins and wounds accrued by the failure of our freedom cannot permanently invalidate the Father's promise to us in our baptism. Penance restores the power of that promise. The same fruitful, Eucharistic sacrifice of Christ which animated the baptismal waters of our adoption here reanimates filial sonship, incorporating it back into full communion with its Eucharistic source, and equipping it for further spiritual warfare and deepened conversion.

In fact, the death-to-life motif of baptism is everywhere expressed in the very shape and rhythm of the liturgical and sacramental rites themselves (at least when they are allowed to be themselves). In their form and faithful expression they tell the story, not only of that relation which is already accomplished in our flesh and which is sealed and consummated in Eucharistic communion, but also of *that relation which is not yet completed,* of the need for constant purification and penance so that the human bride might be made worthy of the divine Bridegroom. In this, the liturgical and sacramental rites are (in their most faithful expression[27]) constituted by an internal irresolution and incompleteness correlative to our own halting and imperfect approach to the mystery. The rites feature starts and stops; tension and release; "clutter," complexity, and repetition; restraint, reserve, and sobriety; petition and humiliation.

27 It is impossible for me to avoid saying something about the situation of Roman liturgy today, non-expert though I am. As indicated previously, it is common knowledge that in recent decades the Church has been torn apart by a crisis — almost a *de facto* schism, one might even say — in Her liturgical practice, and concomitantly, Her belief. Two points seem important. First, much of the Church's worship in the centuries leading up to the Second Vatican Council *already* bore the effects of the self-secularizing and rationalizing tendencies we have already identified in earlier chapters. For example, a certain scholastic penchant for reducing the spirit of the liturgy to questions of validity and invalidity, and a characterization of grace as "medicinal," began to foster a spirit of reductionism and instrumentality in the liturgy. Second, just as attempts to restore a deeper Patristic sense of worship and liturgy along the lines of deification and communion began to pick up steam in the early- to mid-20th century, they were co-opted by an embrace of the *hyper*-instrumentality and reductionism of modernity. Just where the peculiar situation at present regarding the Roman Rite's dual expression in an "extraordinary" and "ordinary" form will end up long-term remains to be seen. Without wanting to enter too deeply into a contentious debate, it seems harder and harder to deny that deep ambiguities, dubious or downright ideological interests, and historically conditioned assumptions, many of which in hindsight have been discredited — not to mention a persistent contemporary horizon of interpretation still bent on perpetuating that particular "spirit" of Vatican II so closely associated with the false assumptions of modernity — haunt the revised order of the Mass. Perhaps only a more baptismal future holds the answers.

Rather than automatically signifying a rigid casuistry, excessive aesthetic ornamentation, or unhealthy insecurity about the state of one's soul, when these characteristics of liturgy are more *baptismally* understood and expressed, they can be perceived as the proper and natural response of one who, having experienced by baptism the unfathomable grace of divine sonship, falls to his knees in gratitude, praise, thanksgiving, and supplication — *worship*. The rites communicate that baptismal adoption is never owed to me, but must always be received as gift. The sober, reserved, and disciplined character of the rites expresses the seriousness of the work of our salvation and adoption and the reverent and contemplative response this gift should provoke, while their complexity expresses the fact that the story of salvation recounted in the liturgy is not something complete, transparent, or simply there for my thoughtless consumption, but rather requires a spiritual labor and apprenticeship whereby I am slowly shaped into the image of the story it tells. More than anything else, then, liturgy should bring us to reverent silence, to a solemn praise and thanksgiving born not from what I can produce or create, but from what is produced and created in me by the sacramental communication of the Father's presence in the rites.

Finally, what Pickstock calls the "haphazard" character of the Roman liturgy (in its extraordinary form) "can be seen as predicated upon a need for a constant re-beginning of liturgy because the true eschatological liturgy is in time endlessly postponed."[28] The "unfinished" character of the rites reminds us that nothing this side of the eschaton can satisfy our quest for meaning. It reminds us that baptismal adoption is aimed towards the fullness of communion only possible in the world to come.

The spousal source and shape of baptismal existence

We have now seen how baptism, the Eucharist, and penance (along with the internal form and logic of the liturgical and sacramental rites) actualize, communicate, and purify the person's baptismal existence within the conditions of space and time, placing him in a horizon beyond the pure "below" of nature and "above" of grace. A final key element, one that pervades and informs all of the liturgical and sacramental themes explored

---

28 Pickstock, *After Writing*, 173. Pickstock also speaks of how what she calls "liturgical stammer" (a complex and incomplete rather than transparent and complete liturgical language) corresponds to an "admission of distance between itself and the transcendent 'real.' It is this very admission of distance which permits a genuine proximity with God" (178).

thus far, is that provided by the sacrament of marriage.

From the strict point of view of marriage as a sacrament, of course, marriage is a state of life or "vocational" sacrament tied to two baptismal persons, a man and woman, who receive in a special way the grace of Christ's union with the Church which enables their union to participate in and embody this "great mystery" (Eph. 5) as a sign of God's love in the world.

However, sacramental marriage first signifies a much broader reality. Contained within it is the grammar and form of that same spousal and filial Love that created and redeemed the world and adopted the creature. At the heart of liturgical and sacramental existence is the highest communication of the love of a husband and a wife, and a father and a mother. God is a *son*, a *husband*, and a *father*. The Church is a *daughter*, a *wife*, and a *mother*. We are baptismally *reborn* from an intimate *spousal* love. The Eucharist is a *spousal* event *par excellence*.

Marriage, then, belongs to the very deepest logic of faith itself, as the grammar that pervades the entire liturgical and sacramental middle occupied by the child of God. Indeed, as pointed out so eloquently and originally by John Paul II, marriage already belongs to the deepest strata of created existence itself, as the "primordial sacrament," an original embedding of the mystery of spousal and filial love in the fabric of existence and experience from "the beginning."[29] In the "one-flesh" union of the first man and woman, created in the image and likeness of God, is concretized a sign, a vision of a reciprocal human love perfectly interwoven with the love of the Creator from which it originated and within which it is sustained, a love that is a sacramental blueprint that communicates, however inchoately (and after sin, *confusedly and brokenly*), something of the God who in Himself is a life-giving "communion of Persons."[30]

In the original horizon of creation, this interweaving of human and divine love suffuses the existential experience of man and woman, an experience that we might call proto-baptismal. Here we see the original instance of what it means to live grace as a personal relation and not mere medicine. Existence itself is thoroughly penetrated and indwelt by the presence of divinity. To be, to exist, is to breathe the clear air of a perfect relation of love. There is no "natural," no "merely human," no conception of the self as divorced from its primary definition in existential union with

---

29 John Paul II, *Man and Woman He Created Them*, 203.
30 Ibid., 163.

the divine and human "other." All of this John Paul II thus calls "primordial," the original form of existence which emerges from the heart of "*the invisible mystery hidden in God from eternity*."[31]

But it is not of course until Christ that we are able to truly see and understand this mystery as it might apply to us after the Fall and after the event of our salvation. The mystery of our primordial beginning is given *definitive* shape in the spousal gift of the Son as Bridegroom to the Church. Here we discover that the beginning *was in fact itself always premised on Christ*. Man and woman, though chronologically prior to the historical revelation of Christ, were already "created through him and for him" (Col. 1:16). The Father had already chosen "us in him, before the foundation of the world.... In love he destined us for adoption to himself through Jesus Christ, in accord with the favor of his will, for the praise of the glory of his grace that he granted us in the beloved" (Eph. 1:3).[32] Christ, the eternal Son of the Father, is also the "firstborn of all creation" (Col. 1:15). In him, in his identity as Son and Bridegroom, is seen the definitive shape of what that primordial sacramentality of the beginning was already signifying and proclaiming.

What we find in the new forms of the sacramental "middle," then, in the baptismal and Eucharistic selfhood discovered in the liturgical action of the Church, is the actualization and re-dimensioning of that which marriage in the beginning already signified: the eternal totality, permanency, fidelity, and fruitfulness in God himself. Here we see the fullest spiritual and eschatological *reality* of what was in the beginning expressed as sign in the man and woman. Baptismal adoption into the divine life "consummates" the reality that the sign of marriage in the

---

31 Ibid., 203.

32 José Granados and Carl Anderson provide a helpful explanation of the paradox that Christ, though chronologically posterior to the original man and woman according to our time, in fact precedes them from the point of view of "God's timeline": "We usually think of time as an arrow flying irreversibly out of the past and into the future. Placed on this standard human time line, Christ's coming looks just like another link in a long chain of historical events stretching back to Adam and Eve. In the Letter to the Ephesians, Paul invites us to look at things the other way around. From God's point of view, Paul is telling us, Christ's coming is not some random event that happened to occur two thousand years ago. For Christ is the origin of all that exists and he brings the whole creation to fulfillment. By the same token, Adam and Eve's one-flesh union may come first in our timeline, but on God's timeline it's Christ and his Church who come first. From God's point of view, in other words, the sacrament of creation gets its existence and meaning from the sacrament of redemption that Christ establishes by his own marriage to the Church." *Called to Love: Approaching John Paul II's Theology of the Body* (New York: Doubleday, 2009), 170–1.

beginning and in Christ points to. This is the new *spiritual* union and fruitfulness that is a foretaste of the marriage of the Lamb (cf. Rev. 19:6–9), of that eschatological time when the sign of marriage will find its *eternal* fulfillment (cf. Mt. 22:30).[33]

By the sign of marriage, then, we can see liturgical and sacramental existence more clearly in its full significance, as a kind of new "primordial" sacramentality; that is, of grace experienced and lived as communion in experience and in time, as a faithful gift to and indwelling with the other. By this, just as we saw how baptism allows one to receive the Eucharist as a child in communion with Father and the Son through the gift of the Spirit, marriage further specifies the nature of the mystical communion experienced therein: "receiving the Eucharist means blending one's existence, closely analogical, spiritually, to what happens when man and wife become one on the physical-mental-spiritual plane."[34]

By the sign of marriage we can also see how past, present, and future belong to the same story, how baptismal adoption does not hang in a void but possesses deep links to an eternal plan of salvation sunk deeply into the earliest moments of human history and carried in the heart and body of every human soul as a yearning for the Eucharistic Christ and full adoption into the Father. As Balthasar expresses it, the "return home" of humanity to its deepest origins "is achieved not by a gnostic form of spiritualization [one that would leave the original bodily archetype of man and woman behind] but by the transformation of the flesh estranged from God through the sacrificial fire of the Cross, in the mystery of the "one" sacrificed flesh of man and woman, Christ and Church."[35]

But the significance of sacramental marriage does not end here. Even after the eschatological fulfillment of the sign of marriage in Christ and the Church, marriage as a vocation in the world is not annulled, but "recharged." Again, baptism into the mystery of Christ and the Church and entry into the Son's relation to the Father does not yet mean departure

33 If *every* believer participates in the anticipation of this state by virtue of his baptism, in the vocation of consecrated celibacy this anticipation acquires the value of a total state of life in its full eschatological radicality in the here and now of historical existence. Cf. John Paul II, *Man and Woman He Created Them*, 379–453.

34 Joseph Cardinal Ratzinger, *Pilgrim Fellowship of Faith: The Church as Communion*, trans. Henry Taylor (San Francisco: Ignatius Press, 2005), 101. For a rich account of the relationship between the liturgy and a theology of the body, see Adam G. Cooper, *Holy Eros: A Liturgical Theology of the Body* (Kettering: Angelico Press, 2014).

35 Balthasar, *Spouse of the Word*, 180.

from this world. Instead, we are sent back to the world to live this mystery and relation in varied ways. In the case of marriage, already a primordial sacrament of creation and now granted its ultimate ecclesial shape in Christ, the baptized who take it up as a state of life do so according to its new specifications. As *sacramental* sign, marriage *now* expresses the totality of both the primordial beginning and the fulfillment of this beginning in Christ, and must be lived as such.

In the married couple, baptismal existence thus acquires new expression. In the totality of their one-flesh union, the couple receives, bears, and expresses the full weight of the spousal and filial story of salvation history. They do so as an extension of the properly ecclesial core of this liturgical and sacramental story into the heart of the world. In the union which becomes the "domestic church" of the family, the communion of husband and wife becomes a microcosm of ecclesial communion and worship, a visible sign of everything given to the baptismal person in the Eucharistic Christ. By cleaving to one another, by living for each other, by generating and raising children in the Lord, by embodying a communion of persons and a domestic church, the couple receives anew the spousal and filial story of the creating, saving, redeeming, electing, and adopting Love of the Father in Christ the Bridegroom, giving witness to it in their union. Their witness thereby serves the building-up of the Body of Christ and the evangelization of the world.[36]

All of this, incidentally, constitutes the ultimate frame through which the "pelvic" liturgies of liberalism might be more effectively out-narrated. A baptismal logic of theological personhood gives the embodied person the absolute "identity" and "orientation" that exceeds all the limitations of a bodily existence shaped only by a nature or a freedom held in bondage to sin and concupiscence. In the redemptive unity of the primordial, ecclesial, and eschatological horizon of baptismal existence, the elements of body, sex, and difference can find their *existential* unification in the absolute identity of the person as son or daughter who cleaves to the crucified and risen flesh of the suffering Son.

From this point of view, it is not enough to approach the pelvic suite of contemporary issues within what I call an "intracosmic" frame, that is,

---

36 Cf. Marc Cardinal Ouellet, *Divine Likeness: Towards a Trinitarian Anthropology of the Family* (Grand Rapids: Eerdmans, 2006); Angelo Cardinal Scola, *The Nuptial Mystery* (Grand Rapids: Eerdmans, 2005); *God and Eros: The Ethos of the Nuptial Mystery*, ed. Colin Patterson and Conor Sweeney (Eugene: Cascade Books, 2015).

solely according to natural and substantialist categories. Nor is it enough to do so only according to a consequential evaluation of these issues within the frame of liberalism, which already largely views the transgressive consequences of the sexual revolution as freedom. If by baptism the person truly becomes a new creation as I have articulated it, then this same logic of total immersion into the mystery extends just as radically to questions of bodily orientation and identity. I am called by baptism to "orient" myself and my desires, not to a law or norm conceived only in intracosmic terms, not only to a divine command, and not only because it might avert negative personal and social consequences. Rather, I am called according to the full measure of an "identity" that I already bear in my flesh, one that rests solely and completely "inside" the infrastructure of the hypostatic union, in the Son's spousal relation to the Church and filial relation to the Father, and that aims toward its ultimate fulfillment in the world to come. It is only here that questions of desire, orientation, and difference can find the redemption they were created and groan for (cf. Rom. 8:22–24).

These remarks can only remain provisional here. Suffice it to say that a theology of body, sex, and difference *after the death of God* must become far more evangelical. We cannot be satisfied with a horizon of operation not prepared to move outside the immanent frame of both nature and freedom.

The sacraments and liturgy as sacred mysteries

In sum, then, through this brief snapshot of the liturgical and sacramental grammar of the sacramental middle, I hope that we can begin to see the true grammar and lifeblood of Christian existence. I hope we can see that baptismal existence finds its ultimate shape from a point inside the Father's communication of love to the world in his Son's spousal relationship to the Church.

And from this point of view we can more clearly see what liturgical and sacramental existence and the communication of sanctifying grace therein *are not*. There is no place for liturgy understood only as an "epic" or "theatrical" spectacle whereby the events of our salvation are told as an objective story to which we are only admitted as spectators, where the quality of my participation and response has little or no bearing on what happens on the altar.

There is no place for a spirit of the bare minimum or legal requirement when it comes to how we conceive of adoptive existence. Sacramental efficacy cannot be conceived according to what Peter Kwasniewski calls "neoscholastic reductionism,"[37] namely, the view that as long as the strict "form and matter" of a sacred rite are correct (you say the right words and use the right things in the rite proper) then the sacrament will be validly "confected" and the grace of the rite produced, such that anything strictly distinct from these essential elements can be regarded as "accidents," or non-essential components of the rite.

The sacraments cannot be understood as mere conduits or "channels" of grace in the abstract. Against the backdrop of some of those tensions explored earlier, grace cannot be thought of only as "medicine" that heals nature as nature, or only as a "power" aimed at rectifying man's moral and juridical irregularity vis-à-vis divine law. Nor can sacramental grace — and here I speak specifically of the grace transmitted and received in marriage and the Eucharist — be thought of as a (magical) power that can overcome contradiction, namely, those situations of moral irregularity whereby what should be my faithful baptismal approach to and participation in the sacrament as a child in full communion with the Church has been truncated or destroyed by my freedom. The sacramental grace of *communion* first presupposes my fidelity to my *baptismal* promises.

Liturgical and sacramental rites cannot be understood as mere ritual markers or signposts of a community's awareness that God is active in their midst. Baptism cannot be conceived as a mere formality, a ritual marking membership in a club or association. The Eucharist cannot be thought of merely as a meal shared in some vague sense of togetherness. There is no place for the quintessentially modern demand for transparency, relevance, and entertainment or the tendency of a celebrant who feels the need to "supplement" a perceived irrelevance or impotence of the rites with his own "personality" or with specific and so often ghastly additions to the liturgical celebration over and beyond the profound mysteries communicated in the rites themselves.

Everything that we have said thus far requires us to resist such reductions and distortions. For what they reduce and distort is the very mystery hidden in God, revealed in Christ, and given to us in baptismal adoption. A reduction and distortion here, in the forms of the living communication

---

37 Peter Kwasniewski, "The Long Shadow of Neoscholastic Reductionism," in *New Liturgical Movement* (blog), July 3, 2017, at http://www.newliturgicalmovement.org/2017/07/the-long-shadow-of-neoscholastic.html#.WYPAc4SGNhE.

of our adoption, will thus betray or truncate the very mystery which they transmit. The dissonance thereby provoked inevitably leads to a loss of credibility for the deepest claims of faith. You become what you eat. It cannot be underestimated how deeply we are shaped by concrete practices, by *doing* things as opposed to *thinking* things. Liturgy that does not express the glory and majesty of the God who gave everything to us will fail at a deep level to *accomplish* and nurture the work that baptism has already begun in us. Or worse, it will cause scandal and dissonance — it will subvert and betray that work, subtly communicating a God who is already dead, a community that believes only in itself, and a faith that is little more than a juvenile superstition that critical reason and secular ideology will easily overcome and in the end seek to destroy.

Being fed by faithful, reverent liturgy is an essential condition of baptismal adoption. Where it is not possible to avoid parish cultures where liturgical rites are so often regarded as embarrassments to get out of the way as quickly and perfunctorily as possible, we must strive to enter into them according to the reality that the rites themselves are in fact constituting and realizing. For in them is the salvation that can be found nowhere else. Let us, at least, treat them as such.

The hope of baptism

It is perhaps the case that this chapter has said both too much and too little. Perhaps there is something here that inspires or provokes possibility. Perhaps it confuses and puzzles, producing more questions than answers. I certainly accept that the broader implications of what I have said likely remain somewhat hazy. What all of this might mean beyond the borders of the person who in his flesh embodies a hypostatic participation in Christ's relation to the Father and who inhabits this relationship in the liturgical and sacramental forms of the Church may not be patently clear, although some more practical indications can be found in the final section of chapter seven.

In the present chapter, my main goal has been to try to *reboot the imagination of the believer*, to place the child of the Father back into existential contact with the fundamental grammar of his baptismal being. The first and primary obligation of the baptized person must always be to read reality *for himself* at all times from its deepest point, that is, from the point of view of a baptismal anthropology. To know myself, and to not betray myself, I must read myself from the central current of *who* — not simply *what*—I am as adopted into the divine life itself. This, I think, we have by and large forgotten how to do. And some imaginative reconnection with this, however imperfect and unfinished, is therefore the desired outcome of this chapter.

The essential point as regards how the baptismal person is then to engage with the world is that if my central claims are true, then this person must become aware that his "secular" pursuits or activities must always be lived from and at a deeper point. I must recognize that my baptismal identity precedes and envelops the multiple forms of my participation and involvement in the world, in personal and social engagements, in public discourse, in other categories of rational thought and fields of research. Even if this identity must not in every instance be fully manifest, it is always there as the silent presence and sanctified horizon of a person who is in Christ. This also means that more conscious or deliberate attempts to witness to the truth must do more than simply point to the structures, natures, essences, and consequences that from the point of view of baptism are only pale elements of what it truly means to be.

We all know that baptism remains a constant struggle. It is hard enough for us to be true to it for ourselves, let alone transmit it as a sign for the redemption of the world. A social context marked by the death of God makes this seem almost impossible. And an ecclesial context marked by its own grave failures and distortions of the liturgical and sacramental mediation of baptismal existence lends a certain morose pathos to everything I have said.

Today, then, amidst fractured and failing Christian worship and practices, the baptism that we carry as a gift in our flesh may be the only effective resource we have in our pursuit of meaning. Yet in it, however degraded and betrayed its mediation, is *everything*. In it is everything that we need, everything we must cling to in difficult circumstances. In it the gift of salvation offered to me remains the hope for a world mired in false liturgies and false stories of emancipation.

The point is not to say that baptism automatically fixes everything. Our existence is still tension, restlessness, and homelessness. It is still a struggle between the old man and the new man. It is still a battle to concretely reconcile and integrate nature and grace, reason and faith, and truth and love. There are at least as many dark nights of the soul, deep existential doubts, and painful trials as flashes of edifying brilliance and heart-warming consolation. The postmodern condition will continue to rage and storm, tempting us to despair and violence.

Even if baptism "out-narrates" postmodernity, it does so only by the *slow* way of love, often in conditions of great suffering and perplexity which it seemingly remains unable to alleviate. To grow in love with a person can never happen spontaneously or in a moment. It requires time: a *life*-time of patience, self-emptying, vulnerability, indwelling, self-examination, devotion, perseverance, stubbornness, apology, humiliation, suffering, reconciliation, purification, conversion. The baptized person is immune to none of this in his or her walk with Christ.

But the difference is that the Son is no ordinary person. We may not yet know him fully, but he knows us and has called us. Our hope is thus in this person, this extraordinary Person both human and divine, this divine Person who breaks open time and space for us, who radiates our adoption to us, who forgives us and loves us in his loving sacramental acts in the Church, and who with the Spirit shows us the Father. Our hope is in this Person who always walks with and before us, who never forsakes us, who is more interior to us than we are to ourselves. This is the great hope of baptism, the great hope of adoption, the great hope of love. We are not alone. The star twinkles even if we do not see it. This is the hope to which we must cling, our *only* hope.

In the next chapter, we shift gears to consider how a baptismal conception of faith as adoption gives way to the question of evangelization.

SIX

The Ambiguities of
Virtual Evangelization

A cold voice answered: "Come not between the Nazgûl and his prey!
Or he will not slay thee in thy turn. He will bear thee away to the
houses of lamentation, beyond all darkness, where thy flesh shall be
devoured, and thy shrivelled mind be left naked to the Lidless Eye."
J. R. R. Tolkien, *The Return of the King*

IF THE PREVIOUS CHAPTER OUTLINES A TENTATIVE baptismal path for how the evangelizer might best confront and out-narrate his or her own postmodern crisis of meaning and discover the deeper meaning of faith, this chapter begins to ask how a baptismal discovery of self and meaning here might then be brought to bear on the world by our witness to and proclamation of the mystery for others in the task and mission of evangelization. Our final chapter will provide a full answer to this question.

At its heart, my take on what constitutes evangelization is that first and foremost it must involve a radiation of the internalization of one's own baptism (and therefore the out-narration of the postmodern condition) to others simply by the bearing of faith in one's own baptized being. The best evangelizer is the saint. For the saint's baptized being radiates the splendor and joy of faith to others inasmuch as it represents an adopted existence that has truly become "first nature." Saints have fully embraced the "oddity" of baptismal personhood. They radiate a baptismal condition which existentially confronts and challenges the violence and despair of the postmodern condition. And in this, they bear the mystery in all its glory in their persons and in their acts.

In a paradoxical sense, then, the most effective evangelizing practice — the practice that should animate and frame all of our positive acts — is

when we *do nothing*. It is when we stop trying to manifest or "prove" God
to ourselves and to others by measures and strategies that move outside
the space of baptismal adoption. It is when we unplug ourselves from the
coercive imperatives of a restless activism which tries to "fill" secular and
technological forms and categories with Gospel content without genuinely
challenging and subverting the former.

The virtual as perverted antitype of baptism

It has become a rote strategy today to frame evangelizing efforts within
the dominant cultural forms of communication typical of late Western
liberal capitalist and technological societies. To "plunder the spoils of
the Egyptians" in the context of evangelization today means, it seems, to
evangelize on Facebook and Twitter, start a blog, run Tony Robbins-like
seminars, programs, and festivals, adopt corporate slogans, logos, brand-
ing, advertising strategies, and the like. Beat the enemy with their own
weapons!

But we have seen how this can be a self-defeating strategy if the "form"
of these practices is already pregnant with a content and allegiance incom-
mensurable with the genuine Christian form (compare the example of
abortion debate based on rights language in chapter three). If the Ring of
power is truly evil, then it is not possible to use its methods and strategies
in the cause of good. The question, however, is to what extent the forms
of virtual and digital evangelization really belong to the logic of the Ring.
And to what extent therefore do they in fact undermine the entire logic
of baptismal faith and thus betray the new evangelization?

This book has suggested that there is something deeply insidious in the
logic that has culminated in the political, social, and economic ideology of
liberalism and the existential crises of the postmodern condition. I have
argued that at the heart of this logic is inscribed a primitive violence that
seeks to impose an order contrary to the mother's smile, an order contrary
to the baptismal logic inscribed in the faith of Jesus Christ.

The case has been made that the seed of this violence begins within
historical Christian theology itself as a self-secularizing impulse that seeks
to "control faith," to explain it by recourse to categories that fall outside
of the baptismal form of love, worship, and beauty. This helped to open
up an imaginative space for the logic of the "secular" properly speaking
that is consummated today in the escalating celebrations of the infinite
possibilities for the self that emerge within a world where God is dead.

The long and short of this is that a postmodern world has created the possibility for a kind of "virtual" reality that is the direct antithesis or the perverted antitype of the baptismal existence of the person in Christ. Baptismal existence represents a new *sacramental* time and a new space outside of the above and the below. By contrast, digitized, virtual, or "hyperreal" reality represents a similar liberation from this binary, but one constituted and consolidated entirely within the categories and technical possibilities of the secular imagination. Both type and perverted antitype imagine something beyond the limits of space and time — but one is the icon, the other the idol. One heals existence, the other destroys it.

With this we see perhaps the ultimate in perverse mutations of a Christian form. Where baptism into Christ places the person in a sacramental world of concrete enfleshed relationships (the Body of Christ, the Fatherhood of God, the motherhood of Mary and the Church), thereby giving the self back to others, to God, to relationships, to the community, to the concrete, and thus to itself, virtual or digital reality promises by contrast the possibility of a self that exists in total freedom from these constitutive relationships and from one's own bodily self. It is a world that is quintessentially *disincarnate*.

Virtual salvation

In this, like Christianity, virtual reality also promises a kind of salvation from the postmodern condition, but one which does not require the individual to embrace real (baptismal) transcendence — the only death which brings life. Even if one cannot *really* escape the conditions of temporality, virtual "reality" perhaps promises the ultimate in therapeutic panaceas. It is of course just another path of violence, despair, alienation, and delusion if one looks here for real salvation, but it has to be admitted that it is a particularly potent one, as can be seen by the addictive patterns of behavior that are associated with digital forms. For once in this world, one is offered a "real" salvation from the limits of bodily and temporal existence, from the despair of a world stripped of mystery. One can create avatars that are the ideal version of the self, to dwell in universes that are places of infinite possibility for that self. *The Matrix* movie plays with this idea: why eat tasteless but real gruel, when one can have a mouth-watering, if virtual, steak?

Even if this limitless virtual freedom is constantly short-circuited by *concrete* reality (in the sense that your virtual identity is dependent on your computer being plugged in, that at some point your bodily needs will kick in and drag you back to the land of the living, and that virtual reality cannot defeat the ultimate death of your body), while you are here, in this virtual world, you are free. Incarnate reality has nothing on you here, as long as you have your internet connection. All the insecurities, anxieties, frustrated desires, physical defects, anger, and violence which belong to the real world can be escaped by the alchemic merging of hands, brain, and technology. And herein seems to lie the immense addictive appeal of virtual activities like gaming.

What we see in virtual reality is thus a particularly sophisticated expansion of the logic of disincarnate relations and radical freedom from said relations and from God that defines the hope of the post-Christian secular. It is made possible by theoretical presuppositions that technology is then able to make "reality," as we saw in chapter three. Heidegger described the essence of technology in terms of what he called "enframing."[1] He used this notion to criticize an understanding of matter in which it essentially consists of mere raw materials ripe for exploitation in a manner that goes far beyond basic needs or natural patterns of use. The material world, stripped of the impulse and symbolics of transcendence, demythologized and disenchanted, remains little more than a "standing reserve" of raw resources waiting to be shaped by my now-limitless (in both theory and practice) freedom. To so "enframe" the world with a gaze of consumptive violence is to regard it as consisting only in mere surfaces to be manipulated and exploited.

It is this that now makes it possible for transhumanism to imagine not just new *virtual* possibilities for the self, but *literal* ones. Technology, the grammar and praxis of enframing, holds out the hope of the *literal* merging of man with machine (not just the conditional or temporary union of hands, brain, and machine), even of the extinction of mortality itself by said merging (as in cryonics and cybernetics). Even if the possibilities of transhumanism are presently restricted to an elite minority, and while it seems unlikely that any future realization of its most ambitious goals could ever be offered to anyone outside this elite, it is nevertheless the case that any number of more practical applications of its logic are already upon us. Note how the mainstreaming of gender-identity fluidity, the perfect expression of a formless freedom in a disincarnate world, has led to a situation where gender reassignment surgery is almost routine.

---

1   Cf. Heidegger, "The Question Concerning Technology."

The evangelizing practices of Facebook

In the meantime, for those of us preoccupied with "softer" forms of virtual reality via our Smartphones, *physical* technical possibility simply fuels the sense that in the end virtual reality is indeed a real possibility beyond space and time, and increasingly perhaps the *preferred* possibility. Here, I can expand the range of possibilities for a self normally constrained by the limits of body and space. I can find the possibility of "globalized" relationships that break space and time, shattering the borders of the given, bringing the world to my fingertips. All of this is possible for anyone with a Smartphone.

It is to this world, broadly speaking, that the dominant forms of social communication today belong (Facebook, Twitter, Instagram, Snapchat, and the almost daily proliferations of new platforms and apps that continue to reimagine the genre). This is to say that these forms belong, genealogically or genetically speaking, to possibilities that emerged from and were generated by a distinctly disincarnate worldview as brought to consummation by technological means. This is not to jump to a premature conclusion that these are therefore necessarily or absolutely "bad" or "godless," but it is to say that whatever they are, *they will not be value-neutral*. And so further interrogation is needed if we wish to assess what role such digital forms might play in the new evangelization.

Two salient features of Facebook in particular illustrate a "form" exhibiting typically modern/postmodern presuppositions which as such would seem to call into question the claim that evangelization can and should uncritically embrace such disincarnate platforms. First, consider the conception of "virtual" time fostered by a digital platform like Facebook. Tan suggests that the "idolization" and "repetition" of the present is characteristic of Facebook time.[2] Peculiar to virtual reality in general is the Facebook timeline's ability to construct a narrative identity outside of an embodied flow of time, "above" or "outside" reality, as it were. That is, the uploading of experiences and images need bear no intrinsic relationship either to each other or to the "real" reality of the person who shares them. They can be purely a fictional product of the imagination, and absent the *real* person, there is no way to tell whether they are in fact a faithful representation of reality.

---

2 Matthew John Paul Tan, "Faith in the Church of Facebook," in *Journal of Moral Theology* (2015), 30.

This means that Facebook promotes a substitute reality consisting of discrete, a-contextual, unconnected, and manipulable moments that simply "hang" outside of any other referent. In Facebook time, you are not the recipient of time, but its master. You construct the images, you control the narrative. You create your own "immersion experience," your own virtualized "baptismal" existence above normal space and time: you create a new self with new coordinates. The narrative produced here, then, need bear no *intrinsic* relationship to incarnate reality, to the fact that you are in reality *not* the master of your destiny but rather the recipient of the mother's smile and the gift of adoption, radically dependent on others and on the *embodied* narrative flow that has shaped your identity.

The virtual narrative promises *freedom from* the embodied narrative. A virtual identity is bound by none of the laws that govern one's real identity (birthplace, family, history, time, location, event) but instead can be a production of the pure present by pure will. This is an idealized vision of the self that need not bear any intrinsic relationship to the real self.

But we could of course imagine possibilities that might lessen the starkness of this picture. It does indeed seem possible to use Facebook or other virtual platforms more "morally," or with a greater degree of fidelity to reality as such, as a kind of faithful extension of your embodied narrative. The capacity of virtual reality to "stretch" space over time makes it possible to stay in contact with loved ones all over the world through the sharing of events and memories that may in fact more or less accurately reflect reality as such. You might simply use Facebook to share pictures of your children with Grandma who lives on the other side of the world.

For the simple, the innocent, the well-grounded, the virtuous, for those grounded in the really real and in real relationships, there will be a degree of insusceptibility to the temptation to treat the virtual as the real. Like hobbits' greater resistance to the corruption of the Ring, those who have a strong connection to reality through the experience and practices of love will always be more resistant to evil and be able to negotiate gray areas and potential pitfalls better than others. But for all the rest of us?

Before we draw any firm conclusions from this, let us consider a second feature of Facebook. If Facebook is premised on the ability to manufacture time and create and control a narrative typified by discrete idealized moments, then it should be no surprise that commodification and consumption seem to belong to the basic ethos of the platform. Regardless of whether an image is placed there innocently and is in fact born from and accurately reflects reality as such, it will have imposed upon it a form premised on the separation of body-person and image. According to the rules of the platform, the viewer of the image is under no obligation to treat the image as a person. The person has been made a digital object, and as such is available for a form of consumption without constraints. The viewer, safe in his own home, distanced from the *real* person, is free to ogle, scorn, criticize, judge, or lust after the digital person under conditions that offer no *internal* limitation on such behavior.

The consumer gaze as form of the virtual

Philosopher Emmanuel Levinas (1906–1995) suggested that what makes a real face-to-face encounter (that is, not between a person and a mere image) so powerful is that the face of the other issues a real-time demand and a summons to the contours of my gaze. The face of the other confronts me with his subjectivity, his identity as a person, his identity (for the believer) as one infinitely loved and valued by God.

For Levinas, the gaze of the other imposes on me the baseline imperative not to murder. It forces me to recognize and respect the subjectivity of the other, to place limits on the objectifying power of my gaze. In this, says Levinas, the "face resists possession, resists my powers. In its epiphany, in expression, the sensible, still graspable, turns into total resistance to the grasp."[3] The "face of the Other at each moment destroys and overflows the plastic image it leaves me...."[4] The point is that when confronted with a living, breathing, feeling person who faces me in *reality*, I am compelled to acknowledge his personhood and his plea for my respect.

Virtual reality by its fundamental nature must be premised on occluding what we might call the "epiphanous" character of genuinely personal encounter and exchange. In reality, the face of the other is an epiphany which challenges and hopefully breaks the utilitarian and calculative tendencies of my gaze. The face is a discipline or praxis that imposes on me the imperative not to gaze exploitatively. The face of the smiling mother forbids utilitarian consumption and the idolization of my own ego and its sovereign gaze. It functions to *break* my ego. In *virtual* reality, by contrast, the face of the other issues none of the demands that it

---

3 Emmanuel Levinas, *Totality and Infinity: An Essay on Exteriority*, trans. Alphonso Lingis (Pittsburgh: Duquesne University Press, 2003), 197.

4 Ibid., 50–51.

otherwise would in a personal encounter. It has become a passive object for consumption.

What virtual reality thus encourages is a "consumption" of persons (and also of all reality) based entirely on the surface of things as read only by the law of my own freedom. It places the image or the text in a non-relational context that is controlled by the user. It does not demand that the user extricate himself from the conditions of his own almighty and imperious gaze.

And what makes all of this doubly insidious is that the highly technologized platform of something like Facebook stimulates the most superficial kind of consumption. Facebook encourages a rapid, vapid, and even manic consumption of an infinity of images from an infinite pool of users. Whereas in the world of concrete reality one would not have access to photo albums in the living rooms of strangers, on Facebook one can in principle "stalk" someone across the world as easily as someone on one's own street.

One can "view," then, not just close friends but casual acquaintances and total strangers, a fact which feeds into increasingly voyeuristic and consumptive activity. Moreover, what the user consumes are often the carefully constructed and idealized versions of the uploader's self, produced with the hope of achieving some kind of online celebrity, merely reinforcing the logic of consumptive viewing. The uploader produces a virtual "product" which the viewer consumes in a manner truly worthy of its utter superficiality and unreality. Behold the empty culture of "celebrity."

The picture I have painted here is admittedly bleak. I mean none of it to take away from the many useful and even community-generating functions and possibilities of digital reality. But I paint it thus to try to show how at a deep level virtual reality is at its best a pallid substitute for baptismal reality. And I think it true that at a deep level it more properly serves another master.

The medium is the message

We would do well to listen to Marshall McLuhan (1911–1980), who coined the famous phrase "the medium is the message"[5]: in other words, the message always follows from and is shaped or "enframed" by the worldview presuppositions inherent in the medium. To adapt a message to a medium

5 Cf. Marshall McLuhan, *Understanding Media: The Extensions of Man* (Cambridge: MIT Press, 1994), 7–21.

other than its native one, then, is to change its content in some way. In light of this, Tan warns, "Anything the church seeks to make manifest through its traversing of cyberspace, in particular the social medium of Facebook, would have to be reformatted to adapt to the timeline platform."[6] In order to evangelize via cyberspace or virtual reality, the Church would have to first *become* it: it would have to translate its message into less than 140 characters (as in Twitter). The body of Christ would have to become a "digital body," as Tan says; it would have to fundamentally *disincarnate* its presence to fit in here. The *body* would have to become the *text*, thus reversing the logic of the Incarnation in which the Word becomes *flesh*. And the ensuing "product" must thus become only a virtual caricature of a genuine embodied faith: faith reduced to gnostic catch-phrases and feel-good memes.

One can thus question the quality and eventual cost of a program of virtual evangelization. First, I suspect that it might be the case that there is a direct correspondence between the cultivation of virtual community and the loss of embodied local community. That is, the more time you spend online looking after your "global" network, the more you neglect the micro-communities of your real time and space that should be your primary responsibility. It risks being a distraction and an excuse for failure in what *really* matters. Again, I do not think it need *necessarily* be an either/or, but my sense is that we are probably too taken today with the disembodied to the detriment of the embodied.

Second, I cannot help but think that online activism in the end more often fosters division and argument than it does genuine dialogue and conversion. More often than not faith becomes the subject of obnoxious and superficial dialectical argumentation and one-upmanship, inasmuch as the disincarnate word rather than the embodied face is the medium of the genre. But, the critic might say, can virtual mediums really be that different from, say, books? Does not the written word feature a similar kind of abstraction from lived reality, a kind of manipulation premised on massaging reality into a different shape? But ask yourself this: were young people ever "slaves" to books as they are today slaves to Facebook, Twitter, Instagram, Snapchat, and the "virtual" in general? Did books ever feed and fuel social pathologies like depression, anxiety, insecurity, and suicidal tendencies?

6 Tan, "Faith in the Church of Facebook," 28.

In a 2017 book, American psychologist Jean Twenge recounts what she describes as an "abrupt" generational shift that she first began to notice in 2012, indicated in line graphs that went from expressing intergenerational cultural and social change in "hills slowly growing into peaks," to "steep mountains" and "sheer cliffs."[7] Why? Her conclusion: "2011–12 was exactly when the majority of Americans started to own cell phones that could access the internet, popularly known as smartphones." She calls this generation "iGen": the generation born and raised with the iPhone.

While Twenge notes that one effect of this phenomenon is that young people tend to lead "physically safer" lives than previous generations, she also points out deepening psychological problems: "Rates of teen depression and suicide have skyrocketed since 2011. It's not an exaggeration to describe iGen as being on the brink of the worst mental-health crisis in decades. Much of this deterioration can be traced to their phones."[8]

Sure, virtual technology cannot account for every social ill that plagues young people and society in general. But it would seem there is something uniquely problematic going on, at least in part traceable back to the medium of virtual communication. There is enough here to question an over-eager embrace of the medium. And so my concern is that rather than *building* community and fostering free and open discussion, online communities too often simply reinforce conformity to the tribal status quo and facilitate the "de-friending" — or bullying — of those who disagree. There would seem to be something uniquely destructive in the way that virtual forms free users from the dialogical demands of the face and gaze of an embodied person who stands before them in the flesh as a concrete person.

I suggested before that the fundamental act of evangelization today in the face of this is when you do *nothing*. To do nothing in this sense is to enact a symbolic praxis of resistance against the idolatry of the virtual, based simply on living out your baptism from within the embodied forms and relationships that it establishes in your embodied sphere of action. Be like Christ. Be a saint. Do the things of baptism well. Anything else will be an organic, faithful extension of fidelity here.

---

7   Jean Twenge, *iGen: Why Today's Super-Connected Kids are Growing up Less Rebellious, More Tolerant, Less Happy — and Totally Unprepared for Adulthood* (New York: Atria Books, 2017), 4.

8   Jean Twenge, "Have Smartphones Destroyed a Generation?" in *The Atlantic* (September 2017).

The challenge for us, however, is that we no longer really know what this might mean. For most of us have only had glimpses of what a baptismally functioning faith might in fact look like. Short of being imprinted by and immersed first-hand in an economy of baptismal practices, we do not really know what it means to live faith in a truly deep and integrated manner. Again, it may rather be the case that we ourselves are more captive to the imperatives and practices of the postmodern condition than we would like to admit.

What might a truly baptismal existence and culture consist of today? How might evangelization pursued on such a basis take shape? We turn in our final chapter to the culture of hobbits for a more concrete and literary fleshing out of the question — a welcome relief, perhaps, from the last two chapters. I maintain that the hobbit may be considered as the archetypical agent of the new evangelization, and thus the one to show us how best to perform the "nothing" that is the *everything* of Christian witness.

SEVEN

How to Evangelize like a Hobbit

"The road must be trod, but it will be very hard. And neither strength
nor wisdom will carry us far upon it. This quest may be attempted
by the weak with as much hope as the strong. Yet it is oft the course
of deeds that move the wheels of the world: Small hands do them
because they must, while the eyes of the great are elsewhere."

J. R. R. Tolkien, *The Fellowship of the Ring*

HOBBITS, SAID THEIR CREATOR J. R. R. TOLKIEN, "love peace and quiet and good tilled earth: a well-ordered and well-farmed countryside was their favourite haunt. They do not and did not understand or like machines more complicated than a forge-bellows, a water-mill, or a handloom...."[1] They live in close contact with the earth, taking pleasure in the slow, the tactile; in craft, fellowship, humor, general merriment, pipe-smoking, and of course, eating and drinking. "Their faces," continues Tolkien,

> were as a rule good-natured rather than beautiful, broad, bright-eyed, red-cheeked, with mouths apt to laughter, and to eating and drinking. And laugh they did, and eat, and drink, often and heartily, being fond of simple jests at all times, and of six meals a day (when they could get them). They were hospitable and delighted in parties, and in presents, which they gave away freely and eagerly accepted.[2]

In short, Hobbits are not "goal or product-oriented," that is, concerned with or motivated by extrinsic measures of value outside a contemplative horizon of meaningfulness. They do not quantify, calculate, and programatize

1 Tolkien, *The Fellowship of the Ring*, 1.
2 Ibid., 2.

their existence with mission statements, project outlines, three-year plans, schemes, policy meetings, productivity reports, cost-benefit analysis, expert consultations, staged rallies, opinion polls, or marketing strategies. They have the most minimal of political structures. Everything about them resists a bureaucratic or calculative mindset, any desire to be somewhere else, something else, or someone else. Nothing about them is fast, hasty, or noisy. Nothing about them is "virtual," specious, artificial.

Rather, everything about their lives is *slow*, ordered by a rhythm that transcends and resists our own capitalist ethic of productivity and efficiency. Rather than fundamentally transforming the world around them by way of technology and force, they instead adapt to and allow themselves to be shaped by — and so learn to collaborate with — their environment.

The evangelizing practices of hobbit culture

And so hobbits embody, one could say, a quintessentially *Catholic* ethos. Catholic philosopher Joseph Pieper (1904–1997) could have been talking about hobbits when he famously called *leisure* the mark of genuine cultures.[3] By this he meant a basic orientation to contemplation rather than to its opposite, activity or *doing*. This is not to legitimate laziness, lethargy, or spiritual torpor (the vice of *acedia*) or to say that Christians ought not to work hard for their own and society's betterment and courageously and actively fight for what is good and true. It is rather to say that all of our work, all of our doing, and all of our making need to be configured by a deeper logic of contemplation and receptivity towards the gift of the smile and presence that precede us.

Pieper claimed that the mark of a culture that prioritized leisure was the festival. What he meant by "festival" was time deliberately hallowed and set aside as the "real time." That is, if capitalist societies today work to be able to "play" from time to time as a "break" from work, work in societies marked by leisure is conceived as subordinate to play. Leisure, symbolically embodied in the festival, is an order and measure of time grounded in the peace and tranquility of a hope for something beyond the grim reality of a fallen world. It is in this sense "sacramental" of the beyond, a reminder that my true homeland is not in the daily struggle and drudgery that the 9–5 often becomes.

---

3 Cf. Joseph Pieper, *Leisure, the Basis of Culture*, trans. Gerald Malsbary (South Bend: St. Augustine's Press, 1998).

In leisure is *hope* and the expansion of heart; and in the festival is the ritual enactment and celebration of that hope, where it is made concrete and thus credible. In Christian "festival" — above all, in the liturgy — a presence of the beyond is given, not so that we can then flee from or denigrate the world, but rather so that we can go back to the world and take up "secular" time, purifying and hallowing it, offering it back to God in all its redeemed splendor.

Hobbits seem to live in precisely this kind of world. The routine and mundane tasks of life that we in our own society would call "secular" are for hobbits anything but secular. Because they make leisure the form or *logos* of their existence, everything else acquires this mark. Work — the doing and making — is itself the extension and "visibility" of hobbits' fundamental "worldview," and in this is no longer "secular." Secular time has been redeemed by *sacred* time, made one of its agents. And thus hobbit "culture" comes to be, a culture thoroughly imbued by an all-pervading ethos of contemplation.

We thus see the paradox that a certain kind of doing "nothing" well — contemplation, leisure, festival, *liturgy* — in fact generates a distinct kind of embodied community and culture. Within this community and culture, hobbits are raised in the long way, the slow way, the way of care and gentleness, the way of stewardship, the way of cultivation, attentiveness, and excellence, the way of tradition and memory, the way of joyful celebration and merriment. This is not just something "morally" or "rationally" proposed to them as an abstract idea with merely utilitarian goods and promises attached to it, but rather something that they unconsciously imbibe simply by being an integral part of a community, and which they intuitively recognize as being worthy of pursuing.

In this way, we can see how a genuine "culture" born out of faith is a key agent of evangelization. The faith is best transmitted within a functioning culture of liturgy, by a "tasting" and "feeling" of faith in the baptismal grammar of the liturgy and the sacraments. This is not to say that intellectual pedagogy is not important; otherwise, why bother reading this book? But intellectual formation, properly speaking, must not be abstracted from the existential horizon of the person. It must not be "virtual." It must flow from, be placed in, and be continually formed by the lived, liturgical center. Short of this, the intellect will lose existential contact with the face and gaze of the other, with the relational pull and challenge of the mother's smile. It is thus only as good as the culture that houses and shapes it.

The point that I am making is that the "cultural" question, or the question of the narrative practices that flow from and in turn reinforce our deepest convictions, is crucial for evangelization and the possibility of the transmission of faith. If an idea is not being expressed on the ground, in lived experience, and in the context of a healthily functioning social and ecclesial milieu, then its ability to impress itself on the person in an integrated and non-dysfunctional way will always be limited. If Christ's love is not being incarnated, its ability to first compel and then actually be lived is reduced.

Before we flesh this out further, let us return to Middle Earth and consider another kind of evangelizing culture and practice, one that brings a very different kind of ethos.

The evangelizing practices of the Ring of Power

If receptivity and contemplation represent the ethos that is imbibed in the hobbit world, it is force and violence that inform and define the *modus operandi* of Sauron and those who give in to his power. The way of Sauron is that of "coercive force."[4] Whereas hobbit culture consists of practices that embody and mediate receptivity and adaptation to the givenness of reality, Sauron's motivation is to draw all things to himself by coercive and manipulative means, to shape reality rather than to be shaped by it. All of this is poured into the ruling Ring, which becomes as it were the "sacrament" of Sauron's coercive force. The Ring's inscription reads: "One Ring to rule them all, One ring to find them; One ring to bring them all and in the darkness bind them."[5] The Ring rules, the Ring finds, the Ring binds.

Those who come into contact with the Ring are pulled into its influence, twisted by its promises, controlled by its power, to the point that their own agency is subverted, weakened, and finally lost. It seems to work on its victims in a subliminal, barely perceptible manner, first presenting itself attractively as a hope and means for good, but then luring the person inexorably into servitude to the dark purposes of Sauron.

The Ring's "evangelization" of the person thus first promises a great redemption in the form of a temptation very like the Serpent's promise to Eve that she would become like God (cf. Gen. 3:5). The Ring appears as a wonderful gift that promises liberation and thus *hope*. For those who resist

---

4 Wood, "'Sad but not Unhappy.'"
5 Tolkien, *The Fellowship of the Ring*, 66.

evil and darkness, it gives the hope of vanquishing Sauron. So Boromir, betraying very early his susceptibility to the temptation of the Ring, says to the council in Rivendell:

> Why do you speak ever of hiding and destroying? Why should we not think that the Great Ring has come into our hands to serve us in the very hour of need? Wielding it the Free Lords of the Free may surely defeat the Enemy. That is what he most fears, I deem. The Men of Gondor are valiant, and they will never submit; but they may be beaten down. Valour needs first strength, and then a weapon. Let the Ring be your weapon, if it has such power as you say. Take it and go forth to victory![6]

Boromir, a great warrior, knows the challenge that faces his men in the fight against the forces of darkness. He is particularly tempted by the Ring's promise for military campaigns. To his logic, the Ring presents itself as a great weapon of military deliverance.

The Ring does not only suggest its power to warriors. It also suggests its powers to the great and the wise, to diplomats and politicians. To these, it suggests itself not as a weapon, but as the power of "office" or rule: with it, one could become the lord of all lands. Upon Frodo's suggestion that Gandalf shoulder the burden of the Ring, the great wizard recoils:

> "No!" cried Gandalf, springing to his feet. "With that power I should have power too great and terrible. And over me the Ring would gain a power still greater and more deadly...the way of the Ring to my heart is by pity, pity for weakness and the desire of strength to do good.... I dare not take it, not even to keep it safe, unused. The wish to wield it would be too great for my strength."[7]

We can see in these examples how the Ring "personalizes" the way it works on each individual, figuring out, as it were, where he is most vulnerable. The corrupting temptation of the Ring brings out the darkest potentialities in each person. The great elf queen Galadriel:

6 Ibid., 348.
7 Ibid., 80–81.

"For many long years I have pondered what I might do, should the
Great Ring come into my hands, and behold!… You will give me
the Ring freely! In place of a Dark Lord you will set up a Queen.
And I shall not be dark but beautiful and terrible as the Morning
and the Night! Fair as the Sea and the Sun and the Snow upon the
Mountain! Dreadful as the Storm and the Lightning! Stronger than
the foundations of the Earth. All shall love me and despair!"[8]

The Ring would work upon Boromir through his valor, upon Gandalf
through his noble pity, upon Galadriel through her captivating beauty
and strength, upon Saruman through his intelligence and cunning. In
other cases, where the Ring evangelizes those who are already weak and
deformed — such as Gollum — its influence is limited to merely super-
charging base characteristics, turning such persons into the worst possible
versions of themselves.

The Ring thus works by parasitizing everything good, subverting it and
gradually replacing it with its antithesis. It births a culture of the practices
of death, hate, fear, threat, violence, jealousy, suspicion, surveillance, and
slavery. The other comes to be viewed as a threat; while under the influence of the Ring, Frodo sees even his greatest friend as an enemy. Even
when one has "head" knowledge that the Ring is toxic or is determined
to use it only for good, it is almost impossible to throw it away or avoid
its cancerous corruption of the best of intentions. By a kind of cultural
osmosis, it has seeped so deeply into the consciousness of this person that
its evangelizing effects are almost impossible to resist. Escape from the dark
practices of Sauron is impossible while under the influence of the Ring.

The Ring is thus analogous to a condition of servitude to the practices of secular culture. To participate in a practice is to participate in
the worldview behind that practice. This is the danger. It is to absorb at
a deep precognitive and subconscious level the implicit commitments
of that worldview, and thus to have one's best intentions subverted and
deformed. To unthinkingly and uncritically participate in *secular* practices
is to celebrate the "sacraments" or "liturgies" of the death of God. As long
as secular culture continues to be the practical benchmark of our actions,
it cannot be expected that faith will inform our existence in any kind of
deep or integrated way.

8 Ibid., 476.

Thus I reiterate my conviction that evangelization can never be conceived along the lines of simply and uncritically "filling" liberal idioms and practices with Christian content. Sooner or later, the Ring *will* find, the Ring *will* bind, and the Ring *will* rule. Perhaps it already has.

One Ring to bind them

The culture most successful at winning converts is the thus one that has the most robust economy of practices operating at a very deep level. The reality today is that there is only *one* functioning culture that generates practices in this sense capable of compelling deep allegiance. The sacramental and liturgical practices of secularity are advertising, consumption, popular entertainment, technologies, virtual reality. These are the stuff of our contemporary social world, the practices that pervade our normal waking hours and imprint their ethos on us at a precognitive level. It cannot be denied that they instill a far more pervasive long-term and wholesale effect than anything the Church currently offers us.

We need to acknowledge that, to a large extent, the Church no longer possesses a functioning culture that could ever hope to compete with the culture and practice-generating machine of secularism. We no longer possess a culture like that of hobbits which would communicate faith to the believer via the long way, the slow way, the liturgical and sacramental way, the bodily way, and that would thus reveal the possibility that faith could become something more than a cognitive idea; that it could become an incarnate and thus credible reality. The way things are now, hobbit culture has been supplanted and out-narrated by the culture of Sauron. The Shire has long been overrun. As a consequence, in a culture dominated by the practices of the Ring, baptism cannot effectively take root, cannot truly become a radiating presence that compels, inspires, and shapes at a deep level.

The real tragedy is that believers in general often seem to operate on the assumption that the Christian task is essentially about trying to "fill" *other* cultural forms and practices with Christian "spirit" or content (usually in incorrigibly mediocre ways), rather than generating a distinctive and formative counter-culture based on a deep self-understanding. Instead of working from the perspective of the baptized existence of the adopted son or daughter, we rather work within — and do not supplant — the "virtual" antithesis of baptismal existence represented by the practices of secular culture. We persist in thinking that making mere mental adjustments or cognitive qualifications could be enough to overcome our captivity to the forms of the secular imagination and the postmodern condition.

If we have discussed virtual reality as the secular antithesis of baptism, we might follow James K. A. Smith in thinking of the shopping mall as the principal *embodied* site of secular "liturgies," one that through a perfecting of the paradigm of consumer capitalism imposes an almost inescapable "pedagogy of desire."[9] Smith suggests that the mall does not represent primarily a *cognitive* stoking of desire, but rather an implicit and unconscious formation of desire: "The pedagogy of the mall does not primarily take hold of the head, so to speak; it aims for the heart, for our guts, our *kardia*. It is a pedagogy of desire that gets hold of us through our body." He goes on to ask a series of pointed questions:

> So what would it take to resist the alluring formation of our desire — and hence our identity — that is offered by the market and the mall? If the mall and its "parachurch" extensions in television and advertising offer a daily liturgy for the formation of the heart, what might be the church's counter-measures? What if the church unwittingly adopts the same liturgical practices as the market and the mall? Will it then really be a site of counter-formation? What would the church's practices have to look like if they're going to form us as the kind of people who desire something entirely different — who desire the kingdom? What would be the shape of an alternative pedagogy of desire?[10]

In principle, of course, the Church already possesses the ultimate in culture-forming potential, of whose foundation we merely scratched the surface in chapter five. For its cultural capital is to be found in the fruitfulness of the Spirit which animates Christ's body, the Church, and creates baptismal time and space. This is the ground of a liturgical and sacramental economy of practices born from Christ's Eucharistic gift of himself, which becomes available to creatures through their adoption as children of the Father in baptism and in the sacraments of the Church and the practices of love in the domestic church. This can become the basis of an ever-expanding culture, of radiating practices of love that seek after the redemption of the world.

9 Smith, *Desiring the Kingdom*, 24.
10 Ibid., 24–25.

The sad reality is, however, as we began to see in chapter two, that we have for centuries been giving this gift away, being unfaithful to it, aligning it with political and worldly interests, failing to embrace and attend to its radicality. We are now at a point where the gift seems worn out, and where many ecclesial authorities currently seem quite happy to give away what's left more or less completely. Like unfaithful spouses, absent fathers, neglectful mothers, and rebellious children, we have failed in our response to the gift of adoption. In our liturgies, in our teaching, in our evangelical discourse (or lack thereof), in our marriages and our families, in our behaviors and our loves, we betray our own withering of conviction, our own lack of faith in anything other than the nominal or superficial. As a consequence, we should not be surprised when we discover that we have no culture or practices of our own that actually embody more than a faith in ourselves and our overriding secular commitments.

The question, then, is how we might best recover such a culture and its practices. For without them, faith remains largely an abstraction that only hovers "virtually" over our embodied lives. Faith *as baptismal adoption* cannot take root. It cannot inspire and convert in the deep sense. It cannot evangelize.

But this again turns the question back on our predicament. If we as a Church are failing to evangelize even our own children, how can we hope to be a light for the rest of the world? This is to say that the task of evangelization which we seek to perform "out there" is only as good as our ability to confront and remedy the extent of our own self-secularization. It is only as good as our willingness to give ourselves over fully to our baptism. As it turns out, doing the deeper "nothing" is in fact much harder than doing the shallower "something." That is, it is easier to be enthusiastic about evangelization if it involves *someone else* and if it involves a busy extrinsic activity that does not really address the deep "cultural" problem within *our own* faith.

What we today call the "new evangelization" — certainly in many of its practical mobilizations — in fact, I suggest, typically lacks the one ingredient essential for truly effective evangelization: our own baptismal conversion. In many respects, rather than deeply and "culturally" addressing this deficit, the whole contemporary project of evangelization seems designed to try to compensate for it through a whole range of programs, and strategies: mission statements, youth conferences, digital productions, catch-phrases, and various financially-driven initiatives, all of which claim to be dynamic, life-changing, and the like, but which instead usually hang in a kind of "virtual" suspension outside of formative daily practices and the actual condition of Catholic Christianity on the ground.

I am not saying that no amount of good can come of these kinds of things. Quite often they may give a person an important first glimpse of meaning and belonging. And perhaps they are better than nothing. But I would say that the extent to which these efforts do not then feed back into the creation of a Christian economy of sustained practices is the extent to which any good generated risks ending up a truncated caricature of what it could be given robust and embodied baptismal coordinates.

Little that we do seems to be creating *integrated* baptismal selves capable of living faith in a genuinely cultural way—that is, a sustained, organic, integrated, and contemplative way—within the challenging situation of the postmodern condition and its liturgies. Little that we do seems to be creating deep liturgical and sacramental practices that might give the evangelized soul a genuine place to have its faith verified and reinforced by *real* practices of love, and that might as such then become the real catalyst for the evangelization of others. Little that we do seems to be really critiquing or challenging people's deep allegiance to secular culture and "rebranding" them in the culture of baptismal faith. Nor are we giving the baptized the ability to negotiate through the malaise caused when ecclesial authorities cease to be faithful to Christ and his Church.

We have failed, in a word, to immerse people in the love that in Christ becomes a practice, a living horizon of a divine presence incarnate in our midst. We have failed at the cultural level.

Perhaps it is true that people are praising and worshipping more; perhaps they have a heightened consciousness for social justice; perhaps they think that the theology of the body is a pretty great idea; perhaps they are out there defending God in the public square. It could be that I am not giving the new evangelization enough time to prove itself. Perhaps the wounds of the post-conciliar experience of faith are still too raw and open.

But my sense is that as long as evangelization looks more like sloganeering and getting young people pumped up at big events, rather than a gentle, thoughtful, imaginative, counter-cultural, non-digital and non-technological, *baptismal* immersion of the person into a genuine culture with genuine practices—the culture and practices of the hobbit, the culture and practices of genuine liturgy and the domestic church—then there is little cause for hope. Virtual evangelization may give you a Christ of a type, for a time, but unless this is *the* Christ *in his baptismal history, in his baptismal time, in his baptismal place and culture*, it will not be a Christ capable of really permeating someone's life. It will not give a Christ who can truly heal the wounds and fractures that come from living within the liturgies of force and violence in the culture of Sauron.

As long as Christianity remains in so great a cultural deficit — as long as we do not have the (suitably scoured) Shire — there will be nothing for evangelized souls to come home to, no sure foundation for the flowering of their first encounter with faith. And there will be no hope of countering the death of God.

Life in the midst of death

In a certain sense, then, we may find ourselves in the position of Sam and Frodo marching into Mordor on our own. All of our hopes seem to have failed. The fellowship of the Ring seems to have unraveled. We find ourselves all alone in a hostile foreign land with new threats popping up by the second.

We have to worry not only about Sauron and the Ring (external secular threats), but also about false prophets and dubious alliances with the powers abounding more than ever in our own communities. The Shire has been overrun by small-minded bureaucrats, managers, and corporate shills. There are more than enough rationalizing pragmatists and opportunists like Saruman, sycophants like Grima Wormtongue, and defeatists like Denethor among us, all of whom are happy to peddle the least prophetic and most mediocre caricatures of Christian faith.

But there is a deep lesson to be learned from the way that Sam and Frodo end up responding to their developing situation. Despite their increasingly dire predicament, they are not cynical, defeatist, fatalistic, or delusional about the pain and horrors that they must face. In their struggle to retain hope, they do not give into to a despair that would make them bitter and angry or cause them to voluntarily hand over the Ring in the futile hope of saving themselves. Nor do they fool themselves that everything will be okay — no glib platitudes about God never giving you more than you can handle. They know that in all likelihood they are marching to a horrific end, and expect nothing less.

Instead of giving in to despair, Sam and Frodo are animated by a hope that comes from two related sources. First, theirs is a hope paradoxically grounded in death. That is, they accept that their mission will end in their death. They do not pin their hopes on any outcome possible from a finite point of view, something that, given their dire circumstances, could only lead to disappointment and despair. They place finitude within an infinite perspective. This does not enervate them, but puts their mission into sharper relief. What matters is not success, but giving yourself to the task with honor, integrity, and love. They realize that in the end success is not up to them. All they can do is keep attempting the task that they have been given, being true to it at all costs even to the bitter end, never giving into the temptation either to flee or to resort to use of the Ring. If they follow this path, win or lose, they will have succeeded at the level that truly matters. With the acceptance of death comes the peaceful realization that this earthly battleground does not in the end determine everything. There is a power beyond this world, and it is to this that we look and hope.

The question is why and how Sam and Frodo are able to make death such a liberating and empowering prospect. That is, how is it that the prospect of death does not crush them? Key here would seem to be that Sam and Frodo carry with them a genuine experience and memory of the good, of real contact with a power strong enough to take the sting and hopelessness of death away. For they carry with them the ethos and formation of the Shire. They carry with them the friendships of the Fellowship.

The point that I am trying to make is that the capacity of hobbits to resist the Ring more strongly than most stems not from their sovereign will or hard work and effort but rather from the deep way in which they have been "evangelized" by the particularly rich and integrated practices of a culture of leisure, contemplation, and hope. Frodo and Sam are willing to die, and are even at peace with their imminent death, because they have experienced something vital and real, something beyond the push and pull of the horizon of finitude.

Perhaps we could say that this comes from the hobbits' basic experience of being *loved*, of concretely encountering an unfailing love in their most basic relationships, such that they therefore truly *believe* in love. As a consequence, it is this that perhaps explains why they have *faith*: they have had a real encounter with a love that does not fail or betray, a love that is therefore credible. And this perhaps explains why they have *hope*: why even in the darkest hour, Sam can look up and see a single star and, being evangelized anew by its light, know that the darkest hour in history cannot ultimately destroy all that is good. Unlike others, they have a certain *childlike* maturity of faith, hope, and love that have never seemed to "mature" into a critical reason that might cause them to *lose* the former virtues, or allow them to attenuate into a thousand impotent nuances.

It is not for nothing, then, that the Council at Rivendell deems the hobbit Frodo worthy to carry the Ring to Mordor. What a risk! But unlike the wise and great, who face the temptations of power in particularly potent ways as a consequence of their status, hobbits are, in the words of Wood,

> worthy opponents of the allurement of the Ring exactly because their life-aims are so very modest. Wanting nothing more than to preserve the freedom of their own peaceable Shire, they have no grandiose ambitions. Their meekness uniquely qualifies them to destroy the Ring in the Cracks of Doom. Theirs is a Quest that can be accomplished by the small even more aptly than by the great—by ordinary folks far more than conventional heroes.[11]

The paradox proposed in the hobbit is nothing less than the great paradox of faith, understood well by St. Paul: "When I am weak, I am strong" (2 Cor. 12:10). One thinks of our Savior's difficult words: "Blessed are the meek, for they shall inherit the earth" (Mt. 5:5). Elrond's suggestion is that power or conventional wisdom alone could not guarantee the success of the quest. Rather, "this quest may be attempted by the weak with as much hope as the strong. Yet such is oft the course of deeds that move the wheels of the world: small hands do them because they must, while the eyes of the great are elsewhere."[12]

Not all those who wander are lost

The hope of this book is that it will help to give an "imaginative" appropriation of the Shire. Even if we ourselves have not had a *real* experience of an integrated "smile" and culture that mediates the radiance of Christ's love through its basic practices, the next best thing is for us to discover a way to *imaginatively* appropriate this culture.

In reality, of course, we remain in a material condition like that of Sam and Frodo, wandering through the wilderness. The sad reality is that if any hope remains for an encounter with faith deeper than a virtual one, it requires that we seriously wrestle with the conditions of this wilderness.

---

11 Wood, "'Sad, but not Unhappy.'"
12 Tolkien, *The Fellowship of the Ring*, 351.

While never eschewing the institutional Church understood in Her deepest identity as the mystical body and bride of Christ, we must be open-eyed about our present situation.

In this kind of setting, believers must think deeply about what kinds of practices and disciplines are necessary to both pursue and avoid for fostering faith for themselves and their families. We must face the fact that, like it or not, *we are already in the wilderness*, and in this environment we cannot take it for granted that the faith we think we have will be strong enough to face the trials that may await.

Rod Dreher, in his articulation of the "Benedict Option," has effectively zeroed in on this essential truth.[13] He has rightly argued that for Christian faith to survive, it must today, more than ever, achieve a new level of critical practical distance from the prevailing secular culture and its liturgies of violence and death. This is not conceived by him as a literal "heading for the hills" or absolute physical separation, but rather as putting the majority of our efforts towards the formation of creative and flexible subcultures, micro-economies of Christian practice shaped by a more conscious and radical commitment to faith. For this to happen, there must be an attendant prudential separation from the cultural status quo. This then leads to a notion of Christian communities typified by a condition of what he calls "exile in place."[14]

I think of my contribution to this endeavor as the provision of an account of faith as baptismal existence that might allow for a more robust evangelical shaping of the structure and practices of any attempt to resist the secular liturgies of the Ring. When one has been consigned to a wilderness where deep sacramental practices of faith are not part of the package deal, one must first learn to appropriate them "imaginatively," at the level of a deep, restrained, and disciplined intellectual pursuit grounded in baptism, going beyond easy devotional excesses and moralistic caricatures, and premised on a sovereign refusal to participate in many of the liturgies of secular culture. Even if this can be no real substitute for first-hand immersion within a real integrated and functioning culture, it is the first critical step that will allow us to inhabit the present wilderness of faith with enough

---

13 Cf. Dreher, *The Benedict Option*. For other considerations of this theme, see Charles J. Chaput, *Strangers in a Strange Land: Living the Catholic Faith in a Post-Christian World* (New York: Henry Holt, 2017); Anthony Esolen, *Out of the Ashes: Rebuilding American Culture* (Washington, DC: Regnery, 2017).

14 Dreher, *The Benedict Option*, 18.

spiritual concentration to enable us to start living our own relationships in truth and love. We must therefore work hard — for leisure.

It is of course true, however, that man cannot live by imagination alone. And herein lies the pathos of my proposal. For imagination to bear real, long-term, and integrated fruit demands *some* degree of existential cognitive and bodily separation from secular culture and practices; it requires its own *real* culture and practices if it is to be a truly sustainable enterprise. What Smith calls "bobblehead" Christianity[15] can never be enough, even if the deeper cognitive or imaginative appropriation of faith that I am suggesting here is one that flows from the baptismal and sacramental font of faith. The communication and transmission of faith requires a micro-culture of practices that express, embody, and inculcate it, that bridge the distance between idea and reality in the baptismal flesh of the person.

But there is always hope. And today, it is perhaps in the practices always possible in the communion of the domestic church that remain the best hope for the hobbit seriously seeking to be faithful. This "primordial" communion, accomplished (like baptism) in the flesh of spouses according to the new sacramental law of Christ and the Church, is itself a culture — a unique sacramental culture of the spousal and filial event of salvation in Christ. It is a culture within *the Culture*, and while it unquestionably draws its efficacy from the mystery of the Church that is its origin and destination (cf. *Familiaris consortio* 49), it is itself also given to the couple as a grace that works in and through the unity of their baptisms in the conjugal bond. It is given to them as the gift of a real presence, a consecration, a ministry; as a grace that they in their freedom and by their baptisms have the capacity to guard, nurture, and enrich.

Because of this intimate proximity to the filial and spousal love that generated and saved the world, the vocation of marriage and family can become one of the fundamental engines of evangelization inasmuch as it provides the first encounter with and mediation of the baptismal destiny of the person. The domestic church is the first and primary hobbit-hole of faith, the first resistance against the coercive and debilitating violence of the Ring. In many respects, a child's experience here determines the extent to which the logic of baptism can appear as real liberation from the postmodern condition for him in his own freedom. A smile that radiates a fully functioning spousal relationship of baptismal and spousal belonging

15 Smith, *Desiring the Kingdom*, 42.

is a first inoculation against a false perception of true reality as a place of violence, chaos, doubt, and despair.

Just how to go about establishing more practical, flexible, and expansive micro-cultures that stretch beyond the foundation of marriage and the family goes somewhat beyond the scope of this book. This is Dreher's particular focus and strength. My effort here has been first and foremost to address the deficit of *baptismal* imagination that I think currently defines the self-understanding and evangelizing activity of the Church. Any hope for a genuinely sacramental culture will require much more than a merely "conservative" response to the situation. It will require more than the mere reassertion of norms or practices that are not first the products of a deep baptismal re-internalization of faith strong enough to resist the forms of the death of God. Only if what we do and how we do it bear the *deep baptismal imprint of our literal transformation in Christ and his sacramental world* will it be possible to do anything both truly evangelical and truly "practical" that does not bear the marks of allegiance to another master.

And this is what I think Sam and Frodo help to give us at the imaginative level. They show us what is at stake and what it means to live radically in the face of certain death. They show us how to live with conviction and faithfulness, not to give way to the "pragmatic" or "political" solutions that mediate the death that truly kills. They thus show us how the very small and indeed death itself can become the hope of life. They show us that not all those who wander are in fact lost.

How to evangelize with baptism

The hope present in the wilderness should never be underestimated. For perhaps a better word for wilderness here is *desert*, the historic site of the contemplative rebirth of Christian faith throughout the ages "to which faith has often found it necessary, at various times, to retreat."[16] To embrace the desert in both a material and spiritual sense is to consciously decouple ourselves from both the debilitating culture and practices of secularity and the bankrupt attempts to overcome that culture and its practices by recourse to the power of the Ring. Embracing the desert means to radically embrace the "nothing." It means to first and foremost embrace and endure prophetic silence[17] and through the radical availability to grace this silence

---

16 Hart, *Atheist Delusions*, 241.
17 Cf. Robert Cardinal Sarah, *The Power of Silence: Against the Dictatorship of Noise*

fosters, to rediscover and witness to an authentic sacramental culture of faith in positive acts and practices shaped, not by fear and force, but by love.

In the end, the hope of Sam and Frodo is borne out with a surprising result. It is precisely their refusal to give into the violence and despair of the Ring that gives them the most complete of victories over the darkness and allows them to be, as it were, the most effective kind of evangelizers. For their subversive and (from the perspective of all things "reasonable") *foolhardy* refusal to do what one might most expect is the very thing that exposes and exploits evil's weak spot and thus wins the day.

Ralph C. Wood notes that Sauron "is intent upon establishing his own supremacy over all things, and he reads all others by his own light. He believes that anyone, having once possessed the virtually absolute power afforded by the Ring, would be determined to use it."[18] Wood notes that this, in the end, is Sauron's undoing—his blind spot. His lack of sympathetic identification with anything outside of himself—his inability to think from any perspective but that of power and force—blinds him to the designs of those who act according to the *good*. His vision is obscured by the evangelizing force of his own false worldview, and becomes victim to its ultimate power over him. His sovereign and seemingly invincible will—embodied in the All-Seeing Eye—is paradoxically undone by its own captivity to an ultimate principle whose *modus operandi* is betrayal. The Eye may *see* all, but it does not truly *understand* all.

What Sauron cannot conceive of is that some of his enemies might want to *destroy* the Ring of Power that he so desperately seeks rather than use it themselves, and might in fact be so foolhardy as to march right under his own nose to the crack of Mount Doom to do so. This is precisely the power of Sam and Frodo's act. They act in a way that evil can never anticipate or understand. Had they and the Fellowship approached the circumstance "rationally," they would have fallen right into the trap of the enemy. It is only by resisting the *modus operandi* of coercive force, by refusing to participate in its liturgies, that evil can be defeated. Evil is vanquished only by facing death with a "smile" in the full knowledge of who you are and what needs to be done.

There is a deep lesson here for how we go about evangelizing others in any context. The *fundamental evangelical act*—the one that must inform

(San Francisco: Ignatius, 2017).
18 Wood, "'Sad, but not Unhappy.'"

all of our positive efforts at the level of action, whatever forum they take place in — is the "nothing." It is the being and doing that is neither calculative nor contrived. It is done for no reason other than that it is good in and of itself. It is the purely positive response, not to some outward provocation or instrumental motivation, but to the gift of divine adoption that now permeates the being of the baptized. It is the radical embrace of the sacramental middle, the in-between space of baptismal existence which is then radiated to the world through the baptized person's flesh.

This is to say that the fundamental evangelical act cannot be simply verbalizing belief, whether on Facebook or in the public square. Anyone can be trained to defend theoretical claims. Anyone can learn formal apologetic skills. Anyone can join public advocacy groups. Rather, true witness is given in the act of *embodying* belief precisely within the "silent" bearing of life's burdens and sorrows in the daily drama of life lived in real and existential contact with faith.

Embodying belief rather than simply verbalizing it reveals the extent to which faith has become a "culture" in your own life: that it has pervaded every nook and cranny of your existence. In this, you embody more than belief: you embody the culture that true belief cultivates. You show others that the gift of faith has created a new world in your life. And in this, *your* world expands into *their* world, simply by the living of your "culture" to its fullest extent.

In all of this, then, evangelization is not primarily activism or something that goes on "out there." It is first and foremost simply *being*, a "foolish" celebration of the baptismal nothing. In its first act it is contemplation, leisure, hope in the Person who truly saves. It is not about quick fixes, easy solutions, or glitzy productions that replace or compete with the genuine practices of life in Christ. It is not about moralizing sound-bites or abstract appeals that hang disconnected from a genuine sacramental life in Christ.

If our attempts to proclaim Christ cannot be made from within the order of contemplation, from inside a genuine and meditative sacramental belonging to Christ and to our brothers and sisters in Him, and if our "apologetic" efforts do not feed the person back into this order and these relationships, then perhaps our evangelizing efforts have already given themselves over to the power of the Ring. They have given in to the temptation of magic, force, and the easy way that does not require genuine conversion, that does not clearly reveal the path of holiness, sacrifice, conversion, and integrated "culture" that life in Christ entails.

As Wood remarks, "The great temptation is to take short-cuts, to follow the easy way, to arrive quickly. In the antique world of Middle-Earth, magic offers the surest escape from slowness and suffering. It is the equivalent of our machines."[19] Christian witness must never give into the temptation to proclaim Christ from outside the conditions of the slow, suffering, and silent journeying through Him, with Him, and in Him.

And so, yet again, this takes us back to ourselves. The battle will not to be won "out there," in the fickleness and betrayals of virtual or political life. Anything out there is only as good as our fidelity to the "in here" of our walk with Christ, as our honest facing of the prospects of death. Virtual arguments and political wins mean nothing if they are not born from and do not proclaim or foster a deep baptismal logic of redemption. The triumph of "conservatism" and conservative politics is not the triumph of Christ. The successes of unqualified and unpurified tradition, of methods and techniques of power, fear, and force, do not create culture. They do not attract people to worship, beauty, and love in baptismal form. Only if the evangelized can witness a culture that fundamentally inverts the logic of the Ring can they truly encounter Christ.

And so if we want to be an effective agent of the new evangelization, it must be we ourselves who are evangelized first. "Only those who have let themselves be profoundly renewed by divine grace," said Benedict XVI, "are able to bear within them — and hence to proclaim — the newness of the Gospel."[20] The only hope we have for bearing the culture of Christ in our person is to have had some genuine encounter with *that* Person in *his* culture. The power of this baptismal encounter, when it is truly allowed to take root, is that it creates a world, or, as I have stressed, a *culture*. Christ's love places the person in a new network of relations that, if given room to breathe and grow, transmits the credibility of the encounter with Christ into the heart of that person's life, and radiates his transformation to others.

Again, all the "virtual" things that we do in the name of the new evangelization may give us Christ, of a type, for a time; but unless this is the Christ revealed and experienced within the fullness of baptismal existence, this is not the Christ who can truly save. And this is why the baptismal "nothing" is so important. Without it, we have only the *false* nothing that kills.

19 Ibid.
20 Address to the Apostolic Penitentiary.

Bringing baptism to the public square

The perennial knock against perspectives like the one just sketched is that they appear to simply give up any form of cultural engagement that is not evangelical in the strict sense, especially when it comes to the broader social forum. That is, they appear to forbid one from engaging in any kind of mediating form of rationality and concrete action not grounded directly in Christ. The bald (and therefore seemingly socially unproductive, divisive, and probably fideistic or "fundamentalist") proclamation of Christ seems the only option left for the Christian. While addressing this critique goes somewhat beyond the scope of the "imaginative" dimension that it is the main intention of this book to help recover, it is impossible to avoid investigating at least *some* of the practical consequences of our fundamental commitment to the baptismal "nothing."

Jeremy Beer has drawn attention to this perceived *aporia* in the context of David L. Schindler's thought. He observes that the usual criticism of Schindler is based on the fact that "he comes to conclusions that are uncomfortable and, from a practical political point of view, seemingly useless. No easy fixes, no programs, emerge from Schindler's work…. In fact, the way in which superficial fixes and programs often conceal and even deepen our predicament is in part what Schindler means to reveal."[21]

The question is this: can a politician, say, faithfully embody the baptismal nothing in his or her profession while using rational and procedural forms other than that nothing? Or is the very notion of a "Christian politician" now oxymoronic in a political context that presupposes the death of God? Can the task of shoring up the *imperium* still be performed?[22]

Let me respond first by sketching a classical account of principles which

---

21 Jeremy Beer, "Philosopher of Love: David L. Schindler," in *The American Conservative* (October 16, 2013), at http://www.theamericanconservative.com/articles/philosopher-of-love-587/.

22 This now famous phrase comes from MacIntyre, who concluded his study of the Enlightenment failure to construct a system of rational ethics on its premises by likening our contemporary situation to that facing Christians during the decline of the Roman empire. While cautioning against drawing "too precise parallels between one historical period and another," MacIntyre nevertheless suggests that "certain parallels are there. A crucial turning point in that earlier history occurred when men and women of good will turned aside from the task of shoring up the Roman *imperium* and ceased to identify the continuation of civility and moral community within the maintenance of that imperium." Alasdair MacIntyre, *After Virtue*, 263. It is this idea, in particular as expressed in MacIntyre's cryptic allusion to the monastic vision of St. Benedict of Nursia (480–547), which in part has been the catalyst for Dreher's "Benedict Option."

have provided one vision for how this class of professions might best operate within a worldly environment. Historically, Catholic Christianity has endorsed an approach to public rationality based on certain assumed broadly shared principles of natural law, itself understood by the Christian as a source of normative value inasmuch as it is the expression of eternal law. That is, even while the unapologetic baptismal proclamation of Christ should be the first and default position for the Christian, the Christian nevertheless remains a citizen of the city of man and as such is called to participate appropriately in that city. The Christian still lives in the world and is subject to the demands of living in community with those who hold different beliefs than he. It is not unfitting then that the Christian join the social conversation about public reason and policy. And this means that a certain tension of pragmatism and compromise will always be involved in the pursuit of a "pure" cultural expression of baptismal existence.

In *principle*, I am happy to ascribe to the above. The reader should not suppose that I am suggesting a baptismal quietism as the *exclusive* element of the new evangelization across the board or in all circumstances. I have of course argued that in the context of the social and cultural death of God, the possibility of a discourse based upon shared universal values will be difficult. Nevertheless, I do accept that the tasks and fronts of evangelization are many and varied and that, especially for those engaged in the public square, in principle some kind of "natural law" argumentation will be inevitable. But several more practical qualifications are needed which may in fact problematize and certainly contextualize aspects of the classical position, at least within the current social context of the death of God and its accompanying secular liturgies.

First, the Christian must always be acutely aware that the linguistic demands and imperatives of public reason can never become a substitute for first-order Christian discourse. We must always remember that the so-called "natural law" is in fact only a pale shadow of the personal and existential radiance of baptismal existence in Christ who is the *fulfillment* of the law. This is particularly important within a context where social discourse has in fact sunk far below a vision of natural law that might still bear some living relationship to eternal law — a fact that makes most current law positivistic in nature, and thus even more of a shadow.

There must therefore be clear limits about how far pragmatism and compromise go in a social setting. Sometimes we are called to choose martyrdom, that is, to bear witness with our blood and suffering instead.

My sense is that Christians in the West have by and large forgotten what it means to make a prophetic stand on the nothing. We have forgotten our responsibility to in fact *eschew* public reason when and if it constitutes an outright celebration of the death of God.

Instead, we keep moving our goalposts. We forever postpone the prophetic stand. This phenomenon has served to erode any prophetic charism potentially borne by Christians in the public sphere. Instead, Christians have today become largely indistinguishable from their secular counterparts, whether they are speaking publicly or privately. The public mode of pragmatism and compromise has become the private mode as well. Second, even if a cultural context were to embody a healthy functioning according to natural law principles, the Christian would still obligated to subvert and unsettle said functioning in some real way. We cannot give the impression that to live according to the perspective of the "goods of human flourishing" or the "natural ends" of man could ever be enough, if by this we practically abstract from their broader foundation in the perspective of eternal law.

This is not to say that shared natural law principles are not important for a society; but the temptation in a hypothetical cultural situation where people appear to be living stable, relatively integrated lives is not to further rock the boat. But, as I think I have made clear in this book, the seed of nihilistic despair is lodged in *any* account of the human good that has not yet discovered or has rejected the call of Christ. The Christian then is called in some way to always proclaim that *nature is never enough.*

Third, and crucially, the fact of the matter is that we are most definitely *not* living today in a cultural situation that exhibits any level of healthy natural flourishing. Instead, as I have argued, we are living in a terminal cultural situation that ritually celebrates the death of God. Any kind of primordial Christian discourse or practices seem to have come to an end. The question is, then, whether natural law, classically or otherwise understood, can gain any purchase at all in such a context.

Already well before the more rapid recent decline of rational discourse in civil society, many Christian attempts to articulate an account of rationality and social good were already shifting away from an emphasis on classical natural law thinking, which placed more stress on said law's theocentric framing. So-called "new" natural law thinking consciously attempted to articulate free-standing general principles (the so-called "goods of human flourishing") in relative independence from a dramatic or sacramental framing of human existence. This was motivated by the desire to gain a more effective voice and hearing within a post-Enlightenment setting which forbids the contributions of a transcendent horizon on principle.

It is telling that in a social setting where God and in fact *any* notion of a generally stable and universal notion of human nature and flourishing have been sacrificed at the altar of *individual* freedom and will, many current articulations of such a denuded notion of natural law have shifted to an *even more* reductive expression, to what I call "social consequentialist" versions of natural law. Here, emphasis has shifted from articulations of human flourishing based on properly positive, principled foundations to ones based on a calculation about what will produce better or worse social consequences. The hope seems to be that if from a public policy and social-scientific point of view we can demonstrate that this or that social ordering has cumulatively better outcomes than other alternatives, then on this basis we will convince people of, say, the importance of something like heterosexual marriage.

The point I make regarding this is twofold. First, what this approach fails to recognize is the level of "worldview" conversion required to take such social-scientific "proof" seriously today. That is, if the liberal is committed to his "faith" — to his individual freedom, choice, and the like — as a horizon of belief, then it will take a lot more than utilitarian and consequential arguments to move him. Rather than submit to adjusting his behavioral and lifestyle choices according to some abstract imperative of "what is best for public policy" generated by his ideological enemy, the liberal is more likely to employ his own engine of social-scientific "proof" to rebut conservative claims to the contrary. Every published study with a conservative conclusion can be met with a similar study with a liberal conclusion. This is not to say that there is ultimately no rational way to mediate between this impasse. But to *actually* overcome it requires an openness to reality not tied to overarching ideological commitments. The point is that in a context of deep ideological motivations, it may not be as easy as simply pointing to the truth as such. One may first have to address the *principles* blocking a different access to the empirical reality.

Second, I do not think it the case that even if you managed to convert someone by your consequentialist argument he would *necessarily* be that much closer to a deeper *baptismal* conversion. For what you would have converted him to in this instance is a public policy argument, not a substantial claim about the human person or good as such. You would have done so, not by appealing to some deeper existential instinct or capacity for truth, goodness, or beauty, but rather perhaps by recourse to fear, threat, and a regime of minimum requirements. This seems to me a pretty desiccated and thus dead-end path, one that risks producing an unstable and narrow idolization of a closed naturalistic system that is much more vulnerable to spiraling distortion and disillusionment.

So what does this all mean for our original question? Of what useful-ness is a mediating discourse based on primordial capacities of human reason possible today within a liberal setting? First off, I think we need to be realistic about expecting to find any kind of silver bullet either way, whether you go maximalist or minimalist in terms of discourse that bears some kind of relation to reason informed by transcendence. Ideological and lifestyle resistance are such that it matters little how an argument is packaged if the conclusion you reach strikes at the heart of liberal beliefs and thus requires a revision of fundamental secular lifestyle choices.

Of course, you might respond to this by appealing to a purported "silent majority" that just needs a rallying point and enough social momentum to shake it out of its slumber. Most of us are not radical secularists at heart. But I am not convinced that in our *deepest* commitments we are not already very nearly there practically speaking. We may carry certain basic moral and metaphysical assumptions that are hangovers from a Christian past, and many of us may still live vaguely "Christian" lives. But if this is grounded in a hangover, not in deep positive belief, and if our basic practices daily commit us to another master, then I am not convinced that any good that does remain in our hearts could in fact ever be activated in a healthy, sustainable manner short of the encounter with Christ in his culture. Sick civilizations do not normally resurrect themselves on the basis of tired ideals only nominally adhered to.

So, on the one hand, hope of influencing the highest levels of policy and law are profoundly limited given the fundamental and pervasive religious commitments of liberalism — commitments shared by the highest political and corporate elites. On the other hand, hope for a silent majority that might rise up in some democratic groundswell underestimates the extent to which this too would carry the twisted ideologies, as well as and the extent of a culture, on both the Left and the Right, broken and fractured by liberalism.

Still, the Christian politician has to say and do something. Here I would suggest that sometimes our aims need to be much lower. In situations where failure is almost certainly guaranteed due to the already "religious" nature of a confrontation with secular norms (as we saw in chapter 3), instead of always whittling away our strategy to the lowest consequentialist denominator and losing the debate from a contrived position of weakness far from the Christian center, perhaps we need to try losing from a position of the best theological strength once in a while.

Take the following example. Imagine that a politician is putting together a bill aimed at placing limits on access to abortion. In Western liberal democracies such efforts are routinely defeated (again, because they strike at the heart of the religious lifestyle choices of liberalism, and any compromise is seen by abortion activists as a slippery slope leading to the overturning of the precedent set by rulings such as Roe vs. Wade). Particularly in cases where the bill is going to be defeated no matter what you do, why not make the defeat that much more complete by consciously subverting the consequentialist arguments normally used to try to gain traction?

Perhaps we should sometimes use such situations as opportunities to signal to our own faith communities and to the world the glorious, first-order Gospel of life spoken, not in the language of pragmatic conservatism, but in the richness of a primordial Christian discourse that far surpasses denuded and shrill arguments based on "rights" or "consequences." Create a bill deliberately designed to spectacularly fail for all the best reasons, for more than "natural" arguments, and make this failure a prophetic act so that people — particularly believers themselves, desperately in need of the full prophetic measure of truth — might witness an example of Christian faith in its fullest non-political and non-ideological articulation and be moved by its beauty.[23]

Maybe this is a rather extreme suggestion. It is certainly not to say that in the domain of jurisprudence we should not be seeking legislation

---

23 After writing this, I came across a piece by Reformed theologian Carl R. Trueman which in a slightly different context comes to a similar conclusion. He makes the following striking and evocative description of the witness that might be produced were the episcopate to take seriously its job of calling to account any Catholic politician who makes "a mockery of Church teaching." "If every Roman Catholic bishop in the country wrote such a letter [of reproof] to every Roman Catholic politician who made a mockery of Church teaching, the effect would be predictably stunning. The scorn and hatred poured down on the hierarchy would be awesome to behold. Christians would be reviled by the media from dawn till dusk. But a terrible beauty would be born, because it would become absolutely clear that the Church stands for something other than the spirit of the age." Carl R. Trueman, "Hey Joe! It's time for bishops to take a public stand on morally bankrupt politicians," in *First Things* (Aug 12, 2016), at https://www.firstthings.com/blogs/firstthoughts/2016/08/hey-joe.

aimed at limiting harm as much as possible. There will remain situations, particularly in the field of law, where it will be important to do anything it takes argumentation-wise to ensure checks and balances on the more egregious moral unravelings in society. But I also want to keep room open for the prophetic moment.

A somewhat more positive and effective way to "aim lower" would be to focus on the local and community level, as many diverse commentators have proposed. Here, in basic relationships and local social engagements, it seems more feasible to speak a language that transcends many of the strictures of higher political and legal registers. Within this environment, speak a language that transcends the dry, formalistic terms and conditions of consequentialist natural law. If you want to do "natural law," do a primordial, existential, experiential kind of natural law, one that accesses the beating heart of the person, not just his intellect; one that encounters him as someone who desires and bears the hope of baptism. Do a natural law born not of stripped-down, rationalistically determined first principles, but rather one gained from the retrospective light of your own baptism radiated into the created structure of reality. In other words, harvest insights from your own baptismal experience and aim them at the experience of others.

My fundamental recommendation would be to consider what is possible from the point of view of the baptized person who now has sharper awareness of what "nature" really wants. It seems to me that the extent to which this person nurtures his own baptism determines the extent to which he will discover the capacity to speak in a creative and dynamic way that goes beyond artificially imposed constraints on the contributions of transcendence to rationality. This is as it were a muscle that we must seek to exercise more. Rather than seeking to speak within the conditions of an airtight system, speak from within your own baptismal "middle." In baptism, the borders between nature and grace have been made permeable for you; show *others* a glimpse of what that could look like for *them*.

I acknowledge that what I have said here remains somewhat abstract and theoretical. I do not have the expertise to be too prescriptive about concrete application of the general principles articulated. Nor do I wish to dump on those courageous souls who do battle in the public square.

My priority is, again, imaginative. I want the Christian to think deeply about the way that baptism changes his existence, and therefore modifies the form of his actions no matter what they are and where they are performed. My hope is that if Christians in various fields and vocations take this seriously, it will enable them to discern for themselves the most effective prudential path for their own particular situation.

Most importantly, we need to cultivate acute awareness for *ourselves* that the social and political discourses which we may be obligated to be involved in at some level can never become a substitute for the fullest gift of identity received within the sacramental forms of the Church. The Christian needs to know that any peacemaking initiative or defense of human rights or social justice, for example, can be no substitute for what the primary language of baptismal faith says about the dignity of the person and love and care for the oppressed child of God the Father. Far too often we assume that the two languages are more or less commensurate.

But if the argument of this book has suggested anything, it is that if we allow baptism to speak on its own terms, it offers something far deeper, richer, and revolutionary — and far more redemptive — than any pragmatic concept dreamed up in liberal theories and aped by liberal theologies. We need to remember that our primary language and identity are baptismal.

Our fundamental task, then, is to personally radiate the mother's smile, to allow others to catch a glimpse of worship, love, and beauty as that which makes the world go 'round, no matter what context we find ourselves in. In some creative way, this must be shown in the various acts which make up our contribution to the public square, a contribution which always remains an imperative for Christians. But we cannot remain content merely to "fill" secular forms with "rational" content. For the medium is the message. This will remain a troubling prudential question, but the defeat of the Ring and the triumph of baptism are at stake.

When the light seems to be fading — when the darkness seems the greatest — hobbits show the way to men. Hobbits show us how we might cast the Ring into the fire. They show us how to stubbornly cling to the things that matter most. They hold out the hope of a culture defined by hope. They resist the violent activist temptation which ultimately gives us over to the power of the Ring. Precisely in all of this, they show us how to destroy the Ring and the shadow of evil. And they thus reveal the possibility of the rising of a new baptismal and evangelical light.

Conclusion

*"I wish it need not have happened in my time," said Frodo.
"So do I," said Gandalf, "and so do all who live to see such times.
But that is not for them to decide. All we have to decide is what to
do with the time that is given us."*

J. R. R. Tolkien, *The Fellowship of the Ring*

THOSE WHO KNOW ME WELL WOULD MOST LIKELY
say that I am a glass-half-empty kind of guy. If you have made it
this far, you might have gained an inkling of why. When others
get excited about quantitative indications of perceived renewed religios-
ity or novel goings-on in the Church, you can find me muttering under
my breath about things like the absence of deep foundations, hype, and
groupthink, the qualitative sacramental criterion for faith and its dis-
cernment, and the long-term conditions needed to sustain and nurture
deep faith. I think one should be more interested in what is to be found
under shiny surfaces, *within* glossy exteriors, and *beyond* fashionable
catch-phrases and platitudes that float above the question of their more
foundational anthropological and linguistic housing, concrete incarnation, and narrative allegiance. I am more interested in the unspoken
foundations of concrete practices than I am in merely verbal, abstract,
or euphoric professions of theoretical belief. When others invoke the
mere fact that something is happening or "trending" as proof that "the
Spirit is moving!" my first response is to suppose that if it is popular it
probably means that it is *not* of the Spirit, or at least, not of the Spirit
in the way that we think.

And yet I have to acknowledge my own faults. In my basic disposition, I
am probably more man (a Boromir, perhaps) than I am hobbit. Meekness,
smallness, and subtlety have never exactly been my strong points. My
visceral response to moments of crisis or injustice is more often than not

markedly *less* than Christ-like, a constant reminder of just how tenuous is my hold on my own violent instincts.

Meanwhile, I must also admit that at least some of my theorizing likely fits quite happily with other somewhat non-evangelical manifestations of a hobbit ethos in my character. My more introverted and quietist dispositions probably most often resemble a kind of dwarfish living under the mountain rather than a kind of radiant baptismal existence that genuinely expands beyond itself to the other. Like Bilbo Baggins, I tend to dread the prospect of an adventure that would take me outside the comfortable confines of my hobbit hole.

And finally, I am sure there is a bit of troll in me as well.

But given the above, all that I have said regarding a hobbit civilization transformed and activated by baptism is thereby directed *as much to myself* as to anyone else. What I think baptism offers is a way to transcend all pathological tendencies. That is, it also forbids us from turning the pursuit of hobbit culture into a merely human "quest for community," just another attempt to reclaim conservative or traditionalist norms and practices for pragmatic purposes (for social survival and stability, or for simply avoiding the fight) but without existential commitment to the living and animating foundations of these norms.

I of course accept that a kind of strategic withdrawal from uncritical participation in the secular liturgies of the Ring, as suggested in particular by someone like Dreher, is essential. As indicated previously, I think that Dreher is absolutely right to suggest that creating much "thicker" Christian micro-communities that inculcate faith through *practices* as much or more so than by cognitive means is essential for the ongoing transmission of faith as we enter what appears to be a new twilight of the institutions and practices of faith in the West. No belief or idea can survive for long without being grounded in a genuine economy of practices, especially in a context dominated by the economy of the practices of the Ring.

My only further qualification, as already indicated, would be that given the pervasive effects of the Ring today, the viability and faithfulness of this project will ultimately require more overt theological specifications. It will require a deep abiding in the baptismal springs of faith, something much more radical than any vision afforded by the fundamental achievements of Western civilization, as essential as many of these achievements remain. The present cultural horizon of the death of God looms as a challenge perhaps unprecedented in the history of challenges to the faith, one in the end answerable only by faith *as faith*.

I am thus at pains to ever more robustly and consciously move towards a deeper *baptismal* specification of the kinds of forms that creative withdrawal and a re-sourcing of the tradition might produce, and the shape that the ensuing practices might take. Without greater baptismal specification, my sense is that the specter of a hollow traditionalism on the one hand or an unstable devotional emotionalism on the other — with all of their respective anthropological and theological dysfunctions and limitations — may more often than not result from attempts to carve out alternative spaces for the cultivation of faith.

Hence my stress on the centrality of the "imaginative" dimension needed to sustain any embodied endeavor that seeks to enact a praxis of resistance against the prevailing secular status quo. This is to say that for Christians, an alternative economy of practices must take conscious and considered theological shape as a *baptismal anthropology* before we can seriously hope for a truly effective "construction of local forms of community within which civility and the intellectual and moral life can be sustained through the new dark ages that are already upon us," as MacIntyre put it.[1]

This may well be a near-impossible or improbable task, given the fundamental importance of practices for forming imagination on the one hand and given the extreme challenge we face in fostering an economy of practices distinct from secularity in both its cultural and ecclesial points of transmission on the other. But this is all the more reason why a deeper "imaginative" imperative must be taken seriously within a postmodern condition where faith has already been colonized by the Ring; where both our imaginations and our bodies (our capacity to think and to act) are in certain unprecedented ways already held captive by the basic nihilism of liberal practices, and where we have by the self-secularizing mediocrity and idolatry of Christian institutions to a large extent already been formally cut off from the genuine sacramental and liturgical practices which give us our own true self.

Under these conditions, we cannot expect to create functioning economies of Christian practice without first addressing the full extent of the amnesia borne by believers who have now for generations, indeed, for *centuries*, been cut off from a genuinely living sacramental and liturgical

---

1 MacIntyre, *After Virtue*, 263.

culture of faith, the kind of expression that would before anything else inculcate faith through a kind of osmosis. My point is that unless we commit seriously to rediscovering faith as faith, beyond the many partial, fractured, or downright false alternatives on offer today, we will not be able to recover and live the genuine practices and communities of said faith in any sustained or integrated way. And so, sketching a vision of personal re-immersion in faith as baptismal adoption has been one of the driving emphases of this book.

Baptismal existence represents the existential challenge to embody faith in a properly sacramental and eschatological, and not just conservative or traditional, manner. A renewed sense of faith born out of the experience of the history of the death of God challenges us to love our spouse, raise our children, drink our beer, smoke our pipes, attend to our gardens, and make gifts of ourselves to our communities in truly existential and sacramental ways. It challenges us to live our marriages and families in a truly sacramental way, not as units of merely natural ends and human flourishing that only facilitate stable societies or protect the rights of our offspring, but as domestic churches, dramatic sacramental and eschatological communities that proclaim the coming Kingdom in all of its tension and radicality.

That is, all of these things that one might call "ordinary" are, properly speaking, no longer natural and secular, or even "human" properly speaking — by baptism they are something more. The acts of our everyday existence are part of the language of our baptismal adoption, our conjugal communion, and our domestic church, whose marks are impressed into our flesh. They are the bodily extensions of our new baptismal identities. They are called into the service of those identities. They are the acts whereby we actualize and make real our adopted existence as children of God. Through them, we bless and sanctify our existence and that of those around us. We become a light for the world. Through our *baptized* bodies — our engaging with time and space from inside the baptismal relation — we proclaim that existence is not secular; we proclaim that being and history are not meaningless; we proclaim that God is *not* dead.

Our micro-communities — our alternative economies of practices — will be everything they can be only when their basic grammar represents the expansion of our baptismal immersion into the history and genealogy of salvation history. They are truly themselves when they are based on the form of our adoption into the Father and the liturgical form of this adoption in the sacramental practices of the body of Christ. To take this seriously is to offer a vision of redemption, not only to the world, but, *even more critically in our own time*, to ourselves and to a deeply wounded, fractured, and dysfunctional institutional Church.

We should be under no illusions about the challenges of performing this "imaginative" task today. It is one thing to attempt to imaginatively conceive a baptismal existence in one's own life in the face of secular coercion; it is quite another even to get to the point where one recognizes the need for such an effort in the first place. And it is yet another thing to concretely live and enact this reality within a culture of secular liturgies. Most will no doubt be happy enough with a safe, mediocre faith that offers little depth or challenge, and that must in the end cede to the creeping power of the Ring. Most will not heed the madman's cry. Perhaps for most he is always come too early. But baptism imposes the true radicality of faith on all of us, whether we like it or not.

In regards to the evangelization to be pursued under contemporary conditions by those who seek to proclaim their faith to the world, the main thrust of this book's argument has been that we must attempt to inoculate ourselves against the temptation to naively yield to the power of the Ring, to unwittingly adopt pseudo-techniques and strategies, pseudo-rationalities, pseudo-spiritualities, and pseudo-communities that depart from the baptismal center. I have tried to show through the genealogies of earlier chapters how "virtual" forms of faith and evangelization can never in fact answer vitally the depth of our self-induced pathologies and the culture of the death of God. Efforts to uncritically "fill" with religious content forms that answer to the Ring in the hope of subverting it fail to perceive the extent to which the medium *is* the message. A form that belongs to another master will inexorably impose itself on the content.

This means that the task of evangelization must be first and foremost about a personal return of each believer to the baptismal font of faith in all its radiant splendor. The act of evangelization itself must be immersed in that font, in the baptismal "nothing" that is total abiding in Christ. It must be purged of the cognitive assumption that it could be superimposed upon dominant secular forms without an effect on its character and integrity. It must be uprooted from the presupposition that history is simply one long march towards progress and enlightenment, a presupposition that uncritically supposes that any and every new development is simply another potential form for the Gospel to express itself in.

I have thus argued that there is something profound to be learned from Tolkien's seminal idea that the trajectory of worldly history is that of a long defeat rather than a triumphant victory. Recall again what he said: "Actually I am a Christian, and indeed a Roman Catholic, so that I do not expect 'history' to be anything but a 'long defeat' — though it contains (and in a legend may contain more clearly and movingly) some samples or glimpses of final victory."[2] We should recognize that there is no real reason why a Christian civilization should not rise, decay, and fall in a manner like any other; that our "progress" could just as easily turn into regress.

I think I have become convinced in principle that once a religious or cultural phenomenon is uprooted from the soil of its origination, at least its *temporal* or *cyclical* death warrant has been signed. I do not deny that it was providential that Christianity moved from the soil of its Jewish roots and was universalized through its encounter with Greek thought, and thus became the foundation of a new civilizational order. But I think that whatever civilizational order it founds at any point in its history will necessarily have the seeds of its own decay written into it, for His "kingdom is not of this world" (Jn. 18:36). For once the fruitful dynamism of the original phenomenon is dissipated within the manifold horizons and concerns that stretch beyond the liturgical center into the world and its ever-changing exigencies, the original message of the primal phenomenon will inevitably be blunted, reduced, and sanitized. (Think of the way that globalization represents the death of the particular, "commodifying" local cultures for universal consumption.) The animating focus shifts from what the baptized Christian *as baptized* needs for eternity to what "all people of good will" need in terms of general principles for building a just society and achieving human flourishing, things that can be comfortably pursued in abstraction from the particular strictures of baptismal belonging. The normal sequence seems to run thus: vibrancy, a stagnant status quo, decline, collapse.

The deeper problem in this quite natural process of civilizational decline is that its effect is not limited to public or social Christianity. The danger is that once Christianity becomes invested in a social order, it is very easy for it to forget, postpone, or water down its own properly unique and eschatological mission to preach the world that baptism grants entry to.

---

2 *The Letters of J. R. R. Tolkien*, ed. Humphrey Carpenter and Christopher Tolkien (New York: Houghton Mifflin Harcourt, 1981), 255.

It is right and good that the Church should care about the world and seek justice and peace. But this can easily become the dominant politicized concern once the Church becomes invested in the institutions and forms of the world. The Church can become more interested in propping up the existing social order and maintaining its privileged place among that order's institutions (even when a social order begins to lose its way) than in preaching a message that may challenge this order at the expense of the Church having to give up its positions (or more often than not today, *delusions*) of influence and prestige.

When this happens, the Church may find Herself proclaiming a message in which the radical particularity and prophetic challenge of Christ's words have been lost in translation as they are fitted to the language of the dominant cultural order, so that what is preached in Her name is no longer unsettling prophetic wisdom, but rather false novelties, clichés, and impotent pandering to the weaknesses of Her members and the spirit of the age.

This is where I think we are today. The fragment has been lost in the whole. The false universal has swallowed the particular. The energy of the core has been dissipated in the peripheries. We would seem to be caught in a long downward slide, moving ever-farther from the most life-giving depth of baptism's font. We have become a world and a faith of Left and Right. Our capacity for baptismal existence from the font has been deadened.

But the hope of history read through Christ is that no earthly condition can ever be the occasion for the loss of hope, even the social and cultural death of God. "Death has been swallowed up in victory" (1 Cor. 15:54). For baptism is the history and genealogy that inserts the person into the long *Victory* of Jesus Christ. The hope for the present and the hope for the future can be found only in baptism. All we have to do is decide what to do with the baptismal time that has been given us in the here and now.

The burden of Tolkien's literary vision is thus to show how the limits of the horizon of temporality and time are surpassed by something far greater. It is this that places existence under the sign of the theological virtue of hope. Violence and despair, no matter how pervasive in this world, carry no power for the one who lives in hope, for the one who has allowed his or her being to be rewoven by the infinite grace of adoption.

Far from making everything out to be just fine, however, Tolkien's particular genius was to grasp keenly that hope is not magic; that it is marked rather by tension, the unexpected and unforeseen, apparent caprice

and chance, struggle, discontinuity, shocks, suffering, and perplexity; by
the risk of living in history. Wood calls Tolkien's vision in the *Lord of the
Rings* "melancholic," marked by "sorrowful joy." On this point, I cannot
recommend enough the reading of Wood's essay.[3] In truly admirable
fashion, he explains how Tolkien's vision resists the temptation to move
too quickly or perhaps *falsely or superficially* to the consummation of our
hope, to paper over the tensions and ambiguities of the present age, to
downplay the personal suffering that the pursuit of good will necessarily
inflict. Tolkien espouses a properly "dramatic" vision of history, one in
which the existential battle between good and evil has not lost its sharp
edge, where faithfulness may demand of us the ultimate sacrifice. Christ
has not yet "closed" history. It still remains determined by evil. Indeed,
we are told by Christ to expect that evil will in fact be the victor in the
temporal order (cf. Mt. 24:9); hence the long defeat.

The power of a baptismal vision is that it resists *both* myopic optimism
and fatalistic pessimism in regard to our life in history. It forbids a blindness
to the reality of evil and its capacity to colonize faith with the enervating
mediocrity of secular practices. It undermines a fear and despair that in
the face of fatalism and determinism would give into violent strategies
and compromises. Instead, baptism invites us into the caprice and chaos
of history with the embodied hope and peace of Jesus Christ, into what
we might describe as a condition of "providential fatalism." This is to say
that we know that existence will not cease to be dominated by evil, but we
also know that this cannot in any way overpower the eventual victory of
good. We know that history is in the end a long defeat, but we also know
that even in the midst of this defeat we have been given the gift that will
enable us to say in the end that "together through the ages of the world
we have fought the long defeat."[4]

The wonder of baptism, then, is that it gives us a graced context or
a lived sacramental world—a "home base," if you will—from which to
negotiate the twists and turns of history and with which to avoid either
underestimating or overestimating its challenges. In our own situation,
it allows us to look on the possibility of looming defeat and recognize it
for what it is. In acknowledging that decline is a normal cycle of history

---

3 Wood, "'Sad, but not Unhappy.'" See also Wood's *The Gospel According to Tolkien:
Visions of the Kingdom in Middle-earth* (Louisville: Westminster John Knox, 2003).
4 Tolkien, *The Fellowship of the Ring*, 464.

and that even a civilization more or less inspired by Christian faith does not stand as an inviolable exception to that rule, we can avoid the pitfall of making a desperate last stand in the hope of propping up an existing order by any idolatrous and soul-destroying means necessary.

The baptized person knows that the kingdom of this world is not *the* Kingdom. He knows his first priority is absolute fidelity to "the God and Father of our Lord Jesus Christ" (Eph. 1:3), and that sometimes this will mean renouncing the world's strategies of consensus and compromise — crucially, even some (many?) of those championed by certain representatives of the Church. Rather than make imprudent alliances and adopt the practices of the Ring, the Christian is given the grace to know when only radically new beginnings remain an option. Perhaps we are closer to this moment than we know. Hart argues that "for us today [the sacrifice and discipline needed to live faith] must involve the painful acknowledgment that neither we nor our distant progeny will live to see a new Christian culture rise in the Western world, and to accept this with both charity and faith."[5]

But it may not be that we are now fighting the last battle in the long defeat. Who knows? Perhaps the end of one phase of a civilization originally inspired by Christ could be followed by the beginning of a brand-new phase, a genuinely new "springtime of faith," a civilization that rises from the ashes, upon a deepened and renewed baptismal foundation, as never before. The hope given to us by baptism is the same hope that animated the first generations of Christians. It pours out the same actualized gift of faith that starts in small cells and grows by slow degrees to cultural expression, not through coercion or tactical compromise, but from the simple, faithful, and holy living as brother and sister, father and mother, husband and wife, or child *in Christ*. As long as we have baptism, we have hope that the cycle can begin anew in every generation. What matters is that we do not let saving the old preclude beginning the new. Only with the right kind of death can come the right kind of life.

In the end, my goal is simple: for each of us to come into more radical and existential contact with the primordial and living radicality that is the Father's love for us. It is to allow this love to shape our walk of faith and our evangelical mission. As children of the Father in the Son and the Spirit, we are given to history to sanctify and redeem time, to abide the

---

5 Hart, "God or Nothingness," 75.

long defeat in joyful witness to the baptism that has saved us. For most of us, our contribution to the sanctification and redemption of time will come in the way of the hobbit more or less literally, via our fidelity to the smallest and most apparently mundane realities. Most of us will not be in a position to influence public policy, to take part in activist crusades, to counsel the wise and the powerful. But being a hobbit is the fundamental vocation for *all* of us, great or small; a fundamental conditioning factor of all action, whether contemplative or active. This is where the true engine of evangelization waits, ready to be started.

But it cannot be started on its own. It demands that each of us come into existential contact with the loving smile of the mother. It requires our own immersion in the fullness of the baptismal smile of the Father, shared with us in Christ and through the Spirit in the culture and practices of sacramental and liturgical faith. It requires that we recognize and understand the ways in which we have been unfaithful to this gift in the long march (or defeat) of history.

My intention has only been to offer some small "imaginative" glimpse of what a baptismal faith and a baptismal culture might look like. The new evangelization must become a *summons* to this faith and culture — to each of us, personally — before it can be a mission "out there." The real work of the new evangelization does not happen "out there." It happens first in our own hearts, in our radical response to a grace that transcends Left and Right, which lives only according to the criteria of its own baptismal logic. It happens in our most fundamental relationships. It happens every time we resist violent practices, and allow truly baptismal practices to transform our hearts and become our *modus operandi.*

And so, I hope that we have discovered a path back to a baptismal future: it is precisely by returning to the small, by becoming a hobbit, by renouncing the various "rings" of power offered by the world, that the future graces of the Kingdom will be poured out for us. Let us pray that each of us may be given the grace to abide the long defeat for the victory of Jesus Christ.

BIBLIOGRAPHY

Anderson, Ryan T. *Truth Overruled: The Future of Marriage and Religious Freedom*. New Jersey: Regnery, 2015.

Anscombe, G. E. M. "Modern Moral Philosophy." *Philosophy* 33 (1958), 1–19.

Arendt, Hannah. *Eichmann in Jerusalem: A Report on the Banality of Evil*. New York: Penguin, 2006.

Bacon, Francis. *The New Organon and Related Writings*. Indianapolis: Bobbs-Merrill, 1960.

Balthasar, Hans Urs von. *Explorations in Theology II: Spouse of the Word*. Translated by A.V. Littledale and Alexander Dru. San Francisco: Ignatius, 1991.

—. "The Fathers, the Scholastics, and Ourselves." Translated by Edward T. Oakes. *Communio* 24 (1997), 347–96.

—. *The Glory of the Lord: A Theological Aesthetics*. Vol 1. *Seeing the Form*. Translated by Erasmo Leiva-Merikakis. San Francisco: Ignatius, 1989.

—. *The Glory of the Lord: A Theological Aesthetics*. Vol. 4. *The Realm of Metaphysics in Antiquity*. Translated by Brian McNeil, Andrew Louth, John Saward, Rowan Williams, and Oliver Davies. San Francisco: Ignatius, 1989.

—. *The Glory of the Lord: A Theological Aesthetics*. Vol. 5. *The Realm of Metaphysics in the Modern Age*. Translated by Oliver Davies, Andrew Louth, Brian McNeil, John Saward, and Rowan Williams. San Francisco: Ignatius, 1991.

—. *Love Alone Is Credible*. Translated by D. C. Schindler. San Francisco: Ignatius, 2004.

—. "On the Concept of Person." *Communio* 13 (1986), 18–26.

—. *Theo-Drama: Theological Dramatic Theory*. Vol. 2. *The Dramatis Personae: Man in God*. Translated by Graham Harrison. San Francisco: Ignatius Press, 1990.

—. *Theo-Drama: Theological Dramatic Theory*. Vol. 3. *The Dramatis Personae: The Person in Christ*. Translated by Graham Harrison. San Francisco: Ignatius Press, 1991.

—. *Theo-Drama: Theological Dramatic Theory*. Vol. 4. *The Action*. Translated by Graham Harrison. San Francisco: Ignatius Press, 1994.

—. *A Theological Anthropology*. Eugene: Wipf and Stock, 1967.

Beer, Jeremy. "Philosopher of Love: David L. Schindler." *The American Conservative* (October 16, 2013). Online: http://www.theamericanconservative.com/articles/philosopher-of-love-587/.

Benedict XVI. Address to the Apostolic Penitentiary, Rome (March 9, 2012). http://www.ewtn.com/library/PAPALDOC/b16intforum.htm.

Benson, Iain T. "That False Struggle between Believers and Non-believers." *Oasis* 12 (2010), 22–5.

Blondel, Maurice. *Action (1893): Essay on a Critique of Life and a Science of Practice*. Translated by Oliva Blanchette. Notre Dame: University of Notre Dame Press, 1984.

—. "History and Dogma." *The Letter on Apologetics and History and Dogma*. Translated by Alexander Dru and Illtyd Trethowan, 221–87. Grand Rapids: Eerdmans, 1994.

Boersma, Hans. *Heavenly Participation: The Weaving of a Sacramental Tapestry*. Grand Rapids: Eerdmans, 2011.

—. *Nouvelle Théologie and Sacramental Ontology: A Return to Mystery*. Oxford: Oxford University Press, 2009.

Boeve, Lieven. *God Interrupts History: Theology in a Time of Upheaval*. London: Continuum, 2007.

Cavanaugh, William T. *Migrations of the Holy: God, State, and the Political Meaning of the Church*. Grand Rapids: Eerdmans, 2011.

—. *The Myth of Religious Violence: Secular Ideology and the Roots of Modern Conflict*. Oxford: Oxford University Press, 2009.

—. *Theo-Political Imagination: Discovering the Liturgy as a Political Act in an Age of Global Consumerism*. London: Bloomsbury, 2002.

Chaput, Charles J. *Strangers in a Strange Land: Living the Catholic Faith in a Post-Christian World*. New York: Henry Holt, 2017.

Cooper, Adam G. *Holy Eros: A Liturgical Theology of the Body*. Kettering: Angelico, 2014.

Crawford, David S. "Gay Marriage, Public Reason, and the Common Good." *Communio* 41 (2014), 380–437.

—. "Liberal Androgyny: 'Gay Marriage' and the Meaning of Sexuality in Our Time." *Communio* 33 (2006), 239–65.

—. "Public Reason and the Anthropology of Orientation: How the Debate Over 'Gay Marriage' Has Been Shaped." *Communio* 43 (2016), 247–73.

Cyril of Jerusalem, St. *Mystagogical Catechesis* I. In *Documents of the Baptismal Liturgy*. Edited by E. C. Whitaker and Maxwell E. Johnson. Collegeville: Liturgical Press, 2003, 30–31.

Daniélou, Jean. *From Shadows to Reality: Studies in the Biblical Typology of the Fathers*. Translated by Wulstan Hibberd. London: Burns & Oates, 1960.

Dawson, Christopher. *Religion and the Rise of Western Culture*. New York: Doubleday, 1991.

Deneen, Patrick. *Why Liberalism Failed*. New Haven and London: Yale University Press, 2018.

Descartes, René. *Meditations on First Philosophy*. Translated by Michael Moriarty. Oxford: Oxford University Press, 2008.

Dogmatic Definition of the Council of Chalcedon. https://www.ewtn.com/faith/teachings/incac2.htm.

Doran, Robert. "René Girard's apocalyptic modernity." *Comunicação & Cultura* 11 (2011), 37–52.

Dreher, Rod. *The Benedict Option: A Strategy for Christians in a Post-Christian Nation*. New York: Sentinel, 2017.

—. "Sex after Christianity." *The American Conservative* (April 9, 2013). http://www.theamericanconservative.com/articles/sex-after-christianity/.

Dupré, Louis. *Passage to Modernity: An Essay in the Hermeneutics of Nature and Culture*. New Haven: Yale University Press, 1993.

Esolen, Anthony. *Out of the Ashes: Rebuilding American Culture*. Washington DC: Regnery, 2017.

Farrow, Douglas. "Why Fight Same-Sex Marriage?" *Touchstone Magazine* 25 (2012). http://www.touchstonemag.com/archives/issue.php?id=166.

Girard, René. *Battling to the End: Conversations with Benoît Chantres*. Translated by Mary Baker. East Lansing: Michigan State University Press, 2010.

—. *I See Satan Fall Like Lightning*. Translated by James G. Williams. Maryknoll: Orbis, 2001.

—. *Things Hidden Since the Foundation of the World*. Translated by Stephen Bann and Michael Metteer. Stanford: Stanford University Press, 1987.

—. "Violence, Difference, Sacrifice: A Conversation with René Girard." Interview with Rebecca Adams. *Religion and Literature* 25 (1993), 9–33.

—. "Violence and Religion: Cause or Effect?" *The Hedgehog Review* 6 (2004). http://www.iasc-culture.org/THR/THR_article_2004_Spring_Girard.php.

—. "On War and Apocalypse." *First Things* (February 2009). https://www.firstthings.com/article/2009/08/on-war-and-apocalypse.

Granados, José and Anderson, Carl. *Called to Love: Approaching John Paul II's Theology of the Body*. New York: Doubleday, 2009.

Habermas, Jürgen. *Legitimation Crisis*. Translated by Thomas McCarthy. London: Heinemann Educational, 1976.

Hanby, Michael. "The Brave New World of Same-Sex Marriage." *The Federalist* (Feb 9, 2014). http://thefederalist.com/2014/02/19/the-brave-new-world-of-same-sex-marriage/.

—. "The Culture of Death, the Ontology of Boredom, and the Resistance of Joy." *Communio* 31 (2004), 181–99.

—. "A More Perfect Absolutism." *First Things* (October 2016). https://www.firstthings.com/article/2016/10/a-more-perfect-absolutism.

Harnack, Adolph von. *What Is Christianity?* Translated by Thomas Bailey Sanders. Philadelphia: Fortress Press, 1986.

Hart, David Bentley. *Atheist Delusions: The Christian Revolution and Its Fashionable Enemies*. New Haven: Yale University Press, 2009.

—. *The Beauty of the Infinite: The Aesthetics of Christian Truth*. Grand Rapids: Eerdmans, 2003.

—. "God or Nothingness." In *I Am the Lord Your God: Christian Reflections on the Ten Commandments*. Edited by Carl E. Braaten and Christopher R. Seitz. Grand Rapids: Eerdmans, 2005, 55–76.

—. "A Philosopher in the Twilight: Heidegger's Philosophy as a Meditation on the Mystery of Being." *First Things* (February 2011). https://www.firstthings.com/article/2011/02/a-philosopher-in-the-twilight.

Hauerwas, Stanley. "The Christian Difference, or Surviving Postmodernism." In *The Blackwell Companion to Postmodern Theology*. Edited by Graham Ward. Oxford: Blackwell, 2005, 144–61.

Heidegger, Martin. "The Question Concerning Technology." In Martin Heidegger, *Basic Writings*. Edited by David Farrell Krell. London: Harper, 2008, 311–41.

—. "The Onto-Theo-Logical Constitution of Metaphysics." In Martin Heidegger, *Identity and Difference*. Translated by Joan Stambaugh. Chicago: University of Chicago Press, 1969, 42–74.

—. "The Way Back into the Ground of Metaphysics." *Existentialism from Dostoevsky to Sartre*. Edited and translated by Walter Kaufman. New York: Meridian Books, 1975, 265–79.

Hume, David. *An Enquiry Concerning Human Understanding, and Other Essays*. Edited by Ernest C. Mossner. New York: Washington Square Press, 1963.

John Paul II. *Man and Woman He Created Them: A Theology of the Body*. Translated by Michael Waldstein. Boston: Pauline, 2006.

Kierkegaard, Søren. *The Diary of Søren Kierkegaard*. Edited by Peter Rohde. New York: Philosophical Library, 1960.

—. *Provocations: Spiritual Writings of Søren Kierkegaard*. Edited by C. E. Moore. Farmington: Plough, 2002.

—. *The Sickness Unto Death: A Christian Psychological Exposition for Upbuilding and Awakening*. Translated by Howard V. Hong and Edna H. Hong. Princeton: Princeton University Press, 1983.

Kwasniewski, Peter. "The Long Shadow of Neoscholastic Reductionism." *New Liturgical Movement* (blog), July 3, 2017. http://www.newliturgicalmovement.org/2017/07/the-long-shadow-of-neoscholastic.html#.WYPAc4SGNhE.

Leithart, Peter J. "Myth of Religious Violence." *First Things* (July 2012). https://www.firstthings.com/blogs/leithart/2012/08/myth-of-religious-violence.

Levinas, Emmanuel. *Totality and Infinity: An Essay on Exteriority*. Translated by Alphonso Lingis. Pittsburgh: Duquesne University Press, 2003.

Lubac, Henri de. *Corpus Mysticum: The Eucharist and the Church in the Middle Ages*. Translated by Gemma Simmonds, Richard Price, and Christopher Stephens. Notre Dame, IN: University of Notre Dame Press, 2006.

—. *The Mystery of the Supernatural*. Translated by Rosemary Sheed. New York: Herder & Herder, 2016.

—. *Surnatural: Études Historiques: nouvelle edition*. Paris: Desclée de Brouwer, 1991.

—. "The Total Meaning of Man and the World." *Communio* 35 (2008), 611–41.

Lyotard, Jean-François. *The Postmodern Condition: A Report on Knowledge*. Translated by Geoff Bennington and Brian Massumi. Minneapolis: University of Minnesota Press, 1984.

MacIntyre, Alasdair. *After Virtue: A Study in Moral Theory*. London: Duckworth, 1990.

—. *Whose Justice? Which Rationality?* London: Duckworth, 1988.

—. *Three Rival Versions of Moral Enquiry: Encyclopedia, Genealogy, and Tradition*. Notre Dame: University of Notre Dame Press, 1990.

Marcuse, Herbert. *One Dimensional Man*. London: Abacus, 1972.

—. "Repressive Tolerance." *A Critique of Pure Tolerance*. Edited by Robert Paul Wolf, Barrington Moore, Jr., and Herbert Marcuse. Boston: Beacon, 1970.

Marion, Jean-Luc. *The Erotic Phenomenon*. Translated by Stephan E. Lewis. Chicago:

Chicago University Press, 2007.

McLuhan, Marshall. *Understanding Media: The Extensions of Man*. Cambridge: MIT Press, 1994.

Melina, Livio. "The Fullness of Christian Action: Beyond Moralism and Antimoralism." *Logos* 8 (2005), 123–40.

—. *Sharing in Christ's Virtues: For a Renewal of Moral Theology in Light of* Veritatis Splendor. Washington, D.C.: CUA Press, 2001.

Milbank, John. "Gay Marriage and the Future of Sexuality." *ABC Religion & Ethics* (March 13, 2012). http://www.abc.net.au/religion/articles/2012/03/13/3452229.htm.

—. "The Impossibility of Gay Marriage and the Threat of Bio-Political Control." *ABC Religion & Ethics* (April 23, 2013). http://www.abc.net.au/religion/articles/2013/04/23/3743531.htm.

—. *Theology and Social Theory: Beyond Secular Reason*. Oxford: Blackwell, 2006.

Nietzsche, Friedrich. *The Anti-Christ*. In Friedrich Nietzsche, *The Anti-Christ, Ecce Homo, Twilight of the Idols*. Translated by Judith Norman. Cambridge: Cambridge University Press, 2005.

—. *Beyond Good and Evil*. Translated by Walter Kaufmann. New York: Vintage Books, 1989.

—. *The Gay Science*. Translated by Josefine Nauckhoff. Cambridge: Cambridge University Press, 2001.

—. *Human, All Too Human: A Book for Free Spirits*. Translated by R. J. Hollingdale. Cambridge: Cambridge University Press, 2005.

—. *Thus Spoke Zarathustra: A Book for All and None*. Translated by Adrian Del Caro. Cambridge: Cambridge University Press, 2006.

—. *The Will to Power*. Translated by Walter Kaufmann and R. J. Hollingdale. New York: Vintage Books, 1968.

Ouellet, Marc Cardinal. *Divine Likeness: Towards a Trinitarian Anthropology of the Family*. Translated by Philip Milligan and Linda M. Cicone. Grand Rapids: Eerdmans, 2006.

Patterson, Colin and Sweeney, Conor, editors. *God and Eros: The Ethos of the Nuptial Mystery*. Eugene: Cascade, 2015.

Pickstock, Catherine. *After Writing: On the Liturgical Consummation of Philosophy*. Oxford: Blackwell, 1998.

Pieper, Joseph. *Leisure, the Basis of Culture*. Translated by Gerald Malsbary. South Bend: St. Augustine's Press, 1998.

Ratzinger, Joseph Cardinal. *"In the Beginning...": A Catholic Understanding of the Story of Creation and the Fall*. Translated by Boniface Ramsey. Grand Rapids: Eerdmans, 1995.

—. "Concerning the Notion of Person in Theology." Translated by Michael Waldstein. *Communio* 17 (1990), 437–54.

—. "Europe in the Crisis of Cultures." Translated by Adrian J. Walker. *Communio* 32 (2005), 345–56.

—. *Introduction to Christianity*. Translated by J.R. Foster. San Francisco: Ignatius, 2000.

—. *Pilgrim Fellowship of Faith: The Church as Communion*. Translated by Henry Taylor. San Francisco: Ignatius, 2005.

—. *The Spirit of the Liturgy*. In *Collected Works: Theology of the Liturgy*. San Francisco: Ignatius, 2014, 3–150.

Ricoeur, Paul. *The Conflict of Interpretations: Essays in Hermeneutics*. Edited by Don Ihde. Evanston: Northwestern University Press, 1974.

Roderick, Rick. "Paul Ricoeur: The Masters of Suspicion." In *The Self Under Siege: Philosophy in the 20th Century*. Audio Cassette, The Teaching Company (1993). http://rickroderick.org/301-paul-ricoeur-the-masters-of-suspicion-1993/.

Rose, Matthew. "The Anti-Christian Alt-Right: The Perverse Thought of Right-Wing Identity Politics." *First Things* (March 2018). https://www.firstthings.com/article/2018/03/the-anti-christian-alt-right.

Rowland, Tracey. *Benedict XVI: A Guide for the Perplexed*. London: T&T Clark, 2010.

Sarah, Robert Cardinal. *The Power of Silence: Against the Dictatorship of Noise*. San Francisco: Ignatius, 2017.

Scola, Angelo Cardinal. *The Nuptial Mystery*. Translated by Michelle K. Borras. Grand Rapids: Eerdmans, 2005.

Schindler, David C. "'Wie Kommt der Mensch in die Theologie?': Heidegger, Hegel, and the Stakes of Onto-Theo-Logy." *Communio* 32 (2005), 637–68.

Schindler, David L. "Christological Aesthetics and *Evangelium Vitae*: Toward a Definition of Liberalism." *Communio* 22 (1995), 193–224.

—. "Grace and the Form of Nature and Culture." In *Catholicism and Secularization in America: Essays on Nature, Grace, and Culture*. Edited by David L. Schindler. Notre Dame: Our Sunday Visitor, 1990, 10–30.

—. "The Repressive Logic of Liberal Rights: Religious Freedom, Contraceptives, and the 'Phony' Argument of the New York Times." *Communio* 38 (2011), 523–47.

—. "Is Truth Ugly? Moralism and the Convertibility of Being and Love." *Communio* 27 (2000), 701–28.

Smith, James K. A. *Desiring the Kingdom: Worship, Worldview, and Cultural Formation*. Grand Rapids: Baker, 2009.

Stark, Rodney. *Bearing False Witness: Debunking Centuries of Anti-Catholic History*. West Conshohocken: Templeton Press, 2016.

Sweeney, Conor. *Sacramental Presence after Heidegger: Onto-Theology, Sacraments, and the Mother's Smile*. Eugene: Cascade, 2015.

Tan, Matthew John Paul. "Faith in the Church of Facebook." *Journal of Moral Theology* (2015), 25–30.

—. *Justice, Unity and the Hidden Christ: The Theopolitical Complex of the Social Justice Approach to Ecumenism in Vatican II*. Eugene: Pickwick, 2014.

Taylor, Charles. "A Catholic Modernity?" In *A Catholic Modernity? Charles Taylor's Marianist Award Lecture*. Edited by James L. Heft. Oxford: Oxford University Press, 1999, 13–38.

—. *A Secular Age*. Cambridge, MA: Belknap Press, 2007.

—. "Two Theories of Modernity." *Hastings Centre Report* 25 (1995), 24–33.

Tolkien, J. R. R. *The Fellowship of the Ring*. New York: HarperCollins, 2011.

—. *The Letters of J.R.R. Tolkien*. Edited by Humphrey Carpenter and Christopher Tolkien. New York: Houghton Mifflin Harcourt, 1981.

Trueman, Carl R. "Hey Joe! It's time for bishops to take a public stand on morally bankrupt politicians." *First Things* (Aug 12, 2016). https://www.firstthings.com/blogs/firstthoughts/2016/08/hey-joe.

Twenge, Jean. "Have Smartphones Destroyed a Generation?" *The Atlantic* (Sept 2017).

— *iGen: Why Today's Super-Connected Kids are Growing up Less Rebellious, More Tolerant, Less Happy—and Totally Unprepared for Adulthood*. New York: Atria Books, 2017.

Tyson, Paul and Tan, Matthew John Paul. "Ecological Disaster and Jacques Ellul's Theological Vision." *Solidarity* 2 (2012), 1–10.

Weber, Max. *The Protestant Ethic and the Spirit of Capitalism*. Translated by Talcott Parsons. New York: Scribners, 1958.

Wood, Ralph C. *The Gospel According to Tolkien: Visions of the Kingdom in Middle-earth*. Louisville: Westminster John Knox, 2003.

—. "'Sad, but not Unhappy': J. R. R. Tolkien's Sorrowful Vision of Joy." *ABC Religion and Ethics* (June 2, 2014). http://www.abc.net.au/religion/articles/2014/06/02/4017211.htm.

Wojtyla, Karol. *The Acting Person*. Translated by Andrzej Potocki. Dordrecht: D. Reidel, 1979.

SUBJECT INDEX

AUTHOR INDEX

.